second edition

interpersonal attraction

second edition

interpersonal attraction

ELLEN BERSCHEID

University of Minnesota

ELAINE HATFIELD WALSTER

University of Wisconsin

ADDISON-WESLEY PUBLISHING COMPANY

Reading, Massachusetts
Menlo Park, California
London · Amsterdam · Don Mills, Ontario · Sydney

TOPICS IN SOCIAL PSYCHOLOGY

Charles A. Kiesler
Series Editor

To Bill and Dewey

This series *Topics in Social Psychology* is directed toward the student with no prior background in social psychology. Taken as a whole, **foreword**
the series covers the ever-expanding field of social psychology reasonably well, but a major advantage of the series is that each individual book was written by well-known scholars in the area. The instructor can select a subset of the books to make up the course in social psychology, the particular subset depending on the instructor's own definition of our field. The original purpose of this series was to provide such freedom for the instructor while maintaining a thoughtful and expert treatment of each topic. In addition, the first editions of the series have been widely used in a variety of other ways: such as supplementary reading in nonpsychology courses; to introduce more advanced courses in psychology, or for the sheer fun of peeking at recent developments in social psychology.

We have developed second editions that serve much the same purpose. Each book is somewhat longer and more open in design, uses updated materials, and in general takes advantage of constructive feedback from colleagues and students across the country. So many people found the first editions of the individual books useful that we have tried to make the second editions even more thorough and complete, and therefore more easily separated from the rest of the series.

This volume centers on interpersonal attraction, running the gamut from attraction and rejection in a group to romantic love. The two authors have published numerous articles on these issues and are well known as leaders in this field of inquiry. I think you will find this edition as exciting as the first one.

Charles A. Kiesler

I knocked on his door and he didn't answer my
knock, so I walked in. And there he was in bed—
a typical bachelor's room, his golf clubs, camera and
everything else all scattered. But then, all around his bed, propped up on
chairs and tables, were pictures of Wallis. I counted sixteen of them. It was
as if he were in a crypt.

And there he was, fast asleep, hugging a small pillow of hers with the
initials "WS" on it. All around him were souvenirs of all their good times
together, everything from rocks to heather. I wanted to bawl! I left the room
stunned, found his newly hired German valet and told him to wake the
Duke and when I walked in, everything—all the pictures, all the souvenirs
—had been cleared away.

I can still close my eyes and see that room!

R. G. MARTIN, *The Woman He Loved*, 1974, p. 344

Of course, the Duke of Windsor was the "sleeping man." A few days
before, he had been King Edward VIII of England. He had renounced his
throne to marry the "scandalous" Wallis Simpson. Now he slept, sick with
loss and loneliness.

King Edward's decision to renounce his throne to marry the woman he
loved is a famous example of how one man's private feelings may have a
cataclysmic effect on affairs of state. History books are replete with other
examples. It would be odd if they were not. Friendship and love, enmity and
hatred, are potent emotions. And they often have potent consequences.

Usually less dramatically, but just as inexorably, our feelings and the
feelings of those around us shape our own lives. We obtain a job because

The writing of this book was facilitated in part by National Science Foundation
Grant GS 35157X to Berscheid and National Institute of Mental Health Grant MH
26681 to Walster.

the interviewer liked us; we lose a court decision because the jury didn't. We take an opportunity to be close to someone we care about; we run away from someone we wish we didn't. We marry for love, or for the hope of it, and some of us create life, others of us take life, in the name of it. The ways in which our affection and enmity for others—and theirs for us—plots the twists and turns of each of our paths are endless. It is not surprising, then, that interpersonal attraction has been an early and endless source of human fascination and speculation.

Theologists and philosophers, anthropologists, ethologists, and sociologists, as well as psychologists of diverse training and specialization, have sought to understand interpersonal attraction. They have taken a multitude of approaches to try to understand interpersonal attraction, in general, and to learn more about some of the specific varieties of attraction, such as friendship or love, in particular.

All of the theory and most of the research reported in this volume represent the effort of just one discipline, social psychology, to understand the causes, effects, and particulars of interpersonal attraction. And, as the Contents indicate, social psychologists have a good deal to say on the subject.

This was not always the case. It was not so very long ago that questions of liking and loving were believed to be the special province of theologians and philosophers: those who have society's license to speak of mystical things, intangibles which can't be studied systematically, things which only can be marveled at, despaired of, and wondered about. Social scientists, of course, must limit their scrutiny to phenomena which are amenable to scientific study, to observation and quantification, to prediction, and, ultimately, to control. These prerequisites certainly excluded the investigation of interpersonal attraction—or at least everyone thought they did.

Everyone, that is, but Kurt Lewin—the German social scientist who fled Germany and came to this country in the 1930s and who founded the discipline of experimental social psychology. Even as a student of psychology at the University of Berlin, learning to measure human reaction times down to a fraction of a second, Lewin envisioned a day in which psychologists would study more than such psychophysical phenomena as reaction times and light thresholds. He foresaw a modern psychology which would remove some of the mystery surrounding phenomena of enormous interest and importance to each of us in our daily lives. As he put it (1940, p. 3):

> The psychologist finds himself in the midst of a rich and vast land full of strange happenings: There are men killing themselves; a child playing; a child forming his lips going to say his first word; a person who, having fallen in love and being caught in an unhappy situation, is not willing or not able to find a way out. . . . It is an immense continent full of fascination

and power and full of stretches of land where no one ever has set foot. Psychology is out to conquer this continent. . . .

And Lewin was convinced that the means of conquest were at hand; that scientific method and analysis could illuminate many of the puzzles and paradoxes of human behavior.

Under Lewin's leadership, social psychologists, first a few and then many, set out on expeditions into the behavioral land of "strange happenings."

In this text, we will take you on a tour of the well-cultivated areas of interpersonal attraction . . . and point out the territories that remain to be conquered along the way.

Overview of Interpersonal Attraction

In Chapter 1, we will pose two basic questions: (1) "What *is* interpersonal attraction?" and (2) "Can one ever really measure such ineffable things as liking and loving . . . enmity and hate?"

"Why are we attracted to one person and not another?" *In Chapter 2*, we will find that a simple principle underlies all attraction: the principle of reinforcement: we like those who reward us and dislike those who punish us. *In Chapter 3*, we'll find that "mere" proximity turns out to be a more important determinant of liking than you'd think. For it is those who are close to us (geographically) that have the greatest opportunity to reward or to punish us—and, thus, become our friends and lovers . . . or our enemies.

While it is true that "we like those who reward us and dislike those who punish us," this principle isn't very useful when we want to predict who will be attracted to whom. Social psychologists have no equation which will permit them to add up all the rewards a person is likely to provide, balance them against the punishments he or she is likely to inflict, and thus arrive at Total Reward Index, which will tell them how much others will like her or him. Thus, researchers have settled on a more realistic goal: to learn what behaviors and events, most people, most of the time, find rewarding.

Which rewards and punishments *are* the most potent determinants of interpersonal attraction and hostility? *In Chapter 4* we will consider one potent reward others can give us: their liking. We'll examine the conditions that make a person unusually receptive . . . or unusually resistant to others' friendly overtures.

In Chapter 5 we consider a second, potent, transsituational reinforcer: similarity. We'll find that the evidence is unclear as to whether or not people like others with *personalities* similar to their own. ("Birds of a feather . . . ?" or, "Opposites attract?") There is voluminous evidence that we all like those who share our *attitudes* . . . and dislike those who don't.

In Chapters 4 and 5, we consider two other transsituational reinforcers . . . and their effect on liking. *In Chapter 6* we find that those who make our life more pleasant in a myriad of little ways—those who reduce our loneliness, fear, or stress—also provide a valuable reward—and endear themselves to us.

Many times people do not reward or punish us directly; rather they help us obtain desired goals . . . or prevent us from obtaining them.

In Chapter 7 we'll review the evidence that indicates that we like those who cooperate with us in our efforts to obtain reward . . . and dislike those who compete against us for rewards.

The reinforcement theorists began with a single principle: people like those who reward them . . . and dislike those who punish them. So far, so good. Equity theorists take things a step further.

In Chapter 8 we'll discuss Equity theory. We'll also present some fascinating evidence that how we treat others has a profound impact on how we feel about *them*. We'll present evidence that we come to like those we benefit . . . and dislike those we harm, as well as the other way around.

Finally, in Chapters 9 and 10, we move from the milder forms of liking into the more profound varieties of Interpersonal Attraction—we'll discuss romantic and companionate love.

In Chapter 9 we focus on passionate love. Schachter has argued that both our minds and our bodies make a unique contribution to our emotions. We will review the evidence which indicates that Schachter may be right. We will examine evidence that: (1) *Mind:* Whether or not we think we *should* be in love has a profound impact on whether or not we *do* fall in love. (2) *Body:* We will review evidence that under the right conditions, *anything* that causes us to become physiologically aroused may deepen our passion.

In Chapter 10 we will focus on companionate love. We will find that equity considerations have a potent impact on whether a passionate relationship blossoms into love . . . and whether or not loving relationships continue . . . or wither and die.

Minneapolis, Minnesota　　　　　　　　　　　　　　　　　　　　　E. B.
Madison, Wisconsin　　　　　　　　　　　　　　　　　　　　　　E. H. W.
December 1977

We would like to thank Darcy Abrahams for her # acknowledgments

delightfully devastating illustrations, and Drs. Ted Huston, Charles Kiesler, George Levinger, and G. William Walster for their thoughtful reviews of this manuscript. We would also like to thank Elinor Loucks and Suzanne Ishmael for editing and typing this manuscript.

Finally, we would also like to thank the following publishers for giving us permission to use quotations, figures, or illustrations from their publications: Academic Press, Inc.; American Psychological Association, Inc.; American Sociological Association; Appleton-Century-Crofts, Inc.; Atherton Press, Inc.; Farrar and Rinehart, Inc.; Field Enterprises, Inc.; Field Newspaper Syndicate; Harcourt Brace and World, Inc.; Harper & Row Publishers, Inc.; King Features Syndicate; J. B. Lippincott Company; *Milwaukee Journal Newspaper*, Inc.; The *New Yorker*; *Scientific American*, Inc.; *The Society for the Psychological Study of Social Issues*; Stanford University Press; Wiley, Inc.; the Yale University Press; and Ziff-Davis Publishing Co.

contents

1

what is interpersonal attraction anyway? can we measure it? *1*

reward theories of interpersonal attraction: an overview *21*

3

rewards and punishments others provide: proximity *29*

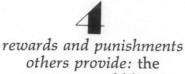

rewards and punishments
others provide: the
reciprocity-of-liking
rule *39*

rewards and
punishments others
provide: similarity   *61*

rewards and punishments
others provide: the
reduction of isolation, fear,
and stress   *91*

rewards and punishments
others provide: cooperation
vs. competition *105*

equity theory
and attraction   *125*

the beginnings:
romantic love   *147*

10

companionate
love   *177*

It is perhaps ironic that to begin to understand the most intimate and touching of human emotions we must retreat to the impersonality and objectivity of the scientific approach. When we do so, we find that our first task is to try to describe and to measure what for so long was believed to be ineffable and immeasurable.

what is interpersonal attraction anyway?
can we measure it?

Interpersonal Attraction: A Conceptual Definition

One might think that it would be easy for scientists to devise a formal definition of interpersonal attraction. The words "like" and "love," "dislike" and "hate" are among the most frequently used in the English language. Everyone knows what they mean; when we say we are "attracted" to someone or "repulsed" by someone, nobody ever asks us to define our terms. Yet scientists have found it impossible to agree on a single definition of attraction. By now an extravagant number of definitions of attraction exist.

Almost all their definitions have one thing in common, however: almost all theorists agree that interpersonal attraction is a positive or negative *attitude* toward another person.

Just what do psychologists mean when they use the term "attitude"?

THE NATURE OF ATTITUDES[1]

You probably already have a fairly good idea of what an attitude is. The word is a part of almost everyone's vocabulary. An attitude simply repre-

---

1. For a more complete discussion of attitudes, see P. Zimbardo, E. E. Ebbesen, and C. Maslach, *Influencing attitudes and changing behavior*, Reading, Mass.: Addison-Wesley, 1977.

sents a person's readiness to respond toward an object, or a class of objects, in a favorable or unfavorable manner. For example, Katz and Stotland[2] (1959, p. 428) define an attitude as "an individual's tendency or predisposition to evaluate an object or the symbol of that object in a certain way."

We might define *interpersonal attraction* (or interpersonal hostility), then, as "an individual's tendency or predisposition to evaluate another person or symbol of that person in a positive (or negative) way." (Walster and Walster 1976, p. 280)

Most investigators have conceptualized an attitude as having three components: a cognitive, an affective, and a behavioral component. The cognitive component of an attitude consists of all our *thoughts* or ideas about the object, or class of objects, in question. The affective component reflects our predisposition to *evaluate* someone or something positively or negatively. (In Chapter 2, we will see that the tendency to categorize other people or situations as good or bad is a very basic one.) The behavioral component of an attitude refers to the individual's tendency to avoid or approach the object; to *behave* in a particular manner toward it.

According to these investigators, when we say that a person has a positive attitude toward President Carter, we might expect to see that attitude reflected in his or her cognitions (the person may believe the President is a decent man and that his proposals are good ones), in the person's emotions (the person may think that anti-Republican cartoons are wildly funny, while anti-Carter cartoons are infuriating), and in the person's behavior (the Carter supporter may attend Democratic fund-raising dinners, while boycotting Republican ones).

Most researchers take it for granted that attitudes really exist. They assume that our "tendencies" and "predispositions" exist somewhere inside the brain (perhaps in a particular pattern of neural connections). They think our attitudes toward President Carter exist even when we are sleeping, or when we're not even thinking about him, or in a situation which would not call for any action toward him.

Is it really necessary to refer to some underlying cognitive organization to predict how individuals will behave in a given situation? Why is it not enough to say that, because individuals behaved in a favorable way toward a person in the past (when we asked them about their attitudes), we predict that they will do the same in the future?

---

2. For a complete list of authors quoted, see the *References* at the end of the book.

Katz and Stotland (1959, p. 428) have argued that the concept of attitude has endured because

> ...the practical need for taking account of behavior does call for some stability and for some identifiable affective–cognitive elements which can be related to social behavior and to social situations. Hence, the concept of attitude is introduced to allow for the fact that cognitive and affective organization can achieve stability and some degree of constancy.

Others might convincingly argue, however, that to treat attitudes as actual entities yields no predictive profit. In fact, they might charge that it promotes confusion concerning the basis on which we are making behavioral predictions. They argue that since an attitude itself cannot be used in the prediction of behavior; we can predict future behavior only from events which we have actually observed.

INTERPERSONAL ATTRACTION: A UNIDIMENSIONAL OR A MULTIDIMENSIONAL VARIABLE?

Most researchers have assumed that attraction is a unidimensional variable (cf. Huston 1974). They assume that attraction and repulsion are mirror images of one another—that the more we like someone, the less we dislike that person. In such a conception of "attraction," one's attraction toward another can vary from extreme attraction to extreme repulsion.

The unidimensional view does not recognize the fact that one's attitude toward another may be extremely complex, that one may both like and dislike another and that one may feel both love and hate for a single individual.

The unidimensional view also fails to recognize the fact that we can feel different *kinds* of attraction for others. On a unidimensional scale of attraction (-10 to $+10$, for example), "respect" for Joe, "gratitude" for Bill, and "admiration" for Harry may all be represented by the same number (say a $+4$).

Thus, the unidimensional view of attraction (which has dominated social psychological attraction research) figures prominently in the lineup of possible culprits for the fact that scientists know little about how we feel about, and react to, those who engender ambivalent feelings in us. The unidimensional view must also bear responsibility for the fact that scientists know little about the kinds of attraction one human may feel for another.

Interpersonal Attraction: Some Operational Definitions

Interpersonal attraction (or interpersonal hostility), then, can be defined as *"an individual's tendency or predisposition to evaluate another person or the symbol of the person in a positive (or negative) way."* Our *conceptual* definition of interpersonal attraction states in general terms what we mean by attraction.

Scientists, however, need both a general conceptual definition of inter-personal attraction and an accompanying precise *Operational definition* of their concept. They need a definition that will allow them to state unequiv-ocally how Person *A's* attraction to Person *B* should be assessed. They need an *operational definition* of attraction, i.e., a definition which consists of the operations or procedures employed in distinguishing the object referred to from others.

Potentially, attraction could be operationally defined in an infinite num-ber of ways. Attraction could be defined as subjects' scores on the *Inter-personal Judgment Scale* of liking (*IJS*), or the frequency with which they have lunch with others, or how wildly the pupils of their eyes dilate when they gaze at others. When scientists choose an operational definition, they are not arbitrarily deciding what attraction *really* means. They are simply settling on a standard operational procedure for defining the term.

How has interpersonal attraction been operationally defined? Have so-cial scientists settled on a single operational measure of attraction—or on several?

Most social scientists insist that interpersonal attraction must be op-erationally defined in a single way. An eloquent spokesman for this position, Donn Byrne (1971, pp. 44–47) states:

> A necessary, though hardly sufficient, condition for progress in research
> is consistency of operations across experiments.... A meaningful and
> cumulative increase in knowledge is possible only if identical or equiva-
> lent operations serve as connecting links across experiments.

Other eminent social scientists staunchly oppose Byrne's point of view. For example, Webb *et al.* (1966) insist that scientists should settle on sev-eral equivalent operational definitions of interpersonal attraction. They ar-gue that one should be less convinced by three experiments demonstrating that "similarity breeds attraction" as measured by the *IJS* than by three ex-periments demonstrating that similarity breeds attraction as measured by the respondent's (1) reaction to the other on the *IJS*, (2) willingness to loan the other money, and (3) pupil size when looking at the other. They argue that any single measure of attraction is bound to be inadequate in some ways. For example, the three operational measures we cited are likely to reflect both the subject's interpersonal attraction and such irrelevant variables as (1) how the respondent thinks he or she should answer the *IJS* in order to make a good impression on the experimenter, (2) how much money he or she has, and (3) whether he or she has just come from a dark movie or a bright beach.

Webb *et al.* (p. 3) say:

> The most persuasive evidence comes through a triangulation of measurement processes. If a proposition can survive the onslaught of a series of imperfect measures, with all their irrelevant error, confidence should be placed in it.

Whether for good or ill, interpersonal attraction has been operationalized in a variety of ways. If social scientists have found it difficult to agree on a Conceptual definition of attraction, they have found it impossible to agree on an Operational one. Let us examine some of the measures that have been used by researchers as indicants of attraction.

Can We Measure Interpersonal Attraction? If So, How?

Elizabeth Barrett Browning could "count the ways" she loved her husband Robert, but the social scientist couldn't and can't. There is no yardstick which allows us to measure the "height and depth and breadth a soul can reach." There is neither calculator nor computer which permits us to quickly and easily quantify one person's statement, "I love you more than I've ever loved anyone," so that we can compare the amount of attraction *it* represents, to the amount underlying another person's shyly spoken, "You're OK."

Although the measurement of attraction is still not quick or easy, it *is* possible. In 1975, one United States Senator made political hay by arguing otherwise. This politician reflected the views of many social scientists of the Victorian era. He denounced the National Science Foundation for encouraging researchers to study love and family relationships. He stated: "No one —not even the National Science Foundation—can argue that falling in love is a science. . . . The impact of love on the heterosexual relationship [is a] very subjective, nonquantifiable subject matter. Love is simply a mystery," he concluded; "it is a waste of time and money to try to study it."

It is odd that the notion that attraction, particularly such intense forms as romantic love, are simply "nonquantifiable" has lingered to the present day. It seems especially strange when we consider that each of us, every day and in a variety of ways, manages to quantify our attraction to others and to measure their attraction for us. Further, we're fairly sophisticated about the measuring devices we construct. The scaling techniques we use to measure attraction, for example, appear to range from simple nominal scaling,

Although the measurement of attraction is not quick or easy, it is possible.

through ordinal scaling, to the more complex interval and ratio scales, just as the social scientists' do.

We use a *nominal scale* when we simply "name," or label, the *kind* of attraction we feel for another. "Like" and "love," for example, are two categories we often use to characterize our attraction for another. Or sometimes a person explains "I *love* Bob, but I'm not *in* love with him;" "love" and "in love" are two separate categories of attraction for the person who takes pains to make this distinction.

In nominal measurement, the numbers we assign to the various categories of attraction (such as "1," "2," or "3") act more as labels than they do as numbers—we cannot order or add the numerical labels we have assigned to the different categories. Nominal measurement requires that we assign the same number to everyone we feel the same way about; all the members of a category must receive the same numeral and no two categories can receive the same number. If we follow these rules of nominal measurement, we know that if two objects do not get the same number, they are not equal; we do not know, however, *how* they are unequal.

We are using *ordinal scaling* whenever we say, "I like Mary more than I like Sue," or "I love George more than George loves me," or whenever we can simply rank people in an order corresponding to the degree to which we feel attracted to them. Ordinal scaling requires that we be able to say that we are attracted to one person "more than" or "less than" another, but we do not have to know how *much* "more than" or "less than."

In *interval scaling*, we do have to answer questions of how much more or less; numerically equal distances on interval scales represent equal distances of the property being measured, such as attraction. Although we probably don't often achieve a true interval scale in our daily life (just as psychologists have difficulty devising true equal-interval scales, as we shall see), we often talk as though we have. Anytime we make such statements as "You laugh at Bill because he loves Sue far more than she loves him . . . but the very same discrepancy exists in your relationship!" we imply that we have rated Bill and Sue's—and you and your partner's . . . attraction on an equal-interval scale.

The highest level of measurement is *ratio scaling*. In addition to possessing the characteristics of nominal, ordinal, and interval scales, a ratio scale has an absolute or natural zero that has true meaning; if an object receives "0" on the scale, then there is a true basis for saying that the object has *none* of the property being measured. Since there is an absolute or natural zero on ratio scales, all arithmetic operations on the numbers objects (including people) receive on the scale are possible, including multiplication and division.

Psychologists almost never are able to devise ratio scales. But we in our daily lives, in the case of our quantification of attraction, speak as though we do. We make such statements as "If you only loved me half as much as I love you" or "Bill loves Barbara twice as much as he loves her."

"No, I am not interested in knowing how you would rate me on a scale of one to ten."

Drawing by Saxon; © 1976. The New Yorker Magazine.

So the quantification of interpersonal attraction not only is *not* "impossible" but it is an operation routinely performed on a daily basis by most everyone. Further, it is a procedure on which people will, on occasion, expend great effort. The following dialogue illustrates the fancy footwork we untrained psychometricians can perform when we are motivated to do so. It can be heard, with some variation, almost anywhere, but especially between couples whose relationship is developing in intensity:

NOMINAL SCALING ⌐ Do you love me?
What category? ⌐ Yes.

⌐ How much?
  Lots.
  How much is 'lots'?
  More than anyone else.
  More than anyone right now?
ORDINAL SCALING   Yes.
More or less   More than anyone ever?
than whom?   No.
  More than you loved Jane?
  Well, no.
  Equally?
└ I think so.

⌐ Well, how much do you love me and did you love Jane?
  It's hard to say.
REACHING FOR   Well, if you had to put it on a −10 to +10 scale, how much do you love me?
INTERVAL AND   What's −10?
RATIO SCALING   You would hate me as much as you could hate anyone?
How much more   What's +10?
or less than?   You'd love me as much as you could love anyone?

FINDING THE MEAN ⊏ I guess I love you +8.

⌐ Do you always love me +8?
  No.
FINDING THE RANGE   What is the least you sometimes love me?
└ −4.

FINDING THE ⌐ How often do you feel that way about me?
STANDARD   Only when you ridicule my intelligence;
DEVIATION └ not very often.

Measures of Attraction

Investigators have devised a number of measures as indexes of the attraction, or the positiveness of the attitude, one person has toward another.

SELF-REPORT MEASURES

Sometimes the simplest, and best, way to find out how a person feels about another is simply to ask him or her. This is one reason why two self-report measures, the *Interpersonal Judgment Scale* and the *Likert* scales, are the most commonly used attraction measures.

The Interpersonal Judgment Scale

The *Interpersonal Judgment Scale* (*IJS*) was developed by Donn Byrne (1971). The *IJS* is comprised of six items. Respondents (usually college students) are asked to estimate another's (1) intelligence, (2) knowledge of current events, (3) morality, and (4) adjustment. They are also asked to indicate (5) their personal feelings of liking or disliking the other, and (6) their feelings about working with him or her in an experiment. It is these last two items which constitute Byrne's measure of attraction:

Personal Feelings (*check one*):

_____ I feel that I would probably like this person very much.
_____ I feel that I would probably like this person.
_____ I feel that I would probably like this person to a slight degree.
_____ I feel that I would probably neither particularly like nor particularly dislike this person.
_____ I feel that I would probably dislike this person to a slight degree.
_____ I feel that I would probably dislike this person.
_____ I feel that I would probably dislike this person very much.

Working Together on an Experiment (*check one*):

_____ I believe that I would very much dislike working with this person in an experiment.
_____ I believe that I would dislike working with this person in an experiment.
_____ I believe that I would dislike working with this person in an experiment to a slight degree.
_____ I believe that I would neither particularly dislike nor particularly enjoy working with this person in an experiment.
_____ I believe that I would enjoy working with this person in an experiment to a slight degree.

———— I believe that I would enjoy working with this person in an experiment.

———— I believe that I would very much enjoy working with this person in an experiment.

Byrne has also developed a version of the *IJS* which attempts to measure romantic attraction. On this extended scale, questions 7 through 10 ask respondents to estimate: (7) How much they would like to date the other person; (8) How much they think they would like the other person as a spouse; (9) How sexually attractive the other person seems to them; and (10) How physically attractive the person is.

The Likert Scales

Perhaps the most popular way to measure attraction is to use a Likert scale. Rensis Likert (1932) proposed a simple procedure for measuring attitudes. The respondent is shown a series of statements, and he is simply asked to indicate the extent to which he agrees with each item. Likert scales have been frequently used to assess such variables as racial and sexual prejudice toward others. Several studies, for example, have assessed whites' attitudes toward blacks by asking them to react to statements such as this:

> Where there is segregation, the black section should have the same equipment in paving, water, and electric-light facilities as are found in the white districts.

(5)	(4)	(3)	(2)	(1)
Strongly approve	Approve	Undecided	Disapprove	Strongly disapprove

A person's attitude score is the sum of his or her individual ratings. (In the example above, the lower a person's score, the more prejudiced against blacks the person would be said to be.)

A number of researchers have developed Likert scales of attraction. Rubin (1970), for example, used a variation of the classical Likert scale to measure liking and love.

Liking Scale

1 I think that ———— is unusually well adjusted.

2 I would highly recommend ———— for a responsible job.

3 In my opinion, ———— is an exceptionally mature person.

4 I have great confidence in ————'s good judgment.

5 Most people would react favorably to ———— after a brief acquaintance.

6 —————————— is one of the most likable people I know.

7 —————————— is the sort of person whom I myself would like to be.

8 It seems to me that it is very easy for —————————— to gain admiration.

Love Scale

1 I feel that I can confide in —————————— about virtually everything.

2 I would do almost anything for ——————————.

3 If I could never be with ——————————, I would feel miserable.

4 If I were lonely, my first thought would be to seek —————————— out.

5 One of my primary concerns is ——————————'s welfare.

6 I would forgive —————————— for practically anything.

7 I feel responsible for ——————————'s well-being.

8 I would greatly enjoy being confided in by ——————————.

9 It would be hard for me to get along without ——————————.

Respondents were asked to consider each item and then to indicate how they felt about the other (a friend vs. a fiancée) on the following scale:

(1)	(5)	(9)
Not at all true; disagree completely	Moderately true; agree to some extent	Definitely true; agree completely

Rubin (1973) found that a couple's score on the *Love Scale* was a good predictor of their subsequent behavior toward each other. "Strong" love couples (as indicated by high scores on the Love Scale), seemed to act more like lovers that did "Weak" love couples. Rubin invited dating couples (who had previously completed the Love Scale) to participate in an experiment. While they were just sitting around waiting for the experiment to begin, Rubin (unknown to the couples) carefully recorded how much time they spent gazing into one another's eyes. As the poets would predict, "Strong" love couples spent significantly more time gazing at each other than did the "Weak" love couples.

Couples' scores on the *Love Scale* also helped predict what later happened to each couple. Six months after they had filled out the *Liking* and the *Love Scales*, Rubin began to wonder what changes, if any, had occurred in the couples' relationships. Which couples were still together? Which had broken up? Which couples' relationships had become more, or less, intense?

Rubin speculated that for many couples, simply being "in love" is reason enough to keep a relationship going. (Such Romantics, as Rubin labeled them, tend to strongly believe that "A person should marry whomever he or she loves regardless of social position" and "As long as they at least love one another, two people should have no difficulty getting together at marriage." Romantics tend to disagree with such statements as "Economic security should be carefully considered before selecting a marriage partner" and "One should not marry against the serious advice of one's parents.") Nonromantics are more practical. They insist that such factors as socioeconomic similarity, personality similarity, and economic security are critical, too.

Rubin predicted that when both partners were Romantics, their *Love* scores should be good predictors of their courtship progress. And they were. The correlations between their score on *Love Scale* and courtship progress was about 0.41 for women and 0.52 for men. When both partners were Nonromantics, however, there was no correlation between the couple's Love scores and whether their relationship had grown more intense, withered, or had simply maintained the status quo.

Although the *IJS* and Likert scales are the most popular ways to measure attraction, other self-report measures are occasionally used. We will briefly review some of these measures.

Guttman's Method of Ordinal Scaling

In 1925, Bogardus developed a scale to measure feelings of "social distance," or "the closeness of the relationship to which a respondent is willing to admit members of various social groups." The Bogardus scale contained seven items, reflecting seven degrees of closeness of the relationship the respondent would permit another, or group of others, to have with him or her. These were:

1 To close kinship by marriage
2 To my club as personal chums
3 To my street as neighbors
4 To employment in my occupation in my country
5 To citizenship in my country
6 As visitors only to my country
7 Would exclude from my country

Bogardus assumed that the items in this scale were ordered as steps along a continuum; that anyone who agreed that "South Vietnamese should be allowed to live on my street as neighbors" (Item 3) would surely be willing to allow them to work in America (Item 4), to become American citizens (Item 5), and would not exclude them from the country, but would allow them to visit America as well (Items 6 and 7).

The Bogardus Social Distance Scale had a unique characteristic. If one knows an individual's "score" on this scale, one can tell precisely how he or she responded to *each individual item*. If one knows an individual obtained a score of "4," one can be virtually certain that he or she did *not* endorse Items 1, 2, or 3, but did endorse Items 4, 5, 6, and 7. (On the other scales, of course, a score of "4" does not reveal *which* items produced that score.) A scale possessing this property is often labeled a *Guttman* scale, in honor of Louis Guttman (1944), a pioneer in the development of scaling techniques.

Using the Social Distance Scale he had devised, Bogardus asked both young businesspersons and public school teachers to indicate "In how many groupings in our country may the members of any race, as a class, be admitted?" It is interesting to note how few opportunities for social contact many groups were perceived as possessing in 1925. From Fig. 1.1 for example, it is evident that in 1925 there was general agreement that an Englishman or a Canadian was much more "socially acceptable" than an Armenian or a Chinese, Negro, Japanese, or Turk.[3]

Ethnic groups	1 To close kinship	2 To club as "chums"	3 To street as neighbors	4 To employment in my occupation	5 To citizenship	6 As visitors only
Armenians						
Bulgarians						
Canadians						
Chinese						
Czechoslovaks						
Danes						
English						
French						
Germans						
Negroes						
Japanese						
Turks						

Fig. 1.1 The reactions of a sample of Americans to selected ethnic groups in 1925. The light area indicates the social distance before contacts are permitted to the given ethnic group. The dark bars denote range of social contacts that were permitted each ethnic group. (From Bogardus 1925.)

3.   E. S. Bogardus, 1925. Measuring social distance. *Journal of Applied Sociology* 9:299–300.

Thurstone's Method of Equal-Appearing Intervals

As the reader will recognize, the Bogardus scale is an *ordinal* scale; it allows us to put respondents in order, from those who are "most accepting" of the person or social group in question to those who are "least accepting." If we use the Bogardus scale, we know that if Joe's score is higher than Tom's, Joe has a more favorable attitude than Tom does. But how *much* more favorable is Joe than Tom? We don't know. We don't know because we have no information about the distance that exists between the items; we don't know precisely how much psychological closeness each item reflects. And, on the Social Distance Scale, it looks as though some adjacent items are closer to each other, in the amount of psychological closeness they represent, than are others. For example, Items 1 and 2 ("I would admit _____ to close kinship" and "I would admit _____ to my club as personal chums") both seem to reflect fairly similar (and extremely high) levels of acceptance. On the other hand, Statements 3 and 4 ("I would admit _____ to my street as neighbors" and "I would admit _____ to employment in my occupation in my country") seem to reflect markedly different levels of acceptance.

Thurstone (1928) was convinced that he could develop a technique to scale attitudes that would be more precise than the Bogardus "Guttman" scale. He argued that it ought to be possible to construct scales in which the distances between adjacent attitude items were roughly equal. If such *equal-interval* scales could be constructed, of course, they would give the investigator a good deal more information about a person's attitude than would an ordinal scale.

Thurstone proposed a procedure for constructing such equal interval scales. First, Thurstone said, the researcher must collect many statement items that seem, at least intuitively, to be related to the attitude he wants to measure. Suppose, for example, the researcher wants to measure "Liking for Gloria" (or for people over 30, or college students, or one's wife or husband). Some items that seem, at least on the face of it, to be relevant to attraction for Gloria are:

1 Gloria can't be trusted.
2 Gloria is no better or no worse than anyone else.
3 Gloria is the kind of person who can get along extremely well with anyone.
4 To know Gloria is to love her.

The next step, according to Thurstone, is to print these attitude statements on small cards and to find some people who are willing to act as judges of the statements. Each judge is asked to sort the cards into 11 evenly spaced piles, ranging from (1) those statements which the judge considers to be most strongly favorable toward Gloria, to (11) those the judge believes are most strongly negative.

After the judges have sorted the statements, the researcher must choose 20 or so of the "best" statements. The best items for the "Liking for Gloria" scale will be those statements which all (or most) judges agree reflect a given degree of favorableness to Gloria; if some judges believe an item is very favorable to Gloria, and others believe it is unfavorable, and still other judges think it is neutral, it will be discarded as a possible item for the final scale. Finally, to construct an equal-appearing interval scale, the researcher must select from the items remaining, a group of statements which are evenly graduated along the dimension of favorableness to Gloria. Having chosen this group of statements, the researcher has a Thurstone Scale of "Liking for Gloria."

The "Liking for Gloria" scale is then simply presented to respondents who are asked to indicate whether they "Agree" or "Disagree" with each of the attitude statements. The more favorable the statements a person is willing to endorse, the higher his "Liking for Gloria" score. We also know that there are equal distances (or intervals) between adjacent items on the scale. This means that if Bob scores 15, Joe scores 10, and Tom scores 5, we know that Bob's liking for Gloria exceeds Joe's to exactly the same extent (+5 units) as Joe's liking for her exceeds Tom's (+5 units).

Evaluation of Self-Report Measures

Investigators who used Thurstone and Guttman scaling techniques believed that these scales would give them more information about a person's attitude than would the simpler Likert scale. Research evidence has somewhat dampened researchers' enthusiasm for Thurstone and Guttman scales over the years. To test the advantages of the Thurstone scale over the Likert scale, Edwards and Kinney (1946) used both techniques to measure the same attitude. Even though the Thurstone scale took twice as much time to construct, the Likert scale was found to be "better" in that it possessed higher reliability. Even more disappointing for advocates of the Thurstone scale was the finding that scores on the two scales were highly correlated (.92); this meant that even though the Thurstone scale took longer to construct, the Thurstone and the Likert scales seem to make equally good predictions. (More recently, Nunnally [1967] has provided still another important reason for measuring attitudes with a Likert scale rather than a Thurstone or Guttman scale; for methodological and statistical reasons too complex to discuss here, it is easier to write items for a Likert scale than for a Thurstone or Guttman scale.) Given the advantages of the Likert scaling technique, the student of attraction is unlikely to encounter either a Thurstone or Guttman scale in modern attraction research.

Other Measures

A variety of other scaling techniques have been developed, such as Osgood's (1957) "Semantic Differential," Coombs's (1950) "Ordered Metric," Lazarsfeld's (1959) "Latent Structure Analysis," or Sherif's *et al.* (1956) "Own Categories" scaling procedures. Since we will not discuss these measures here, students who are interested in learning more about such techniques should consult Fishbein (1967).

UNOBTRUSIVE MEASURES

Although researchers usually assess attraction for another via self-report questionnaires, they have occasionally used a variety of other methods. Some of these techniques for measuring attraction are very subtle.

The investigators who have developed these measures believe that the researcher should use indexes of attitude which can be collected more unobtrusively than can questionnaire measures. There are a variety of arguments which can be advanced for the justification of such measures. To name just one, when persons are forced to consider what their own attitudes are, their introspection may cause them to change their attitude in the process of describing it. Webb, Campbell, Schwartz, and Sechrest (1966), in their valuable and delightful book, discuss several indirect ways of measuring a person's attraction for another.

Tests of Opinion Disguised as Tests of Facts

Sometimes what a person assumes to be the "facts of the matter" about another person tells us more about *him* or *her* (and his or her attitude), than it tells us about the other person. For example, staunch opponents of the Equal Rights Amendment are more likely to subscribe to the *National Review* (which opposes ERA) than to subscribe to *Ms.* and other magazines (which support passage of the ERA). One result of such "selective exposure" is that opponents of ERA are likely to possess an abundance of anti-ERA information—and a paucity of factual information which outlines the favorable consequences of passage of the ERA. Even if an ERA opponent *were* confronted with pro-ERA facts, he or she would be likely to forget or to distort them. (The same selective exposure to facts and selective remembering of facts operates in all groups, of course; pro-ERA persons would also be expected to forget or distort information unfavorable to their position.)

The notion that one tends to forget "unpleasant" facts has been supported by Edwards (1941), Levine and Murphy (1943), Taft (1954), Watson and Hartman (1939), and Weiss (1953).

One way, then, to find out whether a person has a pro-ERA or anti-ERA attitude is to ask him or her to recite the facts of the matter. It is usually easy to guess the person's attitude if we find out what he or she knows—and does not know—about the issue.

Some experimenters have taken advantage of this correlation between factual information and positiveness of attitudes as an indirect way of measuring attitudes (Loeblowitz-Lennard and Riessman 1946; Newcomb 1946; Parrish 1948; Hammond 1948; and Cattell *et al.* 1950). By the "error-choice" technique, Hammond, for example, measured attitudes toward labor and management. The respondent was requested to choose between two alternative answers, each of which was equally wrong, but wrong in opposite directions from the correct answer. One erroneous answer favored labor, the other management. The direction a person's errors took revealed the side he or she favored.

Eye-contact

When two people are engaged in conversation, they look one another in the eye intermittently and for short periods. Argyle (1967) found that the amount of time individuals look at one another varies from 30 percent to 60 percent. One determinant of how long individuals engage in mutual eye-contact appears to be interpersonal attraction. People who like each other tend to look one another in the eye more than do people who feel cooler toward one another. (See Argyle 1967; Exline, 1971; and Rubin, 1970.)

One's "Inclination" toward Another

Galton (1884) was intrigued by the idea that one could assess another's character and personality without the other ever realizing that he or she was being scrutinized. Galton was able to conceive of an amazing array of devices for invading others' privacy without their knowing it. Fortunately for his potential victims, however, he never had time to carry out his luxuriant schemes. Here is how he proposed to measure a couple's attraction for another (p. 184):

> The poetical metaphors of ordinary language suggest many possibilities of measurement. Thus when two persons have an "inclination" to one another, they visibly incline or slope together when sitting side by side, as at a dinner table, and they then throw the stress of their weights on the near legs of their chairs. It does not require much ingenuity to arrange

a pressure gauge with an index and dial to indicate changes in stress, but it is difficult to devise an arrangement that shall fulfill the three-fold condition of being effective, not attracting notice, and being applicable to ordinary furniture. I made some rude experiments, but being busy with other matters, have not carried them on, as I had hoped.

Research by Mehrabian (1968) supports Galton's contention that posture is a "tipoff" to our feelings—we tend to lean toward someone we like and away from someone we dislike.

The Distance One Stands from Another

Members of different nationalities habitually stand different distances apart from one another when conversing (cf. Hall 1968). South Americans, for example, normally stand much closer together when talking with each other than do Americans. How far away from another it seems "correct" to stand is an unconscious social norm; adjustment to the proper distance is made automatically by the participants. When members of different cultural groups get together to talk, the unconscious norm concerning how far apart individuals should stand sometimes becomes a source of awkwardness. In a mixed group of North Americans and South Americans, for example, the South American is likely to keep moving forward to attain the "proper" speaking distance while the American keeps backing up to attain a more comfortable distance. On one occasion, we observed a South American colleague moving forward as he conversed, while his American counterpart moved steadily backward, down the entire length of a corridor. The Ameri-

"Thus when two people have an 'inclination' to one another, they visibly incline or slope together when sitting side by side, as at a dinner table...."

can finally ended up pinned against a file cabinet at the end of the corridor, while the South American had finally attained the speaking distance that was comfortable for him.

Byrne, Ervin, and Lamberth (1970) demonstrated that the distance one stands from another can serve as a useful index of interpersonal attraction. They introduced men and women students to each other and sent each couple out on a 30-minute "blind" coke date. When the couples reported back to the psychologist's desk after their date, he unobtrusively recorded how close to one another they were standing. Their distance from one another was scored on an ordinal scale ranging from 0 (touching one another) to 5 (standing at opposite extremes of the desk). Byrne found that the couple's liking for one another, as measured by the *Interpersonal Judgment Scale*, correlated −0.36 (females) and −0.48 (males) with the physical distance measure; the more the couple liked one another, the closer they stood.

Goldberg, Kiesler, and Collins (1969) and Allgeier and Byrne (1973) have also found proximity to be a useful indicant of liking.

Favor-doing

Other indirect measures of interpersonal attraction that have been used include the extent to which persons will exert themselves to provide benefits for another. Bramel (1969) has observed that:

> If we truly like someone, it pleases us to see him happy and hurts us to see him suffer. If we dislike him, our reaction is just the opposite. If this is so, then the person should be expected to give to those he likes the things he believes they want, and those he dislikes the things he believes they do not want.

Sociometric Choices

It is generally, and most times reasonably, assumed that the more we like someone, the more eager we will be to associate with that person. Thus one's choices as to whom one wishes to spend time with have been used as measures of liking. A sociometric test is a means of obtaining quantitative data on the preferences of group members for associating with other members (cf. Moreno 1934). In this test, an individual may be asked to choose whom the individual wants most (or least) as a roommate or as a partner.

Summary

In this chapter we posed two basic questions: (1) What is interpersonal attraction? (2) How can we measure it?

We defined interpersonal attraction (or interpersonal hostility) as "an individual's tendency or predisposition to evaluate another person or symbol of that person in a positive (or negative) way."

It was relatively easy to settle on a conceptual definition of interpersonal attraction. To decide on an operational definition was harder. Byrne has argued eloquently that interpersonal attraction *must* be defined (operationally) in a single way. Other eminent social psychologists, such as Webb *et al.*, have argued that scientists should devise several equivalent operational definitions of interpersonal attraction. For good or ill, interpersonal attraction has been operationalized in a variety of ways.

What is the best way to measure attraction? We began our discussion by pointing out that several types of scales exist. These range from simple nominal scales, to ordinal scales, to the more sophisticated interval, and ratio scales.

Then we examined the various techniques social psychologists have used to tap interpersonal attraction. They've used such Self-Report measures as the *Interpersonal Judgment Scale* and the Likert scales. They've developed Guttman scales and Thurstone scales. They've also developed a variety of unobtrusive measures for measuring interpersonal attraction. At some time, disguised tests of opinion, eye contact, one's inclination to others, the distance one stands from others, favor-doing, and sociometric choices have all been used to measure attraction.

Introduction

When we're asked *why* we like Joe and why we think Richard is repulsive, we usually have no trouble coming up with an answer. In fact, the readiness with which we can expound on the whys and wherefores of our likes and dislikes suggests that each of us is confident that *we* know why

reward theories of interpersonal attraction:
an overview

we like or dislike others. This suggests that all social scientists would have to do in order to identify the causal determinants of attraction is to follow people around with their tape recorders, pressing the "On" button every time they hear "I love Harriet because. . . ."

If social scientists did, they would probably find when they got back to the laboratory and transcribed their tape recordings that they had obtained a superbly comprehensive collection of all the favorable (and unfavorable) human attributes listed in Webster's dictionary.

For when we are asked why we like Joe so much, we usually answer—"Because Joe is kind and considerate, intelligent and articulate, and also friendly, sincere, and honest, and, besides, he has a terrific sense of humor, an engaging smile, and an endearing cowlick on the back of his head." Similarly, when we are asked why we don't like Jim, we generally itemize the person's "bad qualities"—his dishonesty, or aloofness, or thoughtlessness, or even the shifty ways he clears his throat and parts his hair.

On the pages to follow, we shall see that what our explanations leave out—and what social psychologists have found to be the most important factor of all in the prediction of attraction—is ourselves. In interpersonal attraction, the characteristics of the eye of the beholder must be taken into consideration along with the characteristics of the person beheld; one must refer to the qualities of the *attracted* as well as to the qualities of the *at-*

tractor if we are to understand why a person is "turned on" or "turned off" by another.

The Foundations of Interpersonal Attraction

Probably the most basic of human tendencies is to evaluate things. It's easy to see why this is so. Primitive people had to be "wired up" to categorize the people and things around them as "good" or "bad," as "safe" or "dangerous." They had to be "wired up" to approach the former and to shy away from—or attack—the latter. Otherwise, they wouldn't have been around for long.

Even today, humans are basically evaluators. This pervasive tendency is reflected in their languages. For example, in a cross-cultural study of the world's languages, Triandis and Osgood (1958) conclude that virtually all words in all languages are strongly evaluative. Our own language is similarly evaluative. Most of the 18,000 English adjectives we use to describe each other are either complimentary or insulting. Humans are invariably concerned about whether the things around them are rewarding or punishing.

The general psychological principle which threads throughout virtually all theories of interpersonal attraction is the principle of *reinforcement:* we like those who reward us; we dislike those who punish us.

THE BYRNE-CLORE REINFORCEMENT-AFFECT MODEL

Byrne and Clore (1970) and Lott and Lott (1974) have proposed the most elegant Reinforcement models of interpersonal attraction.

Essentially, their theories propose that our interpersonal likes and dislikes are based on the feelings we associate with other individuals. Baron and Byrne (1976, p. 204) continue:

> To take an obvious example, if a stranger were to walk up to you on the street and give you a swift kick in the shins, negative feelings would be aroused. If you were asked to evaluate the experience, you would say that you didn't like getting kicked and didn't like the person who kicked you. It may be less obvious, but your negative feelings would also be likely to extend to any innocent bystander who happened to be there, to the street where the kicking took place, and to anything else that was associated with the unpleasant interaction. In an analogous way, if on the following day, another passing stranger gave you a year's supply of free movie passes, your feelings would be positive and you would probably express liking toward your surroundings.

MISS PEACH

Courtesy of Mell Lazarus and Field Newspaper Syndicate.

In their recent *Social Psychology* text (1976, p. 204), Baron and Byrne succinctly summarize the Byrne-Clore Reinforcement model's basic principles:

1 Most stimuli to which we are exposed can be identified as either rewarding or punishing. We tend to approach rewarding stimuli such as ice cream or praise or free tickets to the movie; we learn to behave in such a way as to obtain these rewards. We try to avoid coming in contact with punishing stimuli such as electric shock or criticism or a kick in the shins; we learn to behave in such a way as to keep our punishments at a minimum.

2 Rewarding stimuli arouse positive feelings while punishing stimuli arouse negative feelings. These feelings, or affective responses, are believed to fall along a continuum from extremely positive to extremely negative.

3 The evaluation of any given stimulus as good or bad, enjoyable or unenjoyable, depends on whether it arouses positive or negative feelings. The strength of the aroused affect is reflected in how positively or negatively we express our evaluations. The result is that we can order our likes and dislikes along a rough scale. For example, you may like chocolate ice cream better than vanilla, you probably like both of them better than turnip soup, and you dislike having your dentist drill a hole in one of your teeth more than you dislike turnips.

4 Through the process of simple conditioning, any neutral stimulus that is associated with a reward or with a punishment will acquire the capacity to arouse positive or negative feelings, respectively, and therefore will be liked or disliked as a consequence. If the neutral stimulus is a person, he or she will be liked if associated with rewards and disliked if associated with punishments.

In short, we like people who reward us and we dislike people who punish us.

In *The Attraction Paradigm*, Byrne (1971) provides an encyclopedic review of evidence in support of these propositions.

Lott and Lott (1974) have also used the general reinforcement principle to predict who will be attracted to whom. They, too, propose that we grow to like not only those people who directly provide us with rewards in our interaction with them, but we also develop affection for people who are *associated* (even simply by chance) with our experience of reward. They observe, for example, that when we are spending a relaxing evening before the fire, perhaps listening to beautiful music and drinking a fine wine, we often feel special affection for the people who are around us at that time, even if they did not provide us with the rewards of the fire, music, and wine and thus are in no way "responsible" for our pleasure.

In one of their experiments to test whether or not we tend to be attracted to people who just happen to be present at the time we receive a reward, Lott and Lott (1961) formed three-member groups of children who played a game. In the game, some children were rewarded and others were not. Sociometric tests were administered to the children after they had played the game. Each child was asked which two children in the class he or she would choose to take along on the next family vacation.

Lott and Lott found that children who had been rewarded chose members of their three-person groups (who had been present at the time of reward) significantly more often than unrewarded children chose members of *their* groups. Thus, Lott and Lott concluded that the reward which some children had received had become conditioned to the other members of the child's group and this led to increased attraction to these members. The general finding of this study—that reward may increase the attractiveness of previously neutral persons who are simply associated with that reward— has been corroborated by many subsequent studies.

Attraction vs. Commitment

Thibaut and Kelley (1959) point out that liking someone and being committed to someone are two different things. A college beauty may like a fellow a lot, and delight in his company . . . but not enough. She would never consider marrying him. The battered wife may hate her brutal husband, and be totally miserable . . . but not enough. She fears that she and the children would suffer from loneliness, hunger, and poverty if she left.

Thibaut and Kelley argue that we can predict how *satisfied* a person is likely to be with his relationship with us, if we know two things: (1) first, we must find out how much profit he is reaping from interacting with us; (2) second, we need to know how well his profits stack up against the profits he "expects" to get from such relationships; or, as Thibaut and Kelley (pp. 81–82) put it, we need to know the person's *Comparison Level (CL)*.

A person's *CL*, according to Thibaut and Kelley, is:

> ... some modal or average value of all the outcomes known to the person (by virtue of personal or vicarious experience), each outcome weighted by its salience (or the degree to which it is instigated for the person at the moment). A person's *CL* depends not only upon outcomes which he has experienced or seen others experiencing but also upon which of these are actively stimulating to him—are obtruded on him, are vivid and perhaps implicitly rehearsed as he makes an evaluation of his circumstances.

According to these theorists (p. 81), then, how much a person will be attracted to another depends upon whether the outcomes obtained from the other are above or below his or her *CL*:

> If the outcomes in a given relationship surpass the *CL*, that relationship is regarded as a satisfactory one. And, to the degree the outcomes are supra-*CL*, the person may be said to be attracted to the relationship. If the outcomes endured are infra-*CL*, the person is dissatisfied and unhappy with the relationship.

Thibaut and Kelley make a distinction between our liking for another and our commitment to the other. According to Thibaut and Kelley, whether or not people choose to remain in a relationship depends on their *Comparison Level for Alternatives* (or *CL*$_{alt}$). A person's *CL*$_{alt}$ presumably acts as a standard against which a person evaluates whether or not he or she wishes to remain in a relationship with another. It is defined (pp. 21–22) as:

> ... the lowest level of outcomes a member will accept in the light of available opportunities. ... The height of the *CL*$_{alt}$ will depend mainly on the quality of the best of the member's available alternatives, that is, the reward–cost positions experienced or believed to exist in the most satisfactory of the other available relationships.

Thus an individual may abandon a fairly satisfactory relationship simply because a better one comes along. Similarly, even though a person is not attracted to the other (his or her outcomes are below the *CL*), the person may continue to interact with the other simply because nothing better is available (the outcomes he or she obtains in the relationship are above the *CL*$_{alt}$).

In drawing a distinction between a person's happiness with a relationship with another and a person's tendency to maintain that relationship, Thibaut and Kelley provide us with a warning that "attraction" and "association" are not synonymous. This is why the extent to which one spends time with another is an imperfect measure of interpersonal attraction.

While it is generally accepted that "we like those who reward us and dislike those who punish us," this principle isn't very useful when we want to predict who will be attracted to whom. We have no equation which will permit us to add up all the rewards a person is likely to provide, balance them against the punishments which a person is likely to inflict, and thus arrive at a total reward index, which will tell us how much others will like him or her. An individual may find a multitude of things to be rewarding or punishing at any given time. In addition, it is often the case that "one man's meat is another man's poison"; individuals differ in what they find to be rewarding or punishing. And to make prediction even more difficult, what persons find rewarding at one time, they may find punishing at another.

Since it is so difficult to calculate what one individual at one specific point in time will find rewarding or punishing, interpersonal attraction researchers have not even tried to make individual attraction predictions. Rather they have settled on a more realistic goal: to learn which behaviors and events most people, most of the time, find rewarding. By considering some of the specific behaviors that people find rewarding or punishing in a number of different situations—behaviors which appear to be "transsituational reinforcers"—they have won some predictive insight into interpersonal attraction.

Summary

The psychological principle which threads throughout all theories of interpersonal attraction is the principle of reinforcement: we like those who reward us and we dislike those who punish us. The Byrne-Clore Reinforcement paradigm is one of the most elegant Reinforcement models and their theoretical framework has been supported by a great deal of empirical research. Their research, and the research of Lott and Lott, documents that

WINTHROP   **by Dick Cavalli**

Reprinted by permission of Newspaper Enterprise Association.

we like not only those who reward us, but even those who merely happen to be *associated* with reward; we dislike not only those who punish us, but even those who merely happen to be *associated* with punishment.

Thibaut and Kelley point out that liking for another—and commitment to that other are two different things. A person's Comparison Level (*CL*) determines how content he or she is with a relationship. His or her CL_{alt} determines how committed he or she is to it.

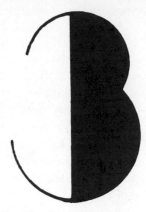

Proximity and Attraction

rewards and punishments others provide:
proximity

Sheer proximity has a strong influence on one's friendship choices. The closer two individuals are located geographically, the more likely it is that they will be attracted to each other. Studies demonstrating the positive relationship between proximity and friendship are so numerous that we will mention only a few.

Several investigators have collected data which indicate that students tend to develop stronger friendships with those students who share their classes, or their dormitory or apartment building, or who sit near them, than with those who are geographically located only slightly farther away (Maisonneuve, Palmade, and Fourment 1952; Willerman and Swanson 1952; Byrne and Buehler 1955; Byrne 1961a, Nahemow and Lawton 1975). Clerks in large department stores and members of a bomber crew have been found to develop closer relations with those who happen to work next to them than with co-workers a few feet away (Gullahorn 1952; Kipnis 1957; Zander and Havelin 1960).

For example, Segal (1974) looked into Maryland State Police trainees' friendship choices, in the hope of finding out which are the most important factors in determining who makes friends with whom. Segal found that "mere" proximity had a stronger effect on attraction than did a host of other characteristics we commonly assume are associated with attraction. Segal (1974) found that the closer together in the alphabet the first letters of the surnames of any two trainees were, the more likely it was that they would name each other as being one of their closest friends on the force. (Since trainees were assigned to seats in classrooms and to rooms on the basis of the alphabetical order of their last names, proximity in the alphabet was a good index of actual proximity of the men.) Segal found that proximity was a better predictor of friendship among the trainees than their similarity of religion, age, marital status, ethnic background, parents' education, organizational memberships, and even leisure activity preferences. See Fig. 3.1.

One of the most interesting studies of the relationship between proximity and friendship choice was conducted by Festinger, Schachter, and Back (1950). These investigators examined the development of friendships in a new housing project for married students. The housing development studied consisted of small houses arranged in U-shaped courts, such that all except the end houses faced onto a grassy area. The two end houses in each court faced onto the street. Festinger (1951) arrived at the intriguing con-

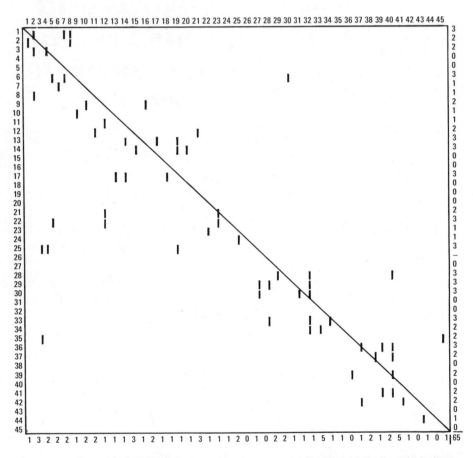

Fig. 3.1 Matrix of friendship choices. Numbers across the top of the matrix indicate place in alphabetic order of *chosen*. Numbers down the left of the matrix indicate place in alphabetic order of *chooser*. (From Mady W. Segal, 1974, *Journal of Personality and Social Psychology* 30: 654–657.)

clusion that to a great extent architects can determine the social life of the residents of their projects. Acording to Festinger (1950, pp. 156–157):

> It is a fair summary to say that the two major factors affecting the friendships which developed were (1) sheer distance between houses and (2) the direction in which a house faced. Friendships developed more frequently between next-door neighbors, less frequently between people whose houses were separated by another house, and so on. As the distance between houses increased, the number of friendships fell off so rapidly that it was rare to find a friendship between persons who lived in houses that were separated by more than four or five other houses. . . . There were instances in which the site plan of the project had more profound effects than merely to determine with whom one associated. Indeed, on occasion the arrangements of the houses severely limited the social life of their occupants. . . . In order to have the street appear "lived on," ten of the houses near the street had been turned so that they faced the street rather than the court area as did the other houses. This apparently small change in the direction in which a house faced had a considerable effect on the lives of the people who, by accident, happened to occupy these end houses. They had less than half as many friends in the project as did those whose houses faced the court area. The consistency of this finding left no doubt that the turning of these houses toward the street had made involuntary social isolates out of the persons who lived in them. . . .

There were still other architectural features which were found by Festinger, Schachter, and Back to have important effects on the social life of the residents. Any architectural feature which brought individuals into proximity with other residents tended to increase their popularity. It was found, for example, that residents whose apartments were located near the entrances and exits of the stairways had more friends than other residents. Similarly, residents whose apartments were located near the mail boxes had more active social lives than did the other residents.

Proximity has also been found to be an important factor in mate selection. A dozen studies have demonstrated that the closer eligible men and women live, the more likely they are to meet and to marry. For example, Clarke (1952) found that more than half of the persons who marry in Columbus, Ohio, live within 16 blocks of one another at the time of their first date together. In 1932, Bossard examined 5000 Philadelphia marriage licenses. He found that 12 percent of the couples were already living at the same address at the time they applied for their license; one-third of them lived within five or fewer blocks of each other. As the distance between the residences of the engaged couples increased, the percentage of marriages decreased steadily and markedly. Corroboration of the importance of propinquity in mate selection comes from Abrams (1943), Kennedy (1943), and Katz and Hill (1958).

Summarizing these studies, Kephart (1961, p. 269) says:

> Cherished notions about romantic love notwithstanding, it appears that when all is said and done, the "one and only" may have a better than 50–50 chance of living within walking distance!

The results of the preceding studies have a number of implications. For some reason, we tend to forget how closely proximity and popularity are linked. You would think that it would be "obvious" to everyone that people who exist in virtual social isolation are going to have trouble making friends, while people who place themselves in the path of other people are likely to be far more popular. It is not. If it were, perhaps people would not be so quick to attribute their unpopularity and loneliness to "deficient personality," "poor social skills," "shyness," and any number of other negative personal characteristics. Perhaps, too, "Dear Abby" would not receive so many worried queries from lonely grade school teachers (who look out over a sea of five-year-old faces), forest rangers (situated in the middle of several thousand vacant acres), or from others, who have not yet realized that one side effect of their choice of occupation, residence, or avocation may be social loneliness.

© 1976 JF.

Many of these studies which have demonstrated the potency of proximity upon friendship formation also have important social implications. It has been found, for example, that white persons who experience increased contact with blacks become less prejudiced after that contact. This finding has been secured in such varied settings as in a meat packing plant (Palmore 1955), a housing project (Deutsch and Collins 1958), and in a university classroom (Mann 1959).

Proximity and Hostility

All of the data cited so far are compatible with the hypothesis that the more closely two people are located in physical space, the more likely it is that they will become attracted to each other. But since these studies have focused upon friendship formation rather than "enemy formation," most of the findings do not disconfirm the equally plausible, but contrary, proposition that the more closely people are located, the more likely it is that they will come to dislike each other.

Evidence that proximity may produce hostility as well as attraction comes primarily from police records, rather than from the social scientist's notebook. The Detroit Police Department's 1976 Annual Report, for example, indicates that in the majority of robberies the perpetrator was either related to, or acquainted with, the victim. It is somewhat surprising to find that thieves are much more likely to rob an intimate than a stranger. It would seem that thieves with common sense would be careful to steal from someone who could not easily identify them. The evidence, however, indicates that individuals are most likely to victimize those in close proximity. Perhaps those of us who fear the intrusion of "thieving maniacs" into our homes can take some comfort from the fact that the intruder is likely to be a friend.

Aggravated assault, like thievery, is also directed toward intimates. Most aggravated assaults occur within the family or among neighbors and acquaintances. In fact, police are especially reluctant to intervene in such quarrels since approximately 40 percent of all police injuries and over 20 percent of deaths in the line of duty occur on family-fight calls. With respect to homicide, FBI statistics reveal that killings within the family make up almost a third of all murders. If one adds killings which occur between "romantic lovers," the figure is even higher.

It seems logically clear, then, that distance per se does not have the strong consequences for positive attraction which the friendship-formation data suggest. While propinquity may be a necessary condition for attraction, it probably is also a necessary condition for hatred.

Perhaps those of us who fear the intrusion of "thieving maniacs" into our homes can take some comfort from the fact that the intruder is likely to be a friend.

Why Does Proximity Breed Strong Feelings?

INCREASED PROBABILITY OF ACQUIRING INFORMATION

What underlies the relationship between proximity and sentiment? Obviously something is made possible, or more likely, with decreasing distance. It seems apparent that what is made possible is an increased probability of receiving information, pro *or* con, about another person and an increased probability of receiving rewards or punishments from the other. Liking and disliking, and especially the strong sentiments of love and hate, are not likely to be felt for people about whom we have minimal information and with whom we have had little experience. What proximity appears to allow, and what distance prevents, is an opportunity to obtain information and accumulate experience regarding the rewards or punishments we are likely to receive from the other person.

Can we conclude, then, that if we know the degree of proximity between two people, but have no knowledge of the content of the information exchange such proximity has made possible, we cannot make a prediction concerning whether a positive sentiment or a negative sentiment will develop? Not necessarily. There are several lines of evidence which suggest that proximity is somewhat more likely to breed attraction than hostility.

Newcomb was one of the first to hypothesize that proximity should produce positive rather than negative attraction. He argues (1956, p. 576) that ". . . when persons interact, the reward–punishment ratio is more often such as to be reinforcing than extinguishing. . . ." Thus, he reasons that the information which comes with proximity is more likely to be favorable than unfavorable and that proximity, therefore, will more often result in liking than disliking. There is little direct evidence to support this proposition. Nevertheless, Newcomb's argument does seem plausible. Since we are dependent upon each other for the satisfaction of our needs, it seems probable that we generally take care to reward others as much as possible in interaction with them. In addition, social canons of courtesy often prohibit dealing out punishments to others even when we are so inclined.

HEIDER'S BALANCE THEORY

There is yet another reason why close proximity with another may favor the development of positive rather than negative affect. The prediction that proximity will more often lead to liking than disliking can be derived from a number of the cognitive-consistency theories. It can perhaps be most easily derived from Heider's (1958) balance theory.

A basic tenet of Heider's theory is that people try to make the *sentiment relationship* which exists between themselves and another person harmonious with the *unit relationship* which exists between themselves and the other.

By "sentiment relationship" Heider simply means the positive or negative attitude we have toward someone—our liking or disliking, gratitude or contempt, love or hate for that person, and so on. The phrase "unit relationship" refers to the degree to which two entities are perceived of as belonging together. The members of a family, for example, are usually perceived of as a unit, as are a person and the person's clothing, a husband and wife, and so on. In his discussion of the conditions which facilitate unit formation, Heider draws upon the principles of perceptual organization which were formulated by the Gestalt psychologists. The Gestaltists discovered that one relationship between objects which is especially likely to lead to unit formation is proximity; objects which are close together spatially tend to be perceived as a unit.

According to Heider's theory, then, if one perceives that a unit relationship with another exists (e.g., the other is in close proximity), this perception should induce a harmonious sentiment relationship (e.g., liking).

To test whether or not the anticipation of being in close social prox-imity with another would increase attraction, Darley and Berscheid (1967) invited college women to discuss their sexual beliefs and experiences with other women. Each woman was shown two folders. The folders (A and B) contained personality data on two other women who were participating in the study. The experimenters told half of the women that their "randomly selected" discussion partner—the woman with whom she was to share her sexual feelings and experiences—was the woman described in Folder A. They told the remaining women that their partner was the woman described in Folder B. (The "other folder," B or A, presumably contained information about a woman who was participating at another time.) The experimenters asked the women to read through both folders, form a general impression of both women, and then rate each of them along a number of dimensions, including likability.

The results of this study make it clear that even the mere *anticipation* of familiarity breeds attraction. The women liked their soon-to-be discus-sion partner, regardless of whether she was woman A or woman B, far more than the woman they knew would always remain a stranger to them.

This study suggests, then, that the factor of proximity, uncontaminated by the specific information which proximity often permits to be exchanged, may make two people feel that they are part of a "unit." This feeling of being in a unit relationship with another may then induce feelings of liking for that other. Knowledge that we will be in close proximity to another may result, then, in our coming to like another before we even meet the other—and *before* we know whether or not we will find their company rewarding.

It is interesting that the mere *anticipation* of interaction may generate liking which is so strong that it will cancel out a person's usual preferences. For example, Berscheid, Boye, and Darley (1968) told some college women that they had been paired with an extremely undesirable partner (a woman who was, among other things, described as "moody," "unclean," and "un-popular"). Evidently, even under these discouraging circumstances, women were able to summon up some enthusiasm for their prospective partner. For, when the experimenter reappeared later and reassured women that he had made a mistake, and she would of course be allowed to *choose* her dis-cussion partner—she could talk with her "moody" partner or with a partner who was "intelligent," "outgoing," popular, and desirable in every way—a surprising number of women chose to stick with their original assignment. In two control conditions (when the women and the undesirable partner had not been told they were a team), women rarely made such an unusual choice.

One of the most intriguing studies in this area was conducted by Berscheid *et al.* (1976). The authors explained to college men and women that they were trying to find out which kinds of romantic relationships work . . . and which just don't. In order to participate in the research, students had to agree to do just one thing—to *exclusively* date whomever the experimenters selected for them for either one week or five weeks. Virtually all students agreed to participate in this unusual project.

After the students had been told who they would be dating and for how long, they were given a chance to view a videotape of a discussion between their anticipated date and several other participants of the opposite sex. The students could monitor only one discussant at a time. (Unbeknownst to the students, the experimenter recorded the amount of time they spent watching each of the discussants.) He found that the longer a student expected to interact with his or her anticipated date, the more the student watched the date-to-be, the more positively the student rated and liked the date, and the more confident the student was in judgments about the date. Thus, not only was there an effort to acquire more information about a person with whom extended and intimate contact was expected, there also was an effort to find positive qualities in him (or her).

There is yet another line of evidence which suggests that increases in proximity probably leads to attraction far more often than it leads to repulsion. Increases in proximity to another usually increase the sheer familiarity of the other, and familiarity, Zajonc (1968) has argued, tends to generate attraction. The results of a series of his own studies, as well as those of others, appear to support the general proposition that mere repeated exposure to another person (or to any other stimulus) results in a more favorable attitude toward that person. Zajonc illustrates the familiarity effect with the following anecdote:

> On February 27, 1967, the Associated Press carried the following story from Corvallis, Oregon:
>
> A mysterious student has been attending a class at Oregon State University for the past two months enveloped in a big black bag. Only his bare feet show. Each Monday, Wednesday, and Friday at 11:00 a.m. the Black Bag sits on a small table near the back of the classroom. The class is Speech 113—basic persuasion . . . . Charles Goetzinger, professor of the class, knows the identity of the person inside. None of the 20 students in the class do. Goetzinger said *the students' attitude changed from hostility toward the Black Bag to curiosity and finally to friendship.* [Italics added.]

Whatever the reason why the students' attitude became more favorable in this particular case, whether the students "became accustomed to her face," or to the lack of one, or whether other factors were responsible, Zajonc and others have demonstrated, with stimuli which include words, names, music, colors, pictures, and human faces, that the more often a person is exposed to a previously novel stimulus, the more the person tends to like that stimulus. Zajonc speculates that a novel and unfamiliar person or stimulus tends to evoke uncertainty and perhaps even some fear and anxiety; with repeated exposure to it, however, these negative reactions tend to dissipate and, thus, our attitude grows more favorable.

Summary

The evidence is clear: the closer our proximity to someone, the more intensely we probably feel about that person. Dozens of studies document that the closer we are to an individual, the more likely we are to end up being friends, dating, or marrying the individual. However, there is also a fair amount of evidence that the closer we are to a person, the more likely we are to hate, maim, or kill that person.

Why are proximity and sentiment so closely related?

Proximity is probably associated with attraction (or repulsion) because proximity allows one (1) to obtain an increased amount of information about the other person, and (2) to experience rewards or punishments from the other.

Although proximity may promote either attraction or repulsion, three lines of evidence suggest that proximity is more likely to produce attraction than its opposite. First, as Heider argues, people try to be cognitively consistent. If people are in a unit relationship with others, they tend to form a positive sentiment relationship with them as well. Second, as Zajonc observes, proximity makes us more familiar with others, and thus may increase our liking for them. Third (and probably most important), as Newcomb observes, people probably reward each other far more than they punish one another. Thus, proximate encounters are likely to be pleasant encounters— and thus friendly encounters.

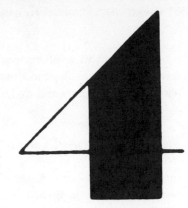

Liking: A Potent Transsituational Reinforcer

rewards and punishments others provide: the reciprocity-of-liking rule

A naive observer from another culture would have little trouble discovering one reward which people in our society spend a tremendous amount of time, money, and effort to obtain. Just a brief glance at a few tele-vision commercials would reveal that the desire for the esteem of others must be a very strong and pervasive motivation, for it is often exploited by those who have something to sell. From girdles to car batteries, mouth-washes to cake mixes, the standard marketing technique is to convince pro-spective buyers that the product will help them win the admiration and affection of others—or, at the very least, help them avoid the others' scorn.

Learning theorists have documented that social approval, like money, is a powerful "transsituational reinforcer." Social approval has been shown to reinforce a wide variety of human activities. For example, experimenters have demonstrated that if we merely nod our head and murmur approval each time another uses a plural noun, we can dramatically increase the fre-quency with which the recipient of our reward of social approval peppers the conversation with plural nouns (e.g., Greenspoon 1955; Dulany 1961). Stronger demonstrations of approval from others—the approving roar of the crowd or another's love—frequently influence lifetimes of activity.

Social approval, again like money, is valuable because if we possess it, we can be reasonably confident that a number of our needs will be satisfied; social censure often forecasts that many of our needs and desires—those which require the good will and cooperation of others for satisfaction—will be frustrated.

According to reinforcement theorists, then, since: "We like those who reward us and dislike those who punish us," we should like those who reward us by liking us and dislike those who punish us with rejection.

The Reciprocity-of-Liking Rule

Most popular advice to those of us who hope to win the affection of another assumes that the reciprocity-of-liking rule will always hold true. For example, Dale Carnegie's injunction to those who want to win friends and influence people—to be "hearty" in their approbation and "lavish" in their praise (1937, p. 51)—is based on this assumption. Although Carnegie's formula captured widespread interest in this country, he was predated by several years by the philosopher Hecato (2nd century B.C.) who wrote:

> I will show you a love potion without drug or herb or any witch's spell; if you wish to be loved, love.

Correlational data, obtained from a wide variety of psychological studies, are often cited in support of the reciprocity-of-liking proposition (e.g., Newcomb 1961; Mettee and Aronson 1974). These data show that we generally believe that those we like, like us. If it is true that we like people who like us, we would expect to find such a correlation. Taken alone, however, these data do not provide conclusive evidence for the existence of a reciprocity-of-liking rule. Either one of two processes, or both, could be responsible for the positive relationship between the extent to which we guess another likes us and the extent to which we like another:

1 As a consequence of our discovery that another likes us, we may become attracted to him or her. (This, of course, is the reinforcement theory prediction; another's liking for us constitutes a reward, and we are attracted to people who reward us.)

2 As a consequence of our attraction to another, we may develop the belief that the other person likes us. In such cases, it is not the reward of another's liking that is producing our attraction to the other, but our attraction that is forming, or distorting, our perception of whether the other person likes us.

To test the first hypothesis, that we come to like those we discover like us, Backman and Secord (1959) formed groups of college students who were strangers to one another. Before the groups actually met, each student was informed that personality test analyses had revealed that certain members of the group would probably like the student very much—and the student was told precisely who these people were.

Courtesy of Mell Lazarus and Field Newspaper Syndicate.

After the group members had chatted with each other for a while, the students were warned that, later, the group might be broken into two-person teams. Each group member was asked to indicate his or her preferences for a team partner. Each group met six times and these sociometric data were collected at the first, third, and sixth sessions.

Backman and Secord found that, by the close of the first session, students preferred over everyone else those people they had been told would like them. (The data obtained from the first session, then, support the reciprocity-of-liking proposition.)

By the third and sixth sessions, however, when students had really gotten to know one another, students no longer preferred those people they had been *told* would like them. The experimenters' bogus information evidently lost its impact, once group members had a chance to find out how the others *really* felt about them. The Backman and Secord experiment, then, indicates that if we think another likes us, we tend to like that person in return.

What about the reverse process? If we like another person very much, are we likely to overestimate how much the other likes us? The evidence suggests that this process also operates (e.g., Tagiuri 1958). Here, too, however, one's tendency to assume that those one likes *must* like one in return probably cannot withstand an abundance of evidence to the contrary. For example, no matter how much a man might wish to convince himself that the woman he loves reciprocates his affection, such a distortion becomes more and more difficult to maintain as she continues to refuse to date him.

SOCIAL DEPRIVATION AND SATIATION

According to Reinforcement theory, people's "need" or "drive" level determines how responsive they are to potential rewards or punishments. A starving man might feel profound gratitude toward the man who offers to share a few scraps of bread with him; a sated man might be disgusted by the same offer.

B.C. by permission of Johnny Hart and Field Enterprises, Inc. (As published in the Wisconsin State Journal.)

Reinforcement theorists, then, would predict that if people are starved for social approval they should be unusually appreciative when they receive some. Similarly, if people are surfeited with social approval and approbation, they should be fairly unresponsive to additional ladles of esteem.

Learning theorists, who have studied the impact of social reinforcement on children's task performance, provide strong support for this hypothesis (e.g., Dorwart, Ezerman, Lewis, and Rosenhan 1965; Gewirtz and Baer 1958a, 1958b; Stevenson and Odom 1962). Social psychologists do, too. In a trio of studies, Dittes (1959), Walster (1965), and Jacobs *et al.* (1971) argued that the strength of our needs and the extent to which our needs are satisfied—or thwarted—by others should interact in determining how much we like the others. They argued:

> When a person's self-esteem is at rockbottom—when his employer has told him that he's an incompetent, his teachers that he's stupid, and his girl friend that he's repulsive—he is in desperate need of a little affection and love. Contrarily, when a person's self-esteem is soaring—when his employer has given him a raise, when he's gotten an A on a tough exam, when his girlfriend says she can make it Saturday night after all—he feels good about himself; he has little need for others' reassurance that he's OK.

Thus, how we feel about ourselves, at any given moment, should have a profound impact on how we react to others who offer us love . . . or who makes it clear they hate us. When our self-esteem is unusually high, we should react calmly to people who accept or reject us. We should like people who accept us, of course . . . but only a little. We should dislike people who reject us . . . but, again, only a little. When our self-esteem is low, our emotions are volatile; we desperately need affection. We should like people who accept us tremendously much. We should dislike people who reject us equally much.

The authors' hypotheses were supported in a trio of experiments (see Dittes 1959; Walster 1965; and Jacobs *et al.* 1971).

Walster (1965) tested the hypothesis that women whose self-confidence had been shattered would be unusually vulnerable to an attractive, accepting man. Women whose self-confidence was at an all-time high, would be far less vulnerable. Other theorists have advanced similar proposals: Reik (1944) argues, for example, that it is when we are dissatisfied with ourselves that we are especially susceptible to falling in love. As evidence he cites the observation that men and women are particularly susceptible to falling in love on the rebound, after they have suffered a severe blow to their egos.

Walster tested her hypothesis in the following way: (1) A woman was introduced to a man (an experimental confederate) who made it clear that

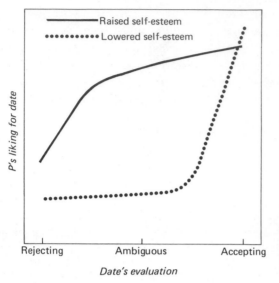

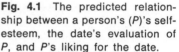

Fig. 4.1 The predicted relationship between a person's (*P*)'s self-esteem, the date's evaluation of *P*, and *P*'s liking for the date.

he was romantically interested in her. (2) The self-esteem of some women was raised by giving them authoritative positive information about themselves. The self-esteem of other women was lowered. Finally, (3) the women were asked how they felt about the date-to-be.

Specifically: The experimenter hired a number of Sanford University women to participate in a research project on personality processes.[1] As each woman was on her way to the testing session, she accidentally bumped into a man. He chatted with her for 15 minutes or so, and then invited her to go to San Francisco for dinner and a show the following week.

Soon after the date had been made, the experimenter arrived, and the experiment presumably began. The woman completed a battery of personality tests, a Word Association test, and the *Rorschach Ink Blot Test*.

When testing was completed the women were handed their "test results." Actually, the women received bogus personality reports. Half of the women received a favorable personality analysis; half received an unfavorable report. (Which report women received was determined by chance.) If the woman had been assigned to the Lowered-esteem condition, the analysis stressed such characteristics as the woman's "immaturity" and her "lack of capacity for successful leadership." If she had been assigned to the Raised-

---

1. Before the women were hired, a clinician reviewed the women's personality test results in order to eliminate any women whom he felt might be hurt by participating in this experiment.

esteem condition, the report stressed the woman's maturity and originality, and stated that she presented "one of the most favorable personality structures analyzed by the staff." (That people will accept false personality descriptions as accurate descriptions of themselves has been established previously (Bramel 1962; Glass 1964). It seems strange that we accept and trust a stranger's description of ourselves rather than our own perceptions, but this is a fact on which fortune-tellers rely.)

How did each woman's momentary self-esteem affect her liking for the man she had met earlier and agreed to date?

A woman whose self-esteem had been temporarily lowered was more receptive to the man's affection than was a woman whose self-esteem had been temporarily raised. The typical Low-esteem condition woman said she liked him "extremely much" or "fairly much." The typical High-esteem condition woman said she felt fairly neutral toward him.

What about the other half of the equation? Is it true that when people's self-esteem has been shattered, they are very touchy about rejection—and especially hostile to anyone who rejects them? When people's self-esteem is unusually high, are they able to take rejection in stride? Evidence from Jacobs et al. (1971) suggests that this hypothesis, too, is true.

In the experiment of Jacobs et al., men from the University of Rochester and Temple University were invited to participate in a computer date-matching program. As before, in an initial session, they took a battery of personality tests. Then a psychiatrist gave them false feedback as to how they had done. In the Raised self-esteem condition, the psychiatrist praised their strong personalities, their open and imaginative minds, their leadership qualities, and their unusual empathy and sensitivity for peers. In the Lowered self-esteem conditions, the psychiatrist liked almost nothing about them.

Once these evaluations had a chance to sink in, Jacobs et al. set out to find out how these men would feel about a woman who was warm and accepting, a woman whose feelings toward them were unclear, or a woman who was cold and rejecting.

As we can see from Fig. 4.2, in the experiment of Jacobs et al., both Raised self-esteem men and Lowered self-esteem men liked the Accepting woman a lot. (In this experiment, both Raised and Lowered self-esteem men seemed to like her equally well.) There was a difference, however, in how Raised self-esteem men and Lowered self-esteem men felt about the Rejecting woman. In general, the Raised self-esteem men could take the rejecting woman or leave her. It was the Lowered self-esteem men who felt the most hostile to her.

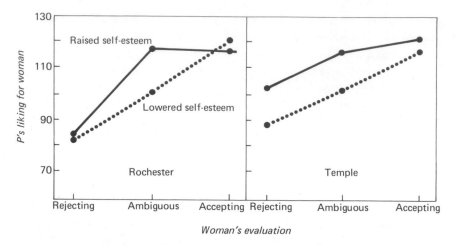

Fig. 4.2 The actual relationship between *P*'s self-esteem, the date's evaluation of *P*, and *P*'s liking for the date.

The Exceptions to the Reciprocity-of-Liking Rule

Although the tendency to like people who like us is sufficiently common-place that the reciprocity-of-liking rule has been cited as a necessary and "nonempirical" principle of human behavior (Ossorio and Davis 1966), life and literature provide a few disconcerting exceptions.

Liking and loving are not *always* reciprocated. If they were, the new kid on the block's friendly overture would never be met with taunts. Love would never be unrequited . . . but it is.

Several researchers have attempted to ferret out the special situations in which liking does not breed liking . . . perhaps even boomerangs and breeds anger and resentment in return. Some of the first to test the Reciprocity-of-liking rule's limits were Deutsch and Solomon (1959). They argued that our self-esteem should affect how receptive we are to love and affection.

Reinforcement theorists, of course, also believe that self-esteem is important. They argue that high self-esteem people have little need for reassurance; their low self-esteem counterparts desperately need reassurance. Ergo, they argue, low self-esteem people are unusually receptive to praise and unusually resentful of censure.

Not so, say Deutsch and Solomon. What matters is not so much whether low or high self-esteem people *need* love . . . but whether or not they think they deserve to get it.

Deutsch and Solomon argue: high self-esteem people (who think they deserve to be loved) are quick (perhaps too quick) to assume that others like them. They're quick to accept the affection of others at face value. Low self-esteem people can't. When others praise them, they feel uneasy. They're suspicious. They suspect their friends' motives, their accuracy, and their sanity.

Two examples: Now and then, a man has so much self-confidence that he tends to assume everyone must love him—the other's vehement denials to the contrary. A woman may insist that he's not her type, she's married to someone else . . . or even screech that she thinks he's ugly, stupid, and arrogant. No matter. "You can always tell when a woman is interested," he says blithely. "She plays hard-to-get."

People with inordinately low self-esteem have the opposite problem. I once had a college mate—good-looking, personable, and witty—who had very low self-esteem. She was in love with a rather inarticulate man. She spent a great deal of time moping around the dorm, crying that he really didn't love her, that the only reason he took her out was because she was sexually "easy." Then, on her birthday, he invited her to dinner, took her to a play, and then dropped her at the dorm with only a chaste goodnight kiss. Was she elated—now confident that he loved the "real" her and not the sexual favors she provided? No. She was hurt. She said, in depression, "I don't even turn him on anymore."

Deutsch and Solomon (1959) argue that it is high self-esteem persons who are unusually receptive to praise, and low self-esteem persons who passively take criticism as their due.

Other Cognitive-consistency theorists would make the same prediction. Heider's Balance theory (1956), for example, predicts that if Person A likes X (any person or object, including Person A), and if Person B also likes X, Person A will tend to like Person B. (This produces a balanced and psychologically comfortable state.)

Ordinarily people do like themselves. (See Fig. 4.3a.) Thus, ordinarily, Reinforcement theorists and Cognitive consistency theorists would agree: people like those who like them and dislike those who don't.

It infrequently may happen, however, that Person A may possess very low self-esteem and may *not* like X (himself) very much. If, in spite of the fact that Person A is convinced he or she is unlikable and unworthy, Person B insists he or she likes Person A very much, this, according to cognitive-consistency theorists, should induce an unbalanced, psychologically uncomfortable state. One way Person A can restore balance and harmony is to decide to dislike Person B. (See Fig. 4.3b.)

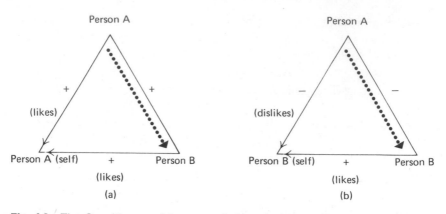

Fig. 4.3 The Cognitive-consistency prediction of an exception to the Reciprocity-of-Liking Rule.

According to cognitive-consistency theory, then, we should like those who like us only if we like ourselves; if we dislike ourselves, we should dislike those whose feelings about us are positive, and thus inconsistent with our own. Although this prediction follows clearly from balance theory, it is not intuitively obvious. It reminds us of Groucho Marx's reasoning: "I wouldn't be caught dead joining any club that would have me as a member."

Deutsch and Solomon (1959) set out to test the hypothesis that we like those who see us as we see ourselves.

They led some women to believe that they were very good at performing group tasks; other women were led to believe that they were poor performers. After the tasks had been completed, each woman received a note from her teammates. In this note, her teammate either raved about her performance and indicated she was a very desirable teammate—or sharply criticized her performance and indicated she was not very desirable. (Which note the women received was randomly determined.)

Deutsch and Solomon predicted that, if the woman believed she had given a successful performance, she would like a teammate who gave a favorable evaluation of her performance more than a teammate who gave her an unfavorable evaluation. Conversely, if the woman believed she had performed unsuccessfully, she would like a teammate who gave her an unfavorable evaluation more than one who gave a favorable evaluation.

In this experiment, Deutsch and Solomon found that the woman's belief as to whether she had given an unusually successful or an unusually dismal performance *did* affect how she reacted to praise or blame: If women thought they had performed well, they liked those who praised their performance and who wanted them as teammates more than those who did not. (Both Reinforcement and Cognitive-consistency theorists would expect this.) However, if women had given an unsuccessful performance, they seemed to like those who praised *and* those who criticized their performance equally well.

Deutsch and Solomon concluded that two things were going on in this experiment: (1) As Reinforcement theory would predict, people—regardless of how they feel about themselves—appreciate praise and resent criticism. (2) However, certain things can dampen the delight we take in praise. For example, in this case, women who thought they did badly—and then were praised—may have felt uneasy (in Heider's terms, they may have experienced Cognitive *im*balance). They may have also had some doubts about their partner's sincerity, intelligence, or sanity.

In this experiment, then, in the Low self-esteem condition, two opposing tendencies may have balanced each other out: i.e., (1) women liked the women who liked them more than the women who did not, and (2) women disliked the women (who praised them) who were "stupid" and "insincere" and liked the women (who criticized them) who were accurate and sincere. And *that's* why praisers and critics were equally well liked.

Additional support for the contention that our self-esteem affects our reaction to praise or blame comes from Dutton (1972). Dutton points out that Deutsch and Solomon—and many of the researchers who followed them—assumed that "High self-esteem" or "Low self-esteem" could easily be temporarily induced in those who participated in their experiments. In these early studies, experimenters simply asked persons to perform a few tasks, gave them some feedback, and then arranged to have someone praise or criticize their performance. This, the experimenters concluded, made some people confident that they were good at a task and others confident they were poor at the same task.

But did it? Did these people really believe the feedback they received? Were they really convinced that forever more, regardless of how hard they tried, they would remain a "superior" performer or an "inferior" one? We do not know. But we can guess. Probably, *most* people who participated in the High self-esteem condition were fairly certain that they were talented; those in the Low self-esteem condition may well have hoped to "show them all."

Dutton argued that whether or not one is certain of one's own ability should have a dramatic impact on how one responds to praise or criticism. Dutton argued that it is only when people are *certain* that they are good or bad that their liking for others should be shaped both by how much the other likes them and by whether the other's evaluative expressions are in accord with their own self-images. When people are *uncertain* about whether they are good or bad performers, the more positive another is, the more they should like the other.

To test his hypothesis, Dutton recruited Canadian students to play eight games of *Wff'n Proof: The Game of Modern Logic*. Afterwards, the students were given information designed to make some students feel *certain* they were better (or worse) than their fellow students; and others merely suspect that they might be better or worse than other group members, and thus *uncertain* of their ability.

After the students had received information from the experimenter about their performances, they received a note from one of the other participants (actually an experimental accomplice). The note that each person received was either positive ("You are the person I most prefer on my team") or it was negative ("You are the person I least prefer on my team"). Then, of course, Dutton measured each person's attraction for the note-writing evaluator.

Dutton's hypothesis received strong support. When students were *certain* they were either far better or far worse than their teammates, they were most attracted to teammates whose evaluation of them—for good or ill—matched their own: If they were sure they were superior, they were most attracted to an approving teammate; if they were sure they were inferior, they were most attracted to a rejecting one. When, however, students were not really quite sure whether they were superior or inferior (although they had a sneaking suspicion as to how they stood), they preferred the positive evaluator regardless of the direction, favorable or unfavorable, of their suspicions. These findings have been reaffirmed by other investigators (e.g., Jones and Schneider 1968).

Most of the time, we probably do not have authoritative information as to how we "stack-up." Thus, most of the time, liking *does* breed liking. However, Dutton's data indicate that when we are certain of our own self-evaluation, the evaluator who tells us we are what we know we are *not* will "lose points."

The Deutsch and Solomon experiment—possibly because its results were so provocative—and so confusing—generated a firestorm of research. Reinforcement theorists contended with cognitive-consistency theorists; neutrals tried to moderate the debate. Now that the dust has settled, we can review what social psychologists have learned from the more than 75 experiments which have investigated the effects another's evaluative appraisals have upon our attraction for the other.

Shrauger (1975) reviewed all of the research which has been conducted on the Reinforcement vs. Cognitive-consistency question. He came to two conclusions: (1) People *do* have a basic desire to think favorably of themselves . . . they try to maintain as favorable an opinion of themselves "as they can get away with." Thus they *do* feel more warmly toward people who praise them than to people who condemn them (even if the condemnation is justified). (2) Nonetheless, people *do* have more respect for consistent evaluations than for inconsistent ones. According to Shrauger, there are several reasons why we prefer people who share our visions of ourselves.

People tend to attribute very different personality and motivational characteristics to consistent vs. inconsistent evaluators. It is natural for us to assume that the consistent observer is responding sensitively and honestly to *us*. It is difficult to guess *what* the inconsistent evaluator is up to. Is the evaluator just uninformed? or insensitive . . . or stupid? Is the evaluator an ingratiator (if the evaluation is flattering) . . . or cruel (if it is not)?

Any time another's appraisal of us deviates from our own, the three factors Shrauger cites—inconsistency, inaccuracy, and ingratiation—are probably inextricably intertwined. So far we have centered on the impact that another's "inconsistency" has on our liking for the other; now we will focus directly upon the effect its frequent companions—inaccuracy and ingratiation—have on our liking for the other.[2]

INACCURACY

Finck (1891, p. 245), writing before the turn of the century, advised his Victorian readers and would-be lovers that:

> Sincerity in compliments is essential, else all is lost. It is useless to try to convince a woman with an ugly mouth or nose that these features are not ugly. She knows they are ugly, as well as Rubinstein knows when he strikes the wrong note.

---

2. For a discussion of the multitude of factors that can affect an evaluator's impact, see S. C. Jones, 1973, Self and interpersonal evaluations: Esteem theories versus consistency theories. *Psychological Bulletin* 79:185–199; and D. R. Mettee and E. Aronson, Affective reactions to appraisal from others. In T. L. Huston (ed.), *Foundations of Interpersonal Attraction*. New York: Academic Press, 1974.

Most social commentators, before and since, have agreed with him; in human relations, it is of paramount importance to be accurate.

The evidence, by and large, is on their side; an evaluator does indeed gain *something* if perceived to be accurate. Consider, for example, an experiment conducted by Berscheid, Walster, and Walster (1969). Students at the University of Minnesota are well aware that the university has a great deal of information on file about their backgrounds, personalities, and grades. The students who participated in this experiment gave permission for four fellow students to look at these data and to guess what they were like (supposedly so that their fellow students could choose a compatible partner for a continuing study). The participants were, of course, allowed to read what the four students had supposedly written. In actuality, the experimenters constructed the evaluations on the basis of a self-concept questionnaire the students had filled out a few weeks before. On this questionnaire, the students had indicated the personal traits they believed they possessed and how positive or negative they believed each trait to be. Thus, the experimenters were able to arrange the evaluations the students received in the following way:

1 The "Accurate-Positive" evaluation was composed of *eight* very positive traits which the students claimed to possess.

...in human relationships, it is of paramount importance to be accurate.

2 The "Accurate-Negative" evaluation was composed of *seven* of these very positive traits and *one* negative trait which students had admitted possessing.

3 The "Inaccurate-Positive" evaluation was composed of *eight* positive traits, but traits students had said were not characteristic of them.

4 The "Inaccurate-Negative" evaluation was composed of *seven* uncharacteristic positive traits and *one* negative uncharacteristic trait.

In each case, the "fellow-student" evaluators concluded their appraisal by saying, in effect, that they thought they would like the students very much.

After reading the evaluations, students were asked what they thought of their four potential partners.

The authors secured the ubiquitous Reinforcement effect: students preferred the students who gave positive evaluations to those who gave negative ones. (The reader might be surprised at this result. Both the Positive evaluations and the so-called Negative evaluations were actually overwhelmingly positive. In addition, all evaluators—both positive *and* (slightly) negative—had concluded by saying that they thought they would like the student very much. But the results of a number of other experiments (e.g., Harvey, Kelley, and Shapiro 1957) also indicate that we are extremely sensitive and responsive to the slightest hint of negativity in others' appraisals. We might speculate that this is because, in our society, people are more often damned by faint praise than they are by out-and-out excoriation. It has been observed, for example, that "Well, well!" are words of malice. Perhaps this is why we learn to become sensitive to a lack of enthusiasm in another's expressions of esteem for us.)

In addition to a Reinforcement effect, the accuracy or inaccuracy of the fellow-students' evaluations also strongly affected attraction for them. Those who gave accurate (and cognitively consistent, in this case) evaluations were liked much more than those who gave inaccurate (and cognitively inconsistent) ones.

This, as well as a variety of other experiments, documents the fact that positive evaluators who are perceived to be both inconsistent and inaccurate do sacrifice some of the "points" they would have otherwise gained in their attempt to win the recipient's affection. (See, for example, Howard and Berkowitz 1958.)

Accuracy Counts . . . A Little

A painstaking review of these studies, however, suggests that although persons who go overboard in praising us lose *some* credibility, they don't lose very much.

It has been observed, for example, that "Well, well!" are words of malice.

(1) The first catch to the general finding that "accuracy counts" is that, after receiving another's appraisals, a person's notions of what is "accurate" or "inaccurate" may undergo swift revision. It is tempting to believe that the compliments we receive are deserved, whether or not they are in reality. That many of us promptly succumb to this temptation was first observed in a study conducted by Jones, Gergen, and Davis (1962). In this experiment, college women were asked to tell an interviewer all about themselves. Some women, those in the *Accuracy* conditions, were requested to give an honest and accurate picture of themselves. (They were asked to imagine that it was a student-counseling interview and that it was to their advantage to be perfectly candid with the interviewer.) The other women, those in the *Ingratiation* conditions, were told to create the most favorable picture they could of themselves. (They were asked to imagine that they were trying to qualify for a fellowship to go abroad for the summer. They were assured that it was their task to impress the interviewer, to figure out the kind of person that the interviewer liked, and to try to act like such a person.) After the interview, the interviewer told each woman what he thought of her. He either said that she created an extremely favorable impression and he liked her, *or* that she created a fairly negative one and he didn't really like her very much.

The Jones *et al.* data yielded a fascinating result. Regardless of whether the women had tried to impress the interviewer or whether they had attempted to present a totally honest picture of themselves, those women who received positive feedback from the interviewer later insisted that their self-representations had been far more *accurate* than did women who received negative feedback. This finding is even more dramatic when we consider that the women in the Ingratiation-Approval condition reported slightly higher accuracy of their self-presentations than did women in the Accuracy-Disapproval condition. Thus the sheer positivity of an evaluation may affect perception of its accuracy which, in turn, may affect the recipient's regard for the evaluator.

(2) There is a second reason why an evaluator's accuracy is often less important than we might expect. A number of theorists have concluded that for maximum effectiveness, a flatterer should not praise persons for those virtues they *know* they possess, but for those they *hope* they possess. For example, Finck (1891, p. 245) (apparently modifying the advice he gave his readers a few pages earlier) states that:

> The most common mistake of lovers is to compliment a woman on her most conspicuous points of beauty. This has very much the same effect on her as telling Rubinstein he is a wonderful pianist. He knows that better than you do, and has been told it so many times that he is sick and tired of hearing it again.

Finck then goes on to quote Lord Chesterfield's dictum,

> "Very ugly or very beautiful women . . . should be flattered on their understanding, and mediocre ones on their beauty."

Jones (1964) suggests that both our self-esteem and the certainty of our self-evaluation affect how we respond to another's compliments. If recipients *wish* to possess some trait . . . but are uncertain whether or not they do . . . they should be especially receptive to compliments. Jones (1964, p. 24) cites Lord Chesterfield's dictum that:

> "Men . . . are most and best flattered upon those points where they wish to excel, and yet are doubtful whether they do or not."

There is *some* experimental support for the notion that we are especially appreciative of people who tell us what we want to hear . . . but are afraid we won't.

(3) There is one final reason why an evaluator's accuracy turns out not to be as critical a determinant of liking as we might expect. Accumulating research suggests that "liking" and "respect" may be two quite independent dimensions of attraction (see Bales 1958; Damrosch 1975; Kiesler and Goldberg 1968, and Mettee, Hrelec, and Wilkins 1971). In an experiment conducted by Dickoff (1961), which we shall discuss at greater length in a

moment, women were asked to describe their reaction to a far-too-positive evaluator and to a totally accurate evaluator. The women liked the far-too-positive evaluator-observer a good deal more than they liked the totally accurate observer. According to the authors "these subjects viewed the over-evaluation as a genuine reflection of something in the observers' personality structure, something which they conceived of as a rather likable set of qualities." Interestingly enough, however, this attraction developed in spite of the fact that some women had limited "respect" for the too-positive evaluator; (in fact, she was judged to be less perceptive and less bright than the accurate evaluator).

All in all, then, the evidence suggests that people do like to be liked. The flatterer—who goes too far in shouting our praises—may lose a few points . . . but not many.

INGRATIATION

People praise us or condemn us for a variety of reasons. When people say they like us, they may be sincere . . . or they may be simply being polite. Or their motives may take on a sinister quality: they may be flattering us in order to manipulate us to serve their own ends. When people admit that they despise us, we are inclined to take their admission at face value. Since it is considered both impolite and impolitic to criticize others, we are generally less suspicious of the critic's ulterior motives. The negative evaluator may have such motives, however; they may be in a bad mood, for example, have problems of their own, be jealous of us, or be trying to prove that they are "sincere friends."

Jones (1964) wrote a fascinating book, *Ingratiation*. ("Ingratiation" can be defined as "saying something you don't really believe, in the hopes of getting something from someone.") Jones (1964) argues (as do such attribution theorists as Jones and Davis 1965; Jones and Wortman 1973; and Kelley 1972) that people most always try to attribute causes to other people's actions—they try to make judgments about why others do and say the things they do. Jones observes our judgment of another's motivation in praising (or condemning) us is inevitably a critical determinant of whether or not we will reciprocate the other's liking (or disliking) us.

There is evidence that when we label another's expression of affection as "ingratiation"—when we believe that the other is flattering us in order to manipulate us into giving the other something—we are reluctant to grant the ingratiator either our esteem or other more solid benefits. Dickoff's study (1961) is typical. She invited women to participate in a study of clinical processes. She began by interviewing them about their personal histories, values, and habits. The women had been told that an observer would

When a person admits that he despises us, we are inclined to take his admission at face value.

watch the interview and record their impressions. The observer had been introduced to the women in one of two ways: (1) In the *Accuracy* condition, she was described as a first-year graduate student in clinical psychology, who was being trained to form accurate impressions of clients; (2) in the *Ulterior Motive* condition, the observer was described as a graduate student who had agreed to serve as an observer for the day, in the hope that she could persuade participants in this experiment to help her out by participating in *her* experiment.

After the interview, the women learned what impression they had made on the observer: (1) In the *Positive* condition, the observer claimed that her impression was extremely positive; (2) in the *Self-concept* condition, the observer's evaluation was very similar to the woman's own; (3) in the *Neutral* condition, the observer was neutral and noncommittal.

After receiving this information, the experimenter asked the woman to give *her* frank impression of the observer. As Fig. 4.4 shows, in the Accuracy conditions, the more positive the observer was, the more the woman liked her.

In the *Ulterior Motive* conditions, however, the extremely positive evaluator lost her appeal. In fact, the suspicious women liked the accurate evaluator more than they liked a positive evaluator.

Note that women in all conditions rated the neutral observer quite negatively. (Once again, we can see that people tend to assume that un-

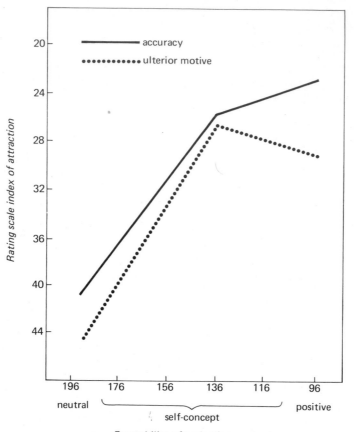

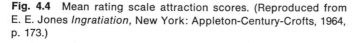

Favorability of evaluation received

Fig. 4.4 Mean rating scale attraction scores. (Reproduced from E. E. Jones *Ingratiation*, New York: Appleton-Century-Crofts, 1964, p. 173.)

enthusiastic evaluations are somewhat negative evaluations.) The Dickoff results have been replicated by Lowe and Goldstein (1970).

It is often difficult, of course, to be certain whether another's liking is given to us with an ulterior motive or not. We try to make, however, an intelligent guess.

One way in which we can determine whether or not an expression of esteem was prompted by an ulterior motive is to evaluate the *grounds* upon which the evaluator ostensibly made the positive evaluation. People seldom simply say "I like you." Rather, they usually follow the "I like you" with "because . . .", or, if not, the recipient is usually aware of the event or circumstances which have prompted the remark. In cases in which the expression of esteem is not followed by a verbal reason for it, and no particular event or bit of behavior seems to have caused the remark, it is customary for the recipient to ask "Why do you say that?" If the grounds upon which the evaluation was ostensibly given are inaccurate—if, for example, others say they like us because we're so beautifully graceful and we have the bumps and bruises to prove we're not, then we may suspect ingratiation.

There are a variety of other factors which may cause people to assume that an expression of esteem is mere ingratiation and, thus, reduce the likelihood that the reciprocity-of-liking rule will hold. For example, when evaluators are in no way dependent on the recipients for satisfaction of their needs (and thus an ulterior motive seems improbable), evaluators' expressions of affection are much more likely to elicit liking in return (e.g., Jones, Gergen, Gumpert, and Thibaut 1965; Jones and Jones 1964; Jones, Jones, and Gergen 1963; Stires and Jones 1969).

Another's expression of attraction for us, then, is a gift horse whose mouth we usually examine quite carefully. If we conclude that ingratiators are trying to "con" us, we like them less than we normally would—perhaps even less than we would have had they expressed more modest liking for.

On the basis of a number of studies, then, we can conclude that expressions of attraction and other positive evaluations do act as rewards and produce reciprocal liking. Overall, the effect seems to be most potent when persons who are evaluated are uncertain of their own self-evaluations. When recipients of the evaluation are certain of their own characteristics, both positiveness *and* consistency become important. There seem to be three main reasons why the consistency of a positive evaluation is important: (1) consistency is rewarding and pleasant in-and-of itself, (2) people may conclude that inconsistent, and thus inaccurate, evaluators are unintelligent and insensitive, which may diminish liking for them, and (3) people may conclude that inconsistent, inaccurate evaluators are ingratiators, which may also depress their liking for them.

Summary

Dale Carnegie advised those who wish to *Win Friends and Influence People* to be hearty in their approbation and lavish in their praise. His advice has merit. Psychologists consistently find that people like people whom they think like them.

There seem to be two reasons for this link: First—as Reinforcement theorists would predict—if we discover others like us, we come to like the others in return. Second—as Cognitive-consistency theorists would predict —if we like others, we are likely to assume, correctly or not, that they like us too.

According to Reinforcement theory, persons' need levels determine how responsive they are to rewards and punishments. Research documents that when our self-esteem is high, we react fairly calmly to the person who accepts or rejects us. We like the person who accepts us . . . a little . . . and dislike the person who rejects us . . . again, only a little. It is when our self-esteem is low that our emotions are at their most volatile. We react with intense affection to those who offer us love . . . and with intense hostility to those who are rejecting.

Finally, we asked: "It is true that people *do* like those who are 'hearty in their approbation and lavish in their praise.' But can we carry this too far? Do flatterers lose *anything* by being too flattering? If their praise is so lavish that it makes us suspect their motives, their accuracy, their intelligence, their sanity, does that dampen our enthusiasm for them?" The answer seems to be "yes"—but not much.

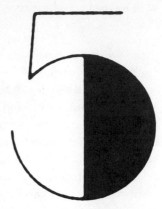

rewards and punishments others provide:
similarity

The idea that we like people who are similar to ourselves is certainly not original with social psychologists. The tired adage, "Birds of a feather flock together," was old in Aristotle's time. Folk psychology, as expressed in such proverbs, is sometimes useful to the social scientist because it may sum up a wealth of human experience and wisdom. More often, however, folk psychology is frustrating. The "birds of a feather" notion is a case in point. As Newcomb (1956) has observed, the usefulness of this particular "law" of human behavior is limited because it is indiscriminate. People may be similar or different on any conceivable dimension upon which humans can be placed, and it seems unlikely that such similarities as length of big toe or social security number generate very much attraction. In addition to being indiscriminate, folk psychology is frustrating for another reason. One no sooner finds a popular maxim which appears to predict for a particular situation, than one finds another which offers contradictory advice—in this case, "Opposites attract."

In this chapter we will discuss varieties of similarity and dissimilarity and their relationship to attraction.

Similarity of Attitudes

The lion's share of researchers' attention has focused upon the relationship between the similarity of people's attitudes and the attraction they have for each other. This research has largely centered on two hypotheses: (a) we *perceive* ourselves to be more similar to those we like (and less similar to those we don't) than we really are; (b) we like those who possess attitudes similar to our own.

Both of these hypotheses—that attraction leads to the perception of attitudinal similarity—and its converse—that perception of similarity leads to attraction—can be derived from a number of cognitive-consistency theories. Perhaps, however, they can be most easily derived from Heider's Balance Theory (1958), which we discussed in Chapter 4.

Heider proposed, it will be recalled, that people strive to make sentiment relationships harmonious with unit relationships. According to Heider, separate entities which are *similar* to one another tend to be perceived as belonging together (as being in unit relationship with one another). According to Heider's theory, then, an harmonious sentiment relationship such as liking should develop between two entities which are perceived to be in unit relationship. The reverse process should also operate: Liking for another should lead to the perception of a unit relationship (e.g., that the liked other is similar to ourself).

EVIDENCE THAT ATTRACTION CAUSES THE PERCEPTION OF SIMILARITY

The evidence suggests that individuals who like one another do indeed perceive themselves as having more things in common than they really do. Investigators have measured both the amount of *perceived* similarity and the amount of *actual* similarity which exists between those who like one another. The findings indicate that we routinely overestimate the extent to which those we like and love share our attitudes. Both Byrne and Blaylock (1963) and Levinger and Breedlove (1966), for example, have found that husbands and wives tend to perceive that they are far more similar to each other than they actually are. Assumed similarity may be greater than actual similarity not only for reasons of cognitive consistency but also because, in the interest of harmony, husbands and wives tend to emphasize their similarities and to conceal or to avoid areas of disagreement.

The proposition that attraction leads to perceived similarity is most strongly supported by studies in which feelings of attraction have been induced on bases other than attitudinal similarity and in which the people involved have not actually interacted with each other. One such study was conducted by Byrne and Wong (1962). People who possessed varying degrees of prejudice against blacks were asked to estimate how similar the attitudes of a black stranger and of a white stranger were to their own. Prejudiced people assumed that the black was less likely to agree with their attitudes than was the white stranger. Unprejudiced persons, however, expected that the black stranger and the white stranger were equally likely to share their attitudes. It appears, then, that peoples' relative liking for blacks and whites may influence their perception of how similar or dissimilar blacks' attitudes are likely to be to their own.

EVIDENCE THAT ATTITUDINAL SIMILARITY CAUSES ATTRACTION

There is a good deal of evidence that the discovery that we share similar attitudes with another generates attraction. The first and classic study of the causal relationship between attitudinal similarity and attraction was conducted by Newcomb (1961) who examined the development of friendship among a group of men attending the University of Michigan. When they arrived at Michigan (and at their assigned dormitory), all of the men were strangers to one another. As the men became acquainted with each other, Newcomb periodically measured their attitudes on a wide variety of dimensions. Then, he assessed their attraction for one another.

As we might expect on the basis of studies mentioned in the previous section, Newcomb found that the more a man liked another resident of his house, the more he tended to *assume* that other shared his attitudes on important and relevant matters.

Newcomb also found that, given an adequate opportunity for the men to become familiar with each other's attitudes, *actual* attitudinal agreement did indeed produce attraction. For example, Newcomb found that the better men got to know one another, the higher the correlation between men's actual agreement with each other's opinions concerning the likability of the other residents, and their attraction for one another. The positive relationship between attitudinal similarity and attraction became statistically significant in the final weeks of the study.

Newcomb found similar relationships between other attitudinal and value similarities and attraction. From knowledge of how similar in attitude

the small society   by Brickman

Washington Star Syndicate, Inc.

the individuals were *before* moving into the dormitory, Newcomb could not predict who would end up friends on short acquaintance. It evidently took the men a fair amount of time to discover which house members shared attitudes similar to their own.

Reinforcement theorists have conducted an avalanche of experimental research designed to document that (1) Attitude similarity is a potent trans-situational reinforcer, and (2) Attitude similarity is a critical determinant of interpersonal attraction. Many of these experiments have been conducted by Byrne and his associates (1971). Byrne *et al.* studied the effect of attitudinal similarity upon attraction in a great number of studies, conducted with diverse populations and under a wide array of conditions. (For a recent and detailed review of this impressive volume of work, see Byrne 1971; or Griffitt 1974.)

Most of these studies have followed the attraction-to-a-stranger procedural paradigm initially developed by Byrne (1961). Typically, the man (whose attraction responses are later to be assessed) is asked to complete an attitude questionnaire, which asks him to indicate his opinions on a wide variety of topics (such as his belief in God, his political preferences, and so on). Later, and seemingly unrelatedly, the man is asked to give his impressions of a stranger simply on the basis of knowledge of a few of the stranger's attitudes. To form his impression of the stranger, the person is given an attitude questionnaire (the same type of survey he filled out earlier) ostensibly as it was answered by the stranger. In actuality, of course, the questionnaire has been filled out by the experimenter in such a way as to vary, in known manner and with reference to the attitude responses made by the person himself earlier, the amount of attitude similarity (or dissimilarity) he shares with the stranger. Finally, after the person has formed a general impression of the stranger, he is asked to fill out Byrne's *IJS* Scale (described in Chapter 1) (which assesses his attraction for the stranger).

Using this general procedure, Byrne and Nelson (1965) compared the effect upon attraction of the *proportion* of similar attitudes expressed by the stranger with the effect of the *number* of similar attitudes expressed. They found it was the *proportion* of similar attitudes the stranger expressed which affected attraction to him. (The greater the proportion of similar, as opposed to dissimilar, attitudes, the greater the liking for the stranger who purportedly filled out the attitude questionnaire.) The sheer number of similar attitudes had no effect upon attraction.

Subsequent studies conducted by Byrne and his associates have corroborated this finding that a person's attraction for the stranger in this experimental situation is a positive linear function of the proportion of attitude statements attributed to the stranger which are in agreement with the person's own attitudes. The effect occurs in this situation with men and women from earliest childhood through old age (see Gaynor, Lamberth, and McCullers 1972; Griffitt, Nelson, and Littlepage 1972). It has been replicated time and again with people of diverse backgrounds and under many different conditions.

On the basis of this combined body of research, Byrne and his associates have proposed that a general "law of attraction": "attraction toward an individual is a positive linear function of the proportion of positive reinforcements associated with him" (Clore and Byrne 1974, p. 158).

At this point, we might consider why attitudinal similarity is generally a transsituational reinforcer. Why should similarity lead to attraction? We previously mentioned one reason: assuming that we like ourselves, we are cognitively consistent if we like those who hold attitudes similar to our own. There are a number of other good reasons why the discovery that we share another's attitudes is often rewarding.

Festinger's theory of social comparison processes (1954), for example, provides insight into the processes which may underlie the relationship between similarity and attraction. According to Festinger, we learn early in life that if our opinions and beliefs are incorrect, we are likely to be punished as a result. In fact, holding inaccurate beliefs—that there are no sharks in the vicinity of this beach or that kind of mushroom is a gastronomical delight—can be fatal.

Most of us, therefore, try to evaluate the correctness of our opinions and beliefs. A belief's "correctness" can be tested against two sources: physical reality or social reality. We may use physical reality to test the correctness of our belief that the mushroom is not poisonous by taking a large bite of it and observing the result. However, it is sometimes safer, and oftentimes easier, to use social reality to assess the accuracy of our beliefs and attitudes. Social reality is, of course, provided by the opinions and attitudes of others. When we find that someone else expresses the same attitudes and opinions we hold on an issue, our conviction that our own attitude is the correct one is supported; our attitude is given social validation. Since it is presumably pleasant to feel that our view of the world is the reasonable and correct one, such social validation should be rewarding. Or, as Byrne (1961, p. 713) puts it:

> Any time that another person offers us validation by indicating that his percepts and concepts are congruent with ours, it constitutes a rewarding interaction and, hence, one element in forming a positive relationship. Any time that another person indicates dissimilarity between our two notions, it constitutes a punishing interaction and thus one element in forming a negative relationship. Disagreement raises the unpleasant

possibility that we are to some degree stupid, uninformed, immoral, or insane.

Attitudinal similarity may help produce attraction for a third reason. If we know a person's attitudes, we can usually guess how that person is likely to behave. If a woman says that she thinks playing mumblety-peg is one of the most fascinating pastimes life has to offer, we may reasonably expect that she will play the game every time she has a chance. Thus, if we ourselves relish mumblety-peg, we may develop an attraction for her—not for reasons of cognitive consistency or for reasons of social validation, but simply because we anticipate many rewarding interactions playing the game with her. If a person feels as we do about things, we feel fairly confident that it would be rewarding to spend some time with that person; if a person despises everything we cherish, we might well be apprehensive about associating with that person.

There is still another reason why attitudinal similarity may lead to attraction. In Chapter 4 we found that people tend to like those who like them. It may be the case that when we learn that others are similar to us, we assume that they are likely to like us; thus, we like them in return.

Evidence that individuals tend to assume that similar others are likely to like them can be gleaned from an experiment conducted by Walster and Walster (1963). They wondered why it is that we so frequently seem to seek

Since it is presumably pleasant to feel that our view of the world is the reasonable and correct one, such social validation should be rewarding.

out similar others and to avoid people who are different from us. It is not intuitively obvious why we should so often prefer the company of similar others. Associating with people very different from oneself has certain advantages—dissimilar others provide new information and new insights into life; they may be unpredictable and thus exciting, for example.

Walster and Walster reasoned that we might choose to associate with dissimilar others more often if one factor were not restraining us: namely the fear that we will not be as well liked by dissimilar others as we are by people who are similar to ourselves. When people are very different from us, their social standards are unclear; we are likely to be afraid that our behavior will be unacceptable if we are not quite sure how we are "supposed" to behave. For example, the gentlemanly Proust (1928) expressed fear that "boors and bounders," unaware of society's rule, would underrate *his* social value. It is probably more usual for us to be afraid of being rejected by those we believe to be superior in some way to ourselves.

Thus, Walster and Walster proposed that if we were confident that everyone we came into contact with would like us, we would not be so hesitant to associate with dissimilar strangers. It is when it is especially important to be liked . . . or when we are unsure of our likability . . . that we will be especially likely to "play it safe"; we will be anxious to associate with similar people.

These hypotheses were tested in the following way: College students were informed that they had been assigned to participate in one of several discussion groups set up to obtain information about why people dream. Students were told that they could participate in any one of five groups. Some groups consisted of very similar people (i.e., fellow students in introductory psychology). Others groups consisted of very dissimilar others (i.e., factory workers, psychologists, etc.).

Students were then led to have different expectations about how much members of *all* groups would probably like them: (1) some were assured that others would be predisposed to like them; (2) some were assured that others would be predisposed to dislike them; (3) some were instructed to choose a group in which others were likely to like them; (4) and some (those who participated in the control group) were given no special instructions.

As predicted, students who had been assured that everyone would find them likable were eager to associate with dissimilar people. In fact, they vastly preferred dissimilar groups to similar ones. If students were told it was important to talk with people who would like them, they more often chose to interact with similar than with dissimilar people. Apparently, they did assume that similar people were more likely to like them than were dissimilar people. Those students who were instructed that they probably would not be liked by any group members were more anxious to talk with similar people than were control subjects. It appears, then, that the more concerned we are about whether others will like us, the more anxious we are to associate with similar others. Presumably, we have more hope of winning over similar strangers than dissimilar ones.

The finding that people who are psychologically secure are especially likely to associate with dissimilar others was corroborated by Goldstein and Rosenfeld (1969). (In this research, psychological security was via the Crowne-Marlowe *Social Desirability Scale* and Maslow's *Security–Insecurity Inventory*.)

Aronson and Worchel (1966) took note of the preceding results, and fired off an attack on Byrne's (1961) explanation of why it is that attitudinal similarity produces interpersonal attraction. Byrne had reasoned that people who tell us we are correct provide a valuable reward—consensual validation; we like them for that. Aronson and Worchel, however, argued that similarity may well produce interpersonal attraction for an entirely different reason: *i.e.*, if people are similar to us, we take it for granted that they will like us, and it is *this*—the anticipation of being liked—that makes us like them.

Aronson and Worchel pointed out that in Byrne's experiments men and women never knew how strangers felt about them—they could only guess. All they knew about the strangers was whether or not the stranger agreed with them. Aronson and Worchel argued that if persons had known how the strangers felt about them, Byrne would have found that *that* was what really mattered; people's discovery that the others agreed or disagreed with their attitudes would have had a negligible impact on their feelings toward the strangers.

To test their hypothesis, Aronson and Worchel led students to believe that their partners in an experiment (who were in reality confederates of the experimenters) possessed attitudes either very similar to or very unlike their own. In some cases students were told explicitly that their partners liked them. (The confederates were said to have stated that they were enjoying working with the students, and that the students seemed to be "really profound and interesting persons, well-informed.") In other cases, the students learned that the others disliked them. (The confederates stated that they had not enjoyed working with the students in the experiment and, further, that the students seemed to be shallow and uninteresting persons.)

Aronson and Worchel found that whether or not the confederate expressed attitudes similar or dissimilar to the students' own had *no* effect upon liking in and of itself. The only thing that mattered was whether or not the confederates said they liked, or disliked, the students.

If it is true that consensual validation is rewarding in and of itself, Aronson and Worchel should have found a positive relationship between attitudinal similarity and attraction. But they didn't.

Byrne and Griffitt (1966) reasoned that Aronson and Worchel's failure to use a wide range of attitudinal similarity and dissimilarity was responsible for their failure to find a link between similarity and attraction. They hypothesized that with a very restricted range of similarity–dissimilarity, the rewarding effect of consensual validation did not have a chance to show itself.

To investigate this possibility, Byrne and Griffitt replicated the Aronson and Worchel design and procedure with only one difference: they extended the range of attitudinal similarity–dissimilarity. Their results indicated that both the confederates' statement of liking or disliking *and* their degree of attitudinal similarity strongly influenced attraction for them. While the results of these experiments indicate that attitudinal similarity may often produce attraction because we anticipate that the similar other will like us, it is clear that attitudinal similarity is rewarding even when such esteem is not forthcoming.

QUALIFICATIONS TO THE RULE THAT ATTITUDINAL SIMILARITY PRODUCES ATTRACTION

Similarity is generally rewarding, and thus it sparks affection. We can all think of some very special circumstances in which similarity is *not* rewarding; circumstances in which similarities are unimportant . . . or, even worse, upsetting and punishing. Under these special circumstances, similarity should not lead to attraction.

One limitation to the rule that attitudinal similarity leads to attraction was drawn by Byrne (1961). Byrne agreed with Newcomb (1961) that we are more likely to develop affection for a person who embraces the views we cherish than for someone who agrees with us on matters we consider relatively trivial.

To test this hypothesis, Byrne, as usual, asked people to complete an attitude questionnaire but, this time, they were also asked to indicate which issues on the questionnaire were most important to them and which were least important. Two weeks later, the experimenter asked them to take a look at a questionnaire that a stranger in another class had ostensibly filled out. The stranger's responses were contrived. (1) Sometimes the stranger seemed to share all of the attitudes they themselves had expressed when they had filled out the questionnaires. (2) Sometimes the stranger seemed to have views opposite to their own. (3) Sometimes the stranger shared their opinions on issues they thought were important—but disagreed on all the trivial issues. And finally, (4) sometimes the stranger seemed to disagree with them on the most important issues—and shared similar opinions only on the least important issues. Each person, again as usual, in this procedural paradigm, then indicated attraction for the stranger.

As we would expect, Byrne found that the stranger who expressed views similar to the person's own was liked a good deal more than the stranger who expressed dissimilar views. (The stranger who expressed similar attitudes was also judged to be more intelligent, better informed, more moral, and better adjusted than the person with dissimilar attitudes.)

Byrne also found that the stranger who agreed on important issues was liked more and was believed to be more moral and better adjusted than was the stranger who agreed only on unimportant issues. (Whether the stranger agreed on important or unimportant issues had no effect on judgments of the stranger's desirability as a work partner, intelligence, or knowledge of currents events.)

Similarities "count" then—especially if they are in important areas. Trivial similarities are a sparse reward—and thus have a trivial effect on liking.

The Similarity–Reinforcement–Attraction link is not an unbreakable one. There is evidence that under certain conditions similarity is anything but rewarding, and that under these special conditions similarity produces repulsion, not attraction.

Two experiments suggest that when the similarities we share with another have disagreeable implications, the usual similarity–attraction relationship may be overturned.

Cooper and Jones (1969) reasoned that the similarities we share with an undesirable person have one type of unpleasant implication, "associative casting." They observe that we often attempt to be seen with the right people and avoid the wrong crowd because we know that others will assume —simply on the basis of our affiliation with the others—that we share their beliefs and values. Thus, they predicted, (and found) that *if people are pleasant*, the more similar we are to them, the more willing we will be to support them publicly. However, *if people are obnoxious and undesirable*, we will react quite differently. The more similar they are, the more worried we will be that we will be socially cast with them—and the more we will publicly disagree with them, in an attempt to disassociate ourselves from them. Taylor and Mettee (1971) secured similar results.

Baron *et al.* (1976) point out that there are still other conditions in which similarity is *not* rewarding, and thus will lead, not to liking, but to repulsion.

Byrne *et al.* (1976, p. 210) ask:

How do you feel when someone just like yourself is more successful than you are? Nadler, Jazwinski, and Lau (1975) hypothesized that similarity in this instance would be more threatening than dissimilarity because it makes one's own failure much more difficult to rationalize. A male subject interacted with a similar or a dissimilar male confederate. Afterward a female confederate was asked to choose just one of them to work with her. When an attitudinally similar confederate was chosen, this made the subjects unhappy, uncreative, and angry, but the choice of a dissimilar other did not have these negative effects.

One might also ask the opposite question: "How do you feel when someone just like yourself turns out to be deranged, degenerate, or deficient?" Theorists have answered that we might not find *that* very rewarding either.

Even Heider (1957, p. 186), whose balance theory predicts a positive relationship between similarity and attraction, took note of this probable exception:

The factor of similarity can . . . evoke disliking when the similarity carries with it disagreeable implications. For example, a person with a disability who wishes to deny it may dislike and even feel hostile toward another person similarly afflicted. The disagreeable similarity may serve as a reminder of the disability, and in other ways emphasize it.

Novak and Lerner (1968) were the first to investigate what happens when the similarity we share with another has "disagreeable implications" for us. As we would expect on the basis of a host of previous evidence, when people were asked to indicate how willing they were to interact with attitudinally similar others or dissimilar others, they were far more willing to associate with the similar persons. When the other persons mentioned that they had histories of emotional disturbance, however, the relationship reversed itself; people showed less willingness to interact with attitudinally similar persons who happened to have histories of emotional disturbance, than with dissimilar others who also had such histories. Novak and Lerner reasoned that the attitudinal similarity shared with the previously disturbed others carried the disagreeable and threatening implication that they, too, could become emotionally disturbed.

Despite these exceptions, there is little doubt that similarity of attitude produces esteem with great consistency. When we meet others who hold attitudes similar to our own, we like them. When the others also discover that our attitudes are similar to *theirs,* and how much we like *them,* their liking for us may be expected to increase. Knowledge that *they* like *us* bolsters, in turn, our esteem for them. In this way, as Newcomb has observed (1956), "attraction breeds attraction."

Similarity and Personality

According to folk psychology, peoples' characters can be judged by the company they keep. Not only are similar individuals assumed to congregate ("Birds of a feather . . .") but individuals are assumed to become like their associates in personal traits and characteristics. ("Keep not ill men company lest you increase the number.") Many a mother, anxious to save her innocent child's character—or at least its reputation—has forbidden the child to keep bad company.

Friends generally agree with this folk wisdom. People usually believe their personalities are more similar to those they count as friends than to those people whom they don't (e.g., Beier, Rossi, and Garfield 1961; Broxton 1963). But are they?

The method generally used to answer the question of whether friends actually do possess similar personality characteristics has been to compare individuals' responses on a personality test with the responses of their friends vs. nonfriends. Reader and English (1947), for example, administered five personality tests to pairs of friends and pairs of nonfriends and computed correlations between the pairs. These investigators found a higher correlation between friends' personality traits than between nonfriends'.

One careful study examined not only the extent to which friends vs. nonfriends thought their own personalities were similar, but the extent to which *others* who were acquainted with them thought their personalities were similar. Miller, Campbell, Twedt, and O'Connell (1966) interviewed students who were living in sororities, fraternities, and dormitories at Northwestern University. They requested students in each group (1) to indicate their five closest friends in the house, and (2) to evaluate themselves and everyone they lived with on a number of personality traits.

Miller et al. (1966) found that friends developed a *reputation* for being very similar. If, for example, residents thought one member of the friendship pair was "conceited," they were likely to assume the other member was, too. Despite the evidence that others take it for granted that friends' personalities are similar, however, the investigators found that the friends, themselves, did *not* see themselves as being very similar in personality.

How does one explain the fact that individuals—who by their own descriptions are unique individuals—are seen by outside observers as being "birds of a feather"? After carefully considering a number of alternative explanations, the authors concluded that the acquaintances were simply wrong. Their perceptions were simply due to a "halo" effect. Miller et al. (1966, p. 11) found:

Those who are friends have been shown to be indeed similar on numerous other dimensions such as attitudes, socioeconomic class, religion, values, interests, etc. (Burgess and Wallin 1953; Byrne and Blaylock 1963; Lindzey and Borgatta 1954; Richardson 1939). With so many dimensions on which true similarity exists, generalization of similarity to personality–trait dimensions could readily occur. The pairs who provided the reputations may have mistakenly rated those who navigate in space and time together and who tend to be similar on a variety of attitudinal, socioeconomic, interest and skill dimensions, as also similar on a variety of personality dimensions.

A few investigators, such as Reader and English (1947) and Izard (1960a), have found positive correlations between friends' personality traits. Generally, however, evidence indicating a positive relationship is not obtained with the regularity with which positive correlations between attitudinal similarity and attraction are found. In addition, correlations between personality similarity and attraction are usually much lower than those between attitude similarity and attraction (cf. Richardson 1939). If personality similarity *is* a factor in attraction, it is perhaps a less important one than attitudinal similarity.

If it is true that friends are at least somewhat more similar in personality than are nonfriends, several questions arise:

1 Do friends *become* similar due to their association? It is easy to imagine, for example, that one might become aggressive if forced to interact continually with an aggressive person. As Plutarch claimed, it may be the case that "if one lives with a lame person, he will learn to limp."

2 Or, do people *select* each other as friends because they share similar personalities?

3 Or, do individuals simply associate with similar people for reasons that have nothing to do with their personal preferences? We discussed the importance of proximity as a determinant of interpersonal attraction in Chapter 2, and the evidence that people are likely to choose their friends from those who happen to be nearby. Due to a variety of reasons, it may be that people tend to be thrown together with those who possess similar personality characteristics. This might be particularly true in cases in which a particular type of personality is drawn to a certain type of occupation.

ASSOCIATION AS A CAUSE OF PERSONALITY SIMILARITY

If it is true that people *become* similar to others as a result of their association with one another, we should expect, say, that married couples should come to resemble one another more and more over time. Do they? The data are somewhat contradictory. Hunt (1935) found no correlation between a

Courtesy of Mell Lazarus and Field Newspaper Syndicate.

couple's similarity in ranking of ideals and the length of time they had been married. Hoffeditz (1934) found no evidence that resemblance on the personality traits of neurotic tendency, self-sufficiency, and dominance increased with duration of marriage; and other studies (e.g., Schooley 1936; Newcomb and Svehla 1937) have obtained mixed results. Thus, it is not clear that frequent interaction produces personality similarity.

ASSOCIATION AS A CONSEQUENCE OF PERSONALITY SIMILARITY

The second notion, that people *select* their friends on the basis of similar personality characteristics, is a more popular explanation of the correlational data which indicate that friends' personalities are more similar than nonfriends' personalities.

Why should personality similarity be a factor in friendship formation? Why should we like people who possess personality characteristics similar to our own? Much of the research investigating the relationship between personality similarity and attraction has been stimulated by a collection of ideas that might be called a "theory of narcissism." It has been hypothesized that people like those who possess personality characteristics similar to their own because of strong narcissistic tendencies. These tendencies presumably lead "the individual to love in another person that which he sees in himself. That which is most like one's self is loved" (Reader and English 1947, p. 216).

The personality similarity-attraction hypothesis is not self-evident, but few of the proponents of the narcissistic point of view elaborate why it is that it should be especially satisfying to behold personality characteristics in another which are similar to our own. If we are irritable and excitable, is it especially satisfying to interact with another who possesses these same unfortunate traits? Is it rewarding simply to know that another person suffers the same loathsome traits we do? Or is it the case that we wish to see only our good qualities reflected in another? But if we are fortunate enough to possess Job's patience and an ethereal calm, for example, wouldn't it perhaps detract from our feelings of self-congratulation to interact with saints, who possess this quality in an even higher degree? Might we not prefer to interact with lesser mortals so that our goodness may shine in comparison?

Although it is not apparent why we should enjoy seeing our own personality characteristics reflected in others, whether we do has been the focus of several studies. Izard (1960b) tested the hypothesis that his subjects would, *prior* to acquaintance, be more similar in personality profile to those people they subsequently came to like, than to those they came to dislike. Izard administered the *Edwards' Personal Preference Schedule* (*EPPS*) to an entire entering college freshman class. Six months later, a number of the freshman women were given a sociometric form requiring them to list the three girls they liked most and the three they liked least. Izard found that the women's prior-to-acquaintance personality profiles were similar to those of their most liked classmates, but not to those of classmates they liked least.

ASSOCIATION WITH SIMILAR OTHERS AS A CONSEQUENCE OF PROXIMITY

In interpreting the results of Izard's study, we can be sure that the friends possessed similar personalities *before* they ever became friends. Nevertheless, we cannot be completely certain that personality similarity was a *cause* of the friendships which formed among the women.

Perhaps women with similar personalities simply happened to be in the same place at the same time; perhaps it was their proximity (not their similarity) which led ultimately to their becoming friends. Unfortunately, we do not know the relationship between similarity of personality and proximity among Izard's subjects. For example, we do not know whether the women who elected to take tapdancing to meet the physical education requirements differed in personality from those who elected to learn judo—or if those who enrolled in home economics differed in personality from those who enrolled in engineering. Therefore, we cannot guess to what extent students selected their "most liked" classmates as friends simply because of the proximity factor rather than for reasons of personality similarity. On the basis of other investigations, which have demonstrated that students who major in similar areas have certain personality similarities (e.g., Goldschmid 1967), we might speculate that proximity was at least partially a factor. To be confident that friends became friends because of personality similarity, frequency of interaction between similar and dissimilar personality types would have had to have been controlled.

Maturity and the Personality–Similarity–Liking Link

Izard (1963) tried to replicate his study. In his second study, he interviewed college freshmen *and* college seniors. Once again, Izard found that the more similar freshmen were in personality, the more they liked one another. When Izard turned to the college seniors, however, he found that the similarity of personality–attraction link suddenly disappeared. Izard reasoned that his failure to replicate his initial results with the older subjects may have been due to the seniors' increased social and emotional maturity. He speculated (1963, p. 600):

> Perhaps the more "mature" person has less need to see his personality characteristics reflected in his friends.

Whether or not this is the true reason for the replication failure, Izard has social support for the notion that mature, mentally healthy persons have less need to see their personality characteristics reflected in their friends. Maslow (1950), for example, has investigated love in "self-actualizing" people through questionnaire data and personal interviews. It was Maslow's impression that in healthy people, homogamy (or the tendency for like to be associated with like) is the rule only with respect to character traits such as honesty, sincerity, and so on. Maslow writes (1953, p. 89):

> In the more external and superficial characteristics..., the extent of homogamy seems to be significantly less than in average people. Self-actualizing people are not threatened by differences nor by strangeness. Indeed, they are rather intrigued than otherwise. They need familiar accents, clothes, food, customs, and ceremonies much less than do average people.

If we can conclude that such traits measured by the *EPPS* as need for "autonomy," "change," or "exhibitionism" are "superficial" traits, Maslow's findings suggest that maturity may indeed make us more tolerant of people who are different from ourselves.

In any case, psychologists are still not sure whether or not people *do* select their friends on the basis of personality similarity. In addition to Izard's failure to replicate his finding with college seniors, several other investigators (e.g., Bonney 1952; Hoffman 1958) have concluded, on the basis of their own investigations, that personality similarity is not a sufficient condition for attraction to take place.

Personality Similarity and Marital Happiness

It has been suggested that similarity of personality, like similarity of attitude, allows two people more easily to reward each other. Thus, it has been proposed that personality similarity should promote marital stability and happiness.

The question of whether actual personality similarities between husbands and wives is associated with marital happiness has not been neglected by researchers. Dymond (1954), for example, found that happily married spouses were more similar to each other than were those of unhappy husbands and wives (in their responses to the *Minnesota Multiphasic Personality Inventory's* (*MMPI*) items concerning interaction with others). Cattell and Nesselrode (1967) published similar findings. These authors investigated the degree to which similarity of personality, as measured by Cattell's

16 Personality Factor questionnaire, is found in stable vs. unstable marriages. They found a great deal of support for the hypothesis that similarity of personality is a characteristic of happily married couples.

THEORY OF COMPLEMENTARY NEEDS

So far, our discussion would suggest that men and women relentlessly seek carbon copies of themselves. However, it's obvious that they don't. Obviously men and women generally look for partners who are *dissimilar* in certain fundamental ways.

For example, as Gerald Marwell (1975) and H. Andrew Michener have wryly observed, most men and women prefer to marry the "opposite"—and complementary—sex. In *traditional* 1950s marriages, men and women were expected to bring different—and complementary—skills to their marriages. Men were expected to perform the "heavy" tasks—like mowing the lawn, shoveling the sidewalks, fixing the furnace, tinkering with the car, and taking out the garbage. Women were supposed to do the "light" work: cleaning the house, cooking, canning, shopping, taking care of the children. These traditional sex-typed roles are changing but the *principle* that "opposites attract" in the division of labor may remain. Women who loathe cooking may find a man especially rewarding who is a culinary genius; men who can't tell a spark plug from a carburetor may find a woman who can very appealing.

Some theorists have even argued that certain patterns of *personality* dissimilarity—rather than detracting from marital happiness—might actually enhance it.

Robert Winch is the leading proponent of the view that "opposites attract." Winch (1958) proposed, in the now classic *Mate Selection: A Study of Complementary Needs*, that (1) men and women are attracted to those friends and lovers who provide them with maximum need-gratification. (2) Thus, men and women prefer those women and men whose needs are complementary to their own.

According to Winch and his associates, a couple's personalities and needs may be complementary in two different ways:

1 The partners' needs may differ in *kind*. (For example, a dominant man or woman may seek out a submissive mate; a nurturant person—who has love to give—may seek out a succorant mate—who needs it.)

2 The partners' needs may differ in *degree*. (The highly dominant person, who enjoys telling other people how to lead their lives, may get along extremely well with a person who has little need to dominate others.)

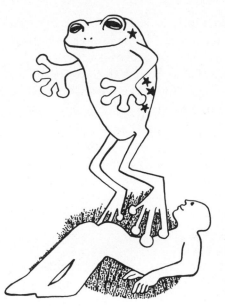

Certain dissimilarities in personality may actually facilitate interpersonal attraction.

Although Winch specifically insists that both friends and lovers look for a "complementary" partner, the lion's share of the research performed to test Winch's theory has been performed with engaged or married couples.

What evidence is there that need complementarity is indeed a factor in interpersonal attraction? Not much.

In a now-classic study, Winch and his associates conducted in-depth interviews with 25 married couples. Winch talked with them about their earliest memories, their experiences growing up, and finally, about their lives at present. After this clinical interview, five analysts met, discussed the interview, and settled on a diagnostic evaluation of the couples' needs. The couples also completed a battery of personality tests (i.e., the *Thematic Apperception Test* and Cattell's *16 PF, Form A*). On the basis of these interviews and tests, Winch *et al.* rated the couples' personality needs.

According to Winch (1954, pp. 245–248), the bulk of this evidence supports the hypothesis that

> . . . persons like our subjects tend to select mates whose needs are complementary rather than similar to their own.

Kerckhoff and Davis (1962) also provide some evidence that people do search for a complementary mate. The authors interviewed college couples. Some of these couples had been going together only a short time (less than 18 months). Some of them had been going together a lot longer. All of the couples were seriously considering marriage.

In early interviews, Kerckhoff and Davis assessed (1) *couples' value consensus* (the extent to which they agreed about the importance of various family values), and (2) the extent to which they shared complementary needs. Kerckhoff and Davis hypothesized that both Value consensus and Need complementarity should have a critical impact on whether a relationship flourished or died. Couples' courtship progress was assessed by asking couples if their relationship had changed in the past seven months (since the study had begun). Couples could give one of three reasons to this question: "Yes, we are nearer being a permanent couple;" "No, it is the same;" or "Yes, we are further from being a permanent couple."

Kerckhoff and Davis found that *early in a relationship* (and only then) Value consensus is of critical importance in determining whether or not a relationship survives. Only *late in a relationship* does Need complementarity become important.

Unfortunately, other researchers have been unable to replicate the Winch *et al.* (1954) and Kerckhoff and Davis (1962) findings. For example, Becker (1964), Bowerman and Day (1956), Murstein (1961), Banta and Heterington (1963), Schellenberg and Bee (1960), and Levinger, Senn, and Jorgensen (1970)—to name a few—tested the Complementarity hypothesis in a series of very careful studies, and secured disappointing results. If anything, these researchers' data indicate that people tend to select mates who possess *similar*, rather than *complementary*, needs.

Winch's original data, then, seem to provide the major support for the need–complementarity hypothesis. And his data analyses have been sharply criticized on methodological grounds (e.g., Tharp 1963; Murstein 1976). As Tharp (1963, p. 107) concludes, after carefully reviewing the avalanche of studies that have been conducted to document that people do so select those with complementary needs:

> It is our judgment ... that the complementarity–need hypothesis as now stated is not tenable.

Even so, psychologists are reluctant to completely abandon the complementarity–need hypothesis. It sounds so reasonable.

Psychologists have argued that the need–complementarity hypothesis can still be saved. They argue that "if only" theorists had formulated the need–complementarity hypothesis a little more precisely ... "if only" they had tested the need–complementarity hypothesis in more sophisticated ways, researchers would surely have found some support for the hypothesis.

For example, Levinger (1964, p. 156) points out that the original need–complementarity hypothesis had two problems: first, men and women's needs can be satisfied in a variety of settings:

Proverbially, it is accepted that the man whose dominance needs are frustrated at the office comes home to release his anger on wife, child, or dog. Or, conversely, the henpecked husband at home goes out to work to boss his employees.

One thing theorists might do, then, is to study not whether or not couples' *general needs* are complementary, but whether or not couples' *marital needs* are.

Secondly, Levinger points out that sometimes a person's needs can best be satisfied by a similar and sometimes by a dissimilar other (e.g., if a shy man is interested in *meeting* people, he might want an outgoing wife. If he's interested in *avoiding* people, he might prefer a reclusive wife). Theorists should provide some guidelines for specifying which needs can best be satisfied by similar friends and lovers and which needs can best be satisfied by complementary ones.

Roscow (1957) has advanced quite a different reason why the need–complementarity hypothesis has received so little support. He has suggested that the need–complementarity hypothesis might be more likely to be confirmed if need–complementarity were analyzed in a framework of more global personality types.

The need–complementarity hypothesis, then, has been critically wounded—but it is not dead. Theorists still hope they can patch up the hypothesis and save it.

THE NEED–COMPLETION PRINCIPLE

Cattell and Nesselrode (1967) have investigated an hypothesis somewhat similar to the need–complementarity proposition. Cattell (1967, p. 351) has reasoned that choice in friendship and in marriage may be directed by:

> ... a desire to possess characteristics (by sharing them in the possessed partner) which are felt by the individual to be necessary to his [or her] self-concept or to his or her social and general life adjustment in marriage. ... For example, a socially awkward person might especially value a partner who is socially adroit and poised.

The need–completion principle differs from the need-complementary hypothesis in two ways: (1) The need–completion principle emphasizes the factor of personal social desirability to a greater extent than does need–complementarity theory. The principle (1967, p. 356) "... states that every person tends to seek in a partner much the same set of desirables—good looks, intelligence, emotional stability, etc.—but more so to the extent that he or she lacks them." (2) The need–completion principle is not particularly concerned with the consequences of the individual's interactions.

This interesting notion has also been advanced, though in slightly different terms, by several psychoanalytic theorists. Theodor Reik, for example, in discussing the origin and nature of romantic love, quickly dismisses similarity as a possible causal factor (1944, pp. xiv–xv):

> As long as one person meets another and does not see him as a different individual with a different makeup, love is psychologically not possible. The difference has to be felt, although it need not become conscious. If the object is exactly like me, where is the necessity to love him? If the other person is precisely as I am, where is the possibility of loving him or her—except in a psychoanalytical theory that we love only ourselves in the other?

Reik persuasively goes on to reject this variant of a theory or narcissism and proceeds to argue that we fall in love with those who possess qualities we envy.

Unfortunately, Cattell and Nesselrode's research dealt yet another blow to the notion that the proper interlocking of a man and woman's personalities leads to love. They found little supporting evidence for the operation of a need–completion principle when they examined the personality responses of stable and unstable married couples.

Nevertheless, the need–completion idea is interesting and some supportive evidence for it is provided by studies in which individuals were asked to describe their friends. When people perceive that their friends are different from themselves, the difference usually is of a specific type: The dissimilar friend is perceived to possess traits which we admire, and wish we possessed, but which we believe we lack. (See Beier, Rossi, and Garfield 1961; Lundy, Katkovsky, Cromwell, and Shoemaker 1955; O'Connor 1956; Reader and English 1947; and Thompson and Nishimura 1952.)

The Beier, Rossi, and Garfield (1961) findings are typical. The people who participated in this experiment completed the *Minnesota Multiphasic Personality Inventory* under three sets of instructions. They first filled out the *MMPI* as they normally would. They then tried to guess how their *best friend* would answer the items. Finally, they tried to guess how their *most disliked acquaintance* would answer the items.

Beier *et al.* predicted that individuals would: (1) project more of their own personal characteristics on friends than on those they disliked, (2) project more socially desirable characteristics to friends than they attributed to themselves; and (3) project more socially undesirable characteristics to disliked persons than they attributed to themselves.

The data confirmed all three hypotheses. The evidence (1961, p. 7) indicated that we assume that our friends are psychologically stronger and better adjusted than we are ourselves.

The friend as compared with the self is seen as more social, less depressed, less susceptible to moods, less concerned with bodily function, less incapacitated by feelings of inadequacy, and generally more active and realistic than oneself. If the individual doing the rating is a male, he sees his male friend as being more interested in masculine activities than himself.

Similarly, Beier *et al.* (1961, p. 7) found that we tend to believe that our enemies are much more psychologically maladjusted than we are.

The disliked person as compared to the self is seen as being more impulsive, more suspicious of others, with more idiosyncratic ideas, and also more aggressiveness. The nonfriend was attributed an excess of almost all the characteristics tapped by the MMPI, i.e., impulsiveness, moodiness, concern with bodily functions, feelings of inadequacy, depression, social isolation, idiosyncratic ideas, and manic activity.

The finding that one tends to suspect the sanity of those people one dislikes can be supported by everyday observation. The "Letters to the Editor" column in any daily newspaper illustrates that irate readers on one side of an issue manage to find clear evidence that their opponents are deranged. The opposition has equal confidence that their supporters possess excellent mental health.

Even psychiatrists are not immune to the temptation to assume that those who agree with them must be mentally healthier than are those who do not share their views. At the time of the 1964 presidential election, *Fact* magazine reported the results of a poll of 12,356 psychiatrists. The poll was designed to assess whether or not Barry Goldwater, the Republican candidate for president, was "psychologically fit" to serve as president. In violation of all reasonable standards, almost half of the psychiatrists who responded—most of whom had never even spoken to Mr. Goldwater—much less examined him—willingly provided their opinion that Mr. Goldwater's state of mental health left much to be desired. He was diagnosed as a "dangerous compensated schizophrenic," a "paranoid," a "severe obsessive–compulsive neurotic," and so it went. One psychiatrist felt so strongly about his mail-order diagnosis of Goldwater as a "dangerous lunatic" that he felt compelled to add: "Any psychiatrist who does not agree with the above is himself psychologically unfit to be a psychiatrist." Needless to say, one can be fairly confident that these same psychiatrists were overwhelmingly for the Democratic candidate at that time. As Mr. Goldwater has grown in stature over the years to become an "elder statesman" of his party and the United States Senate, it would be interesting to know how the same psychiatrists would assess his mental health; undoubtedly, the results of such a poll would suggest Mr. Goldwater has experienced a miraculous "spontaneous remission" and regained his mental health, now that his views are not so divergent from the norm.

CORRELATION IN MENTAL HEALTH

Before leaving our discussion of the role of personality similarities and dissimilarities in interpersonal attraction, we should note that among clinical psychologists and psychiatrists who see many unhappy people—including those enmeshed in marital problems—there is widespread agreement that similarity with respect to the general personality characteristics of neuroticism is a factor in heterosexual attraction. Perhaps Edmund Bergler (1948, p. 11), the psychoanalyst, presents the case most strongly:

> All stories about a normal woman who becomes the prey of a neurotic man, and vice versa, or a normal man who falls in love with a highly neurotic woman, are literary fairy tales. Real life is less romantic; two neurotics look for each other with uncanny regularity. Nothing is left to chance, as far as emotional attachments are concerned.

In addition to the anecdotal evidence upon which many clinicians have advanced this point of view, there are some data which support the proposition that neurotics tend to marry neurotics. Murstein (1967a) administered the MMPI to 99 couples who were either engaged or going steady. Some of the variables subsequently examined were anxiety, ego strength, and repression; in addition a global assessment of all of their MMPI responses were rendered by a clinician. Six months later these couples were asked whether they had progressed in their courtship. Murstein found that the couples showed a significant and positive correlation in mental health. Further, couples who were similar in mental health progressed further in courtship than did dissimilar couples.

Physical Characteristics

According to folklore, people are attracted to people who are similar (or dissimilar, depending upon the particular bit of folk wisdom one reads) in physical appearance. Harris (1912, p. 478) states some common beliefs.

> Weak or little men have a decided inclination for strong or big women, and strong or big women for weak or little men. Blondes prefer dark persons or brunettes; snub-nosed, hook-nosed; persons with excessively thin, long bodies and limbs, those who are stumpy and short, and so on!

Some attempt has been made to investigate the degree to which physical similarities are related to attraction. Unfortunately, most of these studies are correlational, and interpretations of the cause and effect relationships involved are difficult. Again, the existence of attraction has been assumed from evidence that a couple is either married or has shown an intention to marry.

While no one knows if we prefer those whose noses are different from our own, there is evidence that, at least as far as marital selection is concerned, little men do *not* have an affinity for large women and vice versa. Correlations between the stature of husbands and wives are generally positive; short men tend to marry short women (e.g., see Pearson and Lee 1903).

There does appear to be some tendency for those with physical defects to marry those possessing like defects. This may be especially true with respect to deafness. Harris (1912, p. 484), for example, states that "assortative mating for deafness is more nearly perfect than for any other known character." The fact that deaf people do tend to marry one another so impressed Alexander Graham Bell (1883) that he felt compelled to point out the grave consequences of this tendency in an article entitled "Upon the Formation of a Deaf Variety of the Human Race."

There are many reasons why those who are afflicted with a physical defect might marry a person who is similarly afflicted. Perhaps the most compelling explanation of the relationship is that those who possess a defect often spend an unusual amount of time in proximity with others who share their handicaps.

It is interesting, nevertheless, that couples who share the same physical defect may be happier than couples in which one member of the pair does not possess the defect. Harris reports data collected by Fay (1898) which indicate that marriages in which both members are deaf are happier than those in which only one is afflicted. The divorce and separation rate of marriages in which both partners are deaf is lower than that for marriages in which only one partner is deaf.

There is also a good deal of evidence that dating, engaged, and married men and women are similar to one another in the degree to which they are physically attractive. (See Berscheid and Walster 1974.) We shall discuss this evidence in greater detail in Chapter 10. It is clear, however, that such similarity is a consequence, not of preference, but of other factors. The evidence indicates that virtually everyone, male or female, would prefer to date and marry an attractive partner; it is just that, eventually, most people have to "settle" for partners who are no more, and no less, attractive than themselves.

Intelligence and Education

Many investigations have documented that we tend to like and love those who are similar to ourselves in intelligence. The correlations obtained between intelligence of husbands and wives have been approximately of the magnitude +0.40 (e.g., Jones 1929; Reed and Reed 1965). The relationship between the intelligence levels of friends is also positive, but lower (cf. Richardson 1939).

Once again, the fact that the bright birds tend to flock together—and the dull dodos do, too—may be easily explained by propinquity. We know that people are likely to be thrown together with others of like intelligence. For example, if you're a bright teenager, you have a chance to go on to college, where you bump into, meet, and perhaps marry a similarly special person. If you're not, you don't.

It would be interesting to know whether or not people actually seek out those whose intelligence is similar to their own, as well. Is it the case that everyone—intelligent or not—would prefer to date and marry an intelligent partner? Or is it the case that a person of low intelligence finds the company of other unintelligent people most rewarding? This last possibility may also underlie the correlations obtained between intelligence and attraction.

As might be expected, uniformly high correlations have been obtained between husbands and wives on the variable of educational attainment (Garrison, Anderson, and Reed 1968). Again, it is clear that people of like educational level interact with each other more often than do those who are dissimilar. But, in addition, similarity of educational attainment subsumes many cultural and attitudinal similarities which individuals may find attractive in each other.

Other Social Characteristics

The classic study of the similarity of engaged couples along various social dimensions was conducted by Burgess and Wallin (1943). They found that engaged couples were similar on almost every characteristic they examined. Similarity was found with respect to (1) family background, including place lived in childhood, educational level, nativity, income, and social status of parents; (2) religious affiliation; (3) types of family relationships, including happiness of parents' marriage, attitude toward the father when a child, and sex of siblings; (4) social participation, including the tendency to be a lone wolf rather than socially gregarious, leisure time preference ("stay at home" vs. "on the go"), drinking habits, smoking habits, number of friends of same sex, as well as opposite sex, and so on.

Similarity among the couples was found also with respect to their courtship behavior. Variables here included whether or not the person had been previously engaged and the number of people he or she had dated steadily. A similarity of attitude toward marriage was also found among couples, but this, of course, may have come about through their interaction with one another. Burgess and Wallin, then, present overwhelming evidence that like tends to marry like on the basis of social characteristics; homogamy is the rule of dating and mating.

Theorists frequently cite the fact that marriages in our society tend to occur largely within homogeneous segments of the population, as evidence that we *prefer* to marry those similar to ourselves. For example, several social scientists have argued that most groups possess norms which dictate that one should marry a person who is similar to oneself; the inevitable result is homogamous marriages.

Kerckhoff (1974), who has examined some of the reasons which may underlie homogamy, does not find it surprising that scientists have tended to take it for granted that people *prefer* to marry those that they *end up* marrying. He notes that although few of us really believe that there is "one and only one" person in the world with whom we would be happy, our society emphasizes the freedom of the individual to *select* a marriage partner from among a seemingly wide range of candidates. Given the common belief that each of us chooses a mate from a diverse sample of eligible candidates, it seems reasonable to interpret the strong homogamy patterns observed in the United States as an indication of a *preference* for people who are like ourselves in a very wide variety of characteristics.

There are several difficulties with such an interpretation. Perhaps the major one is that, as we have noted, most of us lead circumscribed lives. The common belief that we choose a mate from a wide range of candidates is probably wrong. The "ecology" of mate selection is such that we are preprogrammed to meet and marry those like ourselves. Very few of us ever have an opportunity to meet, interact with, become attracted to, and marry, a person markedly dissimilar from ourselves.

Kerckhoff observes, therefore, that in predicting mate selection it is essential to consider which factors in a society limit contact between groups. In most cases, these forces act to segregate groups of similar people from groups which are dissimilar. Society's "sorting process"—which exerts its influence on the nursery school we first attend, to the neighborhoods in which we live, and which continues throughout our lives—seems to operate principally on the dimension of similarity.

The *experimental* evidence makes it clear that people are attracted to those who share their attitudes. The *correlational* evidence, which suggests that people are likely to *associate* with people who are similar to themselves, cannot provide conclusive evidence that people *prefer* to associate with similar others and avoid those who are dissimilar. In these studies, proximity and similarity are forever confounded.

A recent study conducted by Nahemow and Lawton (1975), which examines the friendship network among residents of a city housing project, sketches the effects of both proximity and similarity on attraction. Friendship between people of *dissimilar* ages and races were found almost exclusively among those who lived very *close* to one another. The investigators found that people will travel greater distances, and generally put themselves out, only to see those people who are *similar* to themselves. Thus, the willingness to endure cost and to expend effort to overcome the barriers of physical distance seem to occur principally when the other is similar to oneself. This provides additional evidence, then, that we may prefer similar to dissimilar others.

Summary

Similarity is often a potent transsituational reinforcer. The answer to the question: "Does *attitudinal* similarity generate liking?" is a resounding "yes." When we discover that others share our beliefs and attitudes, it is satisfying; we like them. When we discover that others disagree with us, it is unsettling; it's hard to like such persons.

Of course, in some very special circumstances, the discovery that we are similar to another may be unsettling. (Say, for example, we discover that our personalities are similar to that of an obnoxious boor—or a mass murderer. In those very special circumstances, similarity will not be reinforcing and will not lead to liking.)

The answer to the question: "Do *personality* similarities lead to liking?" is a resounding "maybe." According to folk psychology, they do. People assume that, initially, individuals *prefer* to congregate with people similar to themselves ("birds of a feather . . .") *and* that people *become* even more like those they associate with, as they continue to interact. The evidence in support of this folk wisdom is sparse. Personality similarity appears to be of only modest importance in determining who likes whom.

If the evidence that personality similarities lead to liking is weak, the evidence that need–complementaries can lead to liking is downright nonexistent. Although it seems reasonable that people should prefer those whose personalities complement their own—that dominant people should like submissive ones, sadists should like masochists, etc.—there is no compelling evidence that they do.

At the present time, the most compelling conclusions seem to be: similarity attracts.

Researchers have amassed a great deal of evidence that we like those who make our lives more pleasant on a day-to-day basis—those who cheer us up . . . and who reduce our loneliness, our fear, and our stress. We will now consider the impact of these more or less specific reinforcers on liking.

rewards and punishments others provide:
the reduction of isolation, fear, and stress

Social Isolation

People do not like to be alone for any length of time. The strength of human desire for the company of others was dramatically demonstrated by the results of a social reform experiment conducted in the early 19th century. As the result of their religious beliefs and a social upsurge of "humanitarianism," the Quakers tried to reform the prison system. They wanted to build a "perfect," "humanitarian" prison. In 1821, they commissioned John Haviland, the great prison achitect of the time, to design it.

The Quaker reformers had observed that mingling among prison inmates produced strong friendships among the inmates—friendships which often continued even after the prisoners were released. Unfortunately, such social bonds often led the ex-criminal back into a life of crime after release. Thus, in the humanitarian reformation, it was decided to build a prison which would prevent contact among the prisoners. Total social isolation, the reformers believed, not only would prevent harmful corruption and protect the criminal's good resolutions, but it would give the prisoner ample opportunity to ponder mistakes and make peace with God. Unfortunately, the means by which the Quakers hoped to reach their admirable goals were based on faulty social analysis. Haviland's architectural design provided for solitary confinement of the prisoners, day and night throughout their incarceration. At first, the new humanitarian prison was extremely popular with wardens and a great many such prisons were built. The prison commissioners, however, soon found that they had to use great ingenuity to keep the prisoners in strict social isolation. New ventilation systems had to be designed, for example, because prisoners soon found that the regular systems could be utilized for purposes of communication.

Ultimately the policy of social isolation was found to be disastrous. Many inmates became physically and mentally ill as a result of their solitary confinement. Their inability to work because of their illnesses eventually forced a change of policy. Current psychological knowledge would have enabled us to foresee this outcome.

By early childhood a person has usually developed a need for the company of people. "Cabin fever" is a familiar expression which epitomizes the discomfort that even brief social isolation brings. Complete social isolation for any period of time is a painful experience. Schachter (1959, p. 6) points out that the autobiographical reports of religious hermits, prisoners of war, and castaways made it clear that social isolation can be psychologically devastating. He found three trends which seem to characterize the experience of individuals enduring absolute social deprivation:

1 The reported pain of the isolation experience seems typically to bear a nonmonotonic relationship to time. At first, isolation becomes more and more unbearable—but then, suddenly, in many cases, the pain of isolation decreases sharply. This decrease in pain is frequently marked by the onset of a state of apathy, sometimes so severe as to resemble a schizophrenic state of withdrawal and detachment. POWs who were isolated from their fellow prisoners for years sometimes lapsed into death.

2 There seems to be a tendency for those in isolation to think, dream, and occasionally to hallucinate about people.

3 Those isolates who are able to keep themselves occupied with distracting activities appear to suffer less and to be less prone to develop apathy.

These data, then, support the conclusion that social isolation is unpleasant. It is evident that others, simply by their sheer physical presence, provide an important reward: they stave off loneliness.

Reduction of Fear

Try an experiment: come to class a few minutes early on a regular school day. You will probably find that few of your classmates approach you.

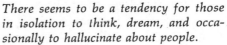

There seems to be a tendency for those in isolation to think, dream, and occasionally to hallucinate about people.

Then, some time when a tough and important exam is scheduled in one of your classes, arrive a few minutes early. You may be surprised to see how many classmates approach you with friendly remarks or joking comments. There is a good psychological explanation for the observation that students seem friendlier on days when an exam is scheduled than on days when one is not. There is experimental evidence that when we feel anxious, afraid, lonely, or unsure of ourselves, the sheer presence of other people is particularly rewarding.

Schachter (1959) was the first to test the hypothesis that fear often produces a desire for the company of others. Schachter explained to the college women who had volunteered to participate in his experiment, that his investigation was concerned with the effects of electric shock. Then he went on to describe the experiment in more detail, but (unknown to the women) he used different descriptions with different groups of women. One description of the shock experiment was designed to make some of the women highly fearful; the other was designed to leave the women who heard it relatively tranquil.

According to Schachter (1959, pp. 12–13), in the "high fear" condition, women:

> ... entered a room to find facing them a gentleman of serious mien, wearing horn-rimmed glasses, dressed in a white laboratory coat, stethoscope dribbling out of his pocket, behind him an array of formidable

electrical junk. After a few preliminaries, the experimenter began: "Allow me to introduce myself. I am Dr. Gregor Zilstein of the Medical School's Departments of Neurology and Psychiatry. I have asked you all to come today in order to serve as subjects in an experiment concerned with the effects of electrical shock.

To make their prospects even more forbidding, Schachter (alias Dr. Zilstein) told the women that the series of electric shocks would probably be extremely painful to them, but added parenthetically that they would leave "no permanent damage."

In the "low fear" condition, the setting of the experiment was designed to avoid arousing anxiety. There was no electrical apparatus in the experimental room. A friendly and benign Dr. Zilstein explained that his experiment was concerned with the effects of extremely mild electrical shock, shocks that would not in any way be painful, but rather would resemble a tickle or a tingle more than anything unpleasant.

After some women had been made more fearful than others, Schachter was ready to examine how fear affected their desire to be with other people. He assessed each woman's desire to affiliate with others in the following way. Dr. Zilstein claimed that there would be about a ten-minute delay while several pieces of equipment were secured. The women were told that during the ten-minute break they could wait in a private cubicle. These rooms were said to be comfortable and spacious; they all contained armchairs and there were books and magazines in each room. Dr. Zilstein also commented that some of them might want to wait with other women. If they preferred to wait with others, they were asked to let him know. He then passed out a sheet upon which the women could indicate whether: (a) they preferred to wait alone; (b) they preferred to wait with others; or (c) they had no preference at all.

Schachter found support for his hypothesis that fearful people will be especially inclined to seek the company of others (see Fig. 6.1). Sixty-three percent of the women in the high-fear condition wanted to wait with the other women in their group. Only 33 percent of the women in the low-fear condition wished to wait with the other women.

Schachter also asked the women to indicate how strongly they desired to be alone or with others. They could give answers varying from "I very much prefer being alone" (scored -2) through "I don't care very much" (0) to "I very much prefer being together with others" (scored $+2$). As the column labeled "Overall Intensity" in Fig. 6.1 indicates, these data also support the notion that affiliative desire increases with fear.

While fear appears to increase our need to affiliate with others, Schachter's subsequent investigations revealed that we apparently do not wish the

| | Number choosing | | | Overall |
	Together	Don't care	Alone	intensity
High anxiety	20	9	3	+.88
Low anxiety	10	18	2	+.35
	χ^2 Tog. *vs.* DC+A = 5.27			$t = 2.83$
	$p < .05$			$p < .01$

Fig. 6.1 Relationship of fear to the affiliative tendency. (Reprinted from *The Psychology of Affiliation*, by Stanley Schachter, p. 18, with the permission of the publishers, Stanford University Press. © 1959 by the Board of Trustees of the Leland Stanford Junior University.)

company of just *any* other person; we are selective about the kind of others we want to be with.

One of the first studies to suggest a limitation to the rule that "misery loves company" was similar in many ways to the experiment described above. Again, Schachter led two groups of college women to anticipate that they would soon receive electric shocks but this time both groups expected severe shock and thus were presumably fearful. Then the women were asked whether they preferred to wait alone or with others. How the "others" were described varied: One group of women was given a choice between waiting alone or waiting with some of the women who were said to be taking part in the same experiment; the other group of women was told they could either wait alone or with women who were waiting to talk to their professors and advisers.

Schachter found that 60 percent of the women who had a chance to visit with *similar* others—women who were also going to receive severe shock soon—chose to spend their time in the company of others rather than alone. But not one single woman who was given the option of waiting with *dissimilar* women—women who were waiting to talk with their professors —chose to wait with others; they all preferred to wait in a room by themselves. Scores on the "Overall Intensity Scale," on which the women indicated the strength of their preference, showed the same effect; women did not seem to be especially anxious to associate with other women unless these other women were in a situation similar to their own. Schachter concludes, then, that misery doesn't love just any kind of company—misery loves only miserable company.

The finding that the anticipation of a frightening experience produces an increased desire to affiliate has been replicated by Darley and Aronson (1966), Gerard and Rabbie (1961), Sarnoff and Zimbardo (1961), and Zimbardo and Formica (1963).

Why do fearful people seem to have a special desire to affiliate with others in situations similar to their own? Schachter considers several possibilities:

1 *Escape* When one is in a stressful situation, perhaps one anticipates that talking to others in the same situation may help one figure out a way to avoid the pain altogether.

2 *Cognitive clarity* There is some evidence that individuals in ambiguous or novel situations will desire to talk with knowledgeable others in order to gain some understanding of an otherwise incomprehensible event. Since receiving severe shock in an experimental setting is probably unique in most people's experience, perhaps the fearful women in Schachter's experiment wanted to associate with others to find out if they knew any more about what was going on than they did.

3 *Direct anxiety reduction* People often comfort and reassure one another. Perhaps the highly anxious women chose to wait with others in the hope that the others would bolster their courage.

4 *Indirect anxiety reduction* An effective device for reducing anxiety is to "get one's mind off one's troubles." People may be seen as more diverting than books or magazines. Perhaps fearful women chose to wait with others in order to prevent themselves from thinking about the shock which would be forthcoming.

5 *Self-evaluation* People often use other people in order to evaluate the reasonableness of their own emotions and feelings. In this novel and emotion-producing situation, an individual probably is not quite sure exactly how she should be reacting. (Should she be angry at the experimenter? Slightly apprehensive about the shock? Terrified? Perhaps high-anxiety women sought out others in an attempt to appropriately label and identify their own feelings.

Schachter concluded that two of these processes were probably operating in his experiments: (1) direct anxiety reduction and (2) self-evaluation. Ingenious experiments by Gerard (1963) and Gerard and Rabbie (1961) also support the notion that the need for self-evaluation is one factor which predisposes fearful individuals to choose to wait with others.

Subsequent experimentation has added two more qualifications to the general conclusion that the more emotionally upset persons are, the more eager they will be to affiliate with others: it depends on *why* they are upset (are they anxious?—or fearful?) and on *how upset* they are (are they moderately upset?—or violently upset?).

ANXIETY VS. FEAR

Sarnoff and Zimbardo argued that "anxiety" and "fear" might have markedly different effects on one's desire for company. They hypothesized (1961, p. 357):

> The greater the fear aroused, the more the subjects should choose to be together with others while they await actual contact with the fear arousing object. Conversely, the greater the anxiety elicited, the more the subjects should choose to be alone while they await contact with the anxiety arousing object.

The authors' reasoning was as follows: *Fear* is stimulated by inherently dangerous external objects or events. Fearful persons have good reason to be upset. They assume that others will sympathize with them, and thus they are eager to share their feelings with others. *Anxiety* is typically aroused by stimuli which, objectively considered, are innocuous (i.e., the sight of snakes, the idea of flying, leaving the house, etc.). Anxious persons are uncomfortably aware that their feelings may be inappropriate. Since they suspect that others will not sympathize with them, the last thing they want to do is to confide in others.

The authors tested their hypothesis in a simple experiment. In the High Fear conditions, they attempted to replicate Schachter's original experiment. They frightened men by telling them they would soon receive severe electric shock. As they had expected, they found that the High Fear men were unusually eager to affiliate with others.

In the High Anxiety conditions, the authors tried to make men anxious. They told them that they would soon be required to suck on a number of objects associated with infantile oral behavior: nipples, baby bottles, and pacifiers. Again, just as they had expected, they found that High Anxiety men were *less* willing to wait with others than were men who were not about to undergo such an embarrassing experience.

This experiment suggests that when we are upset about an impending stressful experience, but are ashamed of our reaction and suspect our response is inappropriate, we may avoid—rather than seek—the company of others.

VIOLENT VS. TEMPERED EMOTIONAL REACTIONS

There is still another qualification to the general relationship between the anticipation of a stressful experience and affiliation. There is evidence that people, who are experiencing extremely violent emotional upset, prefer to be alone rather than in the company of others. Sheatsley and Feldman (1964), for example, report that people who were most emotionally upset after the

. . . High Anxiety men were less willing to wait with others than were men who were not about to undergo such an embarrassing experience.

assassination of John Kennedy were most desirous of being alone in the days following the events. Latané and Wheeler (1966), who interviewed young naval recruits after they had participated in clean-up operations at the site of the wreckage of a commercial airplane, found that while non-emotional men indicated a desire to talk about their experiences, highly emotional men who had participated in the body search had little desire to talk to others in the week following the crash. Reviewing these and other studies, Wheeler (1974) concludes that strong emotion may lead to social isolation rather than affiliation due to: (1) a desire to avoid embarrassment or a depressive reaction; (2) the absence of any need to reduce uncertainty about the appropriateness of one's emotional upset; (3) a desire to avoid having the emotional response heightened by interaction with others who are also fearful.

Ordinal Position, Fear, and Affiliation

In examining his data on the relationship between fear and affiliative tendency, Schachter uncovered a surprising result. First-born children seemed to respond differently from later-borns under high-fear conditions. First-borns seemed both more fearful than later-borns and more desirous of associating with others when they were fearful than were later-borns.

To try to explain this finding, Schachter speculated about the ways in which the early experience of first-born and later-born children might differ. He proposed two possible reasons why first-borns might learn, to a greater extent than later-borns, that when they are distressed other human beings can reduce their distress and thus should be sought out.

First, mothers might be more responsive to the fears and distress of their first child than they are to the distress of their later children. They might "respond to more signals, respond more quickly, stay longer, and generally do a more effective all-round job of reducing anxiety with the first child than with later children." By the time subsequent children are born, mothers might well be more blasé and sophisticated about child rearing. Thus they may respond more slowly to the second child's every cry of distress and move less rapidly to calm the second-born's fears. And by the time the fourth or fifth child arrives, mothers might be so sophisticated—or so worn out—that they no longer care very much. If this scenario has any validity, it is reasonable that first-born children would come to associate the experience of distress with its reduction by other humans to a much greater extent than would later-borns.

Second, Schachter observes, younger children may have more threatening and fearsome persons in their immediate environment than do first-borns—namely, their older brothers and sisters. Schachter comments that "by reputation at least, older children get their exercise by knocking the younger ones about." For this reason, later-borns might be less likely than first-borns to develop the expectation that others are a frequent source of comfort and support.

On the basis of such reasoning, Schachter suspected that under fear-provoking conditions, first-born and only children might manifest stronger affiliative needs than later-born children. A reanalysis of the data from the experiments discussed above supported his hypothesis. First and only children strongly preferred to wait with others in the high-fear condition, whereas later-born children did not. (This difference was not due to a general higher sociability level of first-born children, since under low-fear conditions, there were no differences between the choices of first-born and later-born children.)

Schachter cites two possible reasons for this finding. First, it is possible that the same frightening situation might arouse considerably more fear in early-born children than in later-born children. Second, even if all individuals are made equally (and highly) fearful, first- and only-borns might still choose to be together more often than later-borns (the early-borns to a greater extent than later-borns, having learned that other people often help reduce fear). Schachter found support for both of these interpretations. Fear-arousing situations did seem to frighten first-borns more than later-borns, *and* even when first-borns and later-borns were equally frightened, the first-borns were *still* more anxious to affiliate with others than were their later-born counterparts.

In recent years, researchers have found that only children and first-borns differ from their fellows in a variety of ways. Adams (1972) provides a good review and critique of this research.

Reduction of Physiological Stress

There is some evidence that individuals who are placed in a stressful situation show less severe physiological disturbance if there are other people present than if there are not. (See Epley, 1974) Bovard (1959) developed an intriguing theory concerning the effect social stimuli have upon an individual's physiological response to stress.

Bovard (1959, p. 267) first presents data (from Selye 1950) that noxious stimuli, which produce physical stress, induce a systematic, nonspecific response in the vertebrate organism.

> This response involves release of adrenocorticotrophic hormone (ACTH) from the anterior pituitary and the consequent release of adrenal cortical hormones (cortisone, 17-hydroxycorticosterone) into the blood stream. Their effects are in general protein-catabolic, involving conversion of protein into glucose, and specifically include maintenance of blood-pressure and blood-sugar (glucose) levels under shock.

Psychological stress, like physical stress, also produces a pituitary–adrenal response, stimulating carbohydrate metabolism and protein breakdown. However, Bovard says (p. 267):

> ... the important difference between psychological and physical stress is that the former does not directly affect the body cells and, hence, must be mediated by the central nervous system.

There is a serious question as to whether the organism's pituitary–adrenal response to psychological stress has survival value. Bovard reports that experiments by Bartlett and his colleagues (Bartlett, Bohr, Helmendach, Foster, and Miller 1954; Bartlett, Helmendach, and Bohr 1953; Bartlett, Helmendach, and Inman 1954) indicate that animals subjected to emotional stress (restraint) *and* physical stress (extreme cold) maintained body temperature far less adequately than animals subjected to physical stress alone. Since the pituitary–adrenal response to psychological stress seems to be maladaptive, Bovard (p. 268) concludes that:

... the inhibition or dampening of the emotional-excitement component of the response to physical stress should have survival value for the organism.

Since psychological stress, unlike physical stress, must be mediated by the central nervous system, Bovard proposes a technique for preventing such stress from adversely affecting the organism. He suggests that if an animal must confront a stressful situation, we can increase its chance of survival if we place it in the company of other animals of the same species (particularly *familiar* animals of the same species). If the animal happens to be us, we can reduce the adverse effects of the stressful event by surrounding ourselves with familiar people.

Bovard (p. 269) argues that the presence of a familiar animal in the same stressful situation "calls forth in the organism a 'competing response' which inhibits, masks, or screens the stress stimulus, such that the latter has a minimal effect." This "inhibiting effect" is said to be produced in the following ways:

> A number of recent studies ... have suggested a reciprocal inhibitory effect between the posterior hypothalamus ... and the anterior hypothalamus and parasympathetic centers. ... Stimulation of the latter region would appear to inhibit activity of the former. ...
>
> The simplest hypothesis to account for the observed phenomena at the human and animal levels is, therefore, that the presence of another member of the same species stimulates activity of the anterior hypothalamus and thus, as a byproduct, inhibits activity of the posterior hypothalamus and its centers mediating the neuroendocrine response to stress. Previous interaction with the other person or animal, as the case may be, could be assumed to accentuate this effect.

Bovard's hypothesis is supported by a result of an experiment conducted by Back and Bogdonoff (1964). These investigators observed that small groups of friends who together experienced the physical stress of venipuncture and withdrawal of a blood sample showed a lower resultant level of free fatty acids in their blood streams than did comparable groups of strangers who underwent the same experience. Since the free fatty acid level of the blood is a function of sympathetic autonomic activity, this experimental finding indicates that the presence of persons with whom one has previously interacted, such as a small group of friends, inhibits the posterior hypothalamic, and hence the sympathetic autonomic, response to stress.

Several other studies provide suggestive evidence that Bovard's general hypothesis may be correct. For example, combat studies indicate that a small group (a platoon bomber crew) is very effective in sustaining members under severe battle stress (e.g., Mandlebaum 1952), and other studies also suggest that the small groups to which individuals belong provide a great deal of support to them when they are under stress.

How persons react to drugs is known to depend to a large extent on the setting in which they take the drug. Staff members at Boston Psychopathic Hospital (1955) report that most individuals who tried LSD in the hospital setting experienced stressful psychotic reactions. According to their report, however, those who took LSD in a group situation had a more pleasant experience than did those who tried the chemical individually. Group participation appeared to relieve the tension associated with the stressful LSD experience.

Several animal studies suggest that the presence of other animals diminishes an animal's disturbance in a stressful situation. Studies conducted by Arsenian (1943), Conger, Sawrey, and Turrell (1957), Davitz and Mason (1955), Liddell (1950), and Mason (1960) support such a conclusion, as does an investigation by Latané and Glass (1968). In the latter experiment, rats were placed in a fear-arousing situation. Some rats were entirely alone as they faced the stressful circumstances; others had the company of a little red toy car which simply sat immobile in their cage; for still other rats, the toy car cruised around the cage; and, finally, in one of the two remaining conditions, the rat experienced the fear-arousing stimuli in the presence of another, anesthetized rat who, of course, was completely immobile; rats in the remaining condition were each given a normal, and thus animate, rat companion. Latané and Glass found that rats who had the benefit of a "buddy," the presence of another normal rat companion, were the least fearful of all the rats who participated in the experiment; in fact, even those rats whose rat partner was immobile and unconscious showed less fear than the rats who faced the stressful stimuli alone or with the toy car.

This accumulating evidence, that the presence of others may help reduce the discomfort produced by stress, provides an additional reason why individuals might learn to affiliate with others when they find themselves in stressful circumstances.

Summary

In this chapter, we considered three additional reinforcers that have been found to have strong impact on liking. People find it upsetting—or terrifying—to be isolated, and to be facing frightening, or stressful, events. Those who, by their mere presence, soften these feelings, come to be liked.

The Reduction of Social Isolation

At first, social isolation is merely unpleasant; in time, it become unbearable. If it continues interminably, it can lead to apathy . . . and death. It is evident that others, simply by their sheer physical presence, provide an important reward: they stave off loneliness and social isolation.

Reduction of Fear

Schachter proposed that when we feel unsure of ourselves, anxious, or afraid, the sheer physical presence of others is particularly rewarding. Schachter found that "misery *does* love company" . . . but not just any company . . . "misery only loves miserable company."

Other researchers have added a few qualifications to the "misery loves company" hypothesis. They point out that, under very special circumstances, the fearful person is hesitant to associate with others. Sarnoff and Zimbardo found that fearful people, who know they have good reason to be upset, expect others to sympathize with them and thus are eager to share their feelings with them. However, anxious people, who are uncomfortably aware that their feelings might not be appropriate, are hesitant to spend time with others who might or might not share their feelings.

Other authors have found that when people feel *somewhat* upset, they're eager to be with others who share their feelings. When people feel that their feelings are *extreme* and out of control, however, they tend to prefer to be alone.

The Reduction of Psychological Stress

There is considerable evidence that individuals who are placed in a stressful situation become less disturbed physiologically when there are people present than when there are not.

The accumulating evidence, then, suggests that when we are lonely, fearful, or under stress, the presence of others is extremely rewarding. It is no wonder then that we often come to like—or to love—those who make our hard times a little better.

rewards and punishments others provide:
cooperation vs. competition

Many times people do not reward or punish us directly; rather, they are instrumental either in helping us obtain desired goals or in blocking our progress toward need gratification. As we might expect, there is a great deal of evidence which indicates that we tend to like those who cooperate with us in our attempts to obtain rewards for ourselves (e.g., Berkowitz and Daniels 1963; Goranson and Berkowitz 1966). There is also evidence that we tend to dislike those who frustrate our attempts to obtain rewards, whether they do so because of maliciousness or because they find themselves competing against us for rewards (e.g., Burnstein and Worchel 1962).

Naturalistic Study of Cooperation vs. Competition

Perhaps the most interesting and best known studies of the relationship between cooperation, competition, and interpersonal attraction were performed under the direction of Muzafer Sherif (e.g., Sherif, Harvey, White, Hood, and Sherif 1954). Boys of about twelve years of age who attended a summer camp run by the experimenters participated in this series of field experiments. None of the boys knew each other before they attended the camp.

Although the camps were ostensibly set up to study "camping methods and group living in general," the investigators were primarily interested in the latter, especially intergroup relations and the effectiveness of various techniques for reducing hostility between groups. The camp setting, isolated from outside influences, afforded the experimenters a unique opportunity to vary the conditions and circumstances of interaction between the camp members. Such control was necessary for the creation of hostility between campers, and then for subsequent examination of the efficacy of various hostility-reduction techniques.

The initial steps the experimenters took to organize the summer camp (which will be seen to be not uncommon in terms of how such camps are frequently organized), illustrate how hostility and divisiveness may be generated among groups. The experimenters' first step was to divide the campers into separate groups and to instill a sense of camaraderie and esprit de corps within each group. Each boy was assigned to one of two separate living groups in the camp, and each group was given a name (e.g., "Bull Dogs" and "Red Devils").

In an attempt to assure that a feeling of "we-ness" would develop within each living group, the daily activities of the group members were planned in such a way that interdependent, coordinated activity among the members was necessary to the achievement of desirable goals. The food, for example, was unprepared. In order to eat, coordinated activities, such as building a fire and apportioning the food, were required.

DEVELOPMENT OF ANTAGONISM

Following the successful development of two "in-groups" within the camp, each characterized by mutual good feeling between in-group members, the experimenters attempted to induce animosity between the two living groups. The Bull Dogs and Red Devils, for example, were often brought together to participate in competitive and mutually frustrating activities in which the securing of rewards by one group necessarily frustrated the other group's desire to obtain the same rewards.

The effects of the competitive games were not immediate at first. Initial good sportsmanship on the part of both groups, for example, resulted in the winning group spontaneously giving a cheer for the losers and the losers responding with a cheer for the winners. However, fortunately for the experimenters (Sherif and Sherif 1956, p. 294), the effects of competition evidenced themselves in time:

> . . . as the series of contests progressed, this cheer changed from "2–4–6–8, who do we appreciate," followed by the name of the other group, to "2–4–6–8, who do we apprecihate."

Winning points could be accumulated in the series of competitive games and camp contests, and in one camp the series culminated in the award of a prize to the members of the winning group, the Bull Dogs. By this time, the hostility of the Red Devils toward the Bull Dogs was not restricted to a subtle change in the wording of a cheer. The Bull Dogs were often accused of cheating during the contests and were frequently the targets of other verbal abuse.

Following the series of competitive games, and the awarding of the prize, plans were made for a party. The Bull Dogs and Red Devils were told by the camp managers (the experimenters) that the party would help them rid themselves of all the bad feelings which had developed toward the other group. Both the Bull Dogs and the Red Devils agreed to attend the party.

Although it had been represented as a peacemaking party, the experimenters had not finished their tension-creating manipulations. They placed the party refreshments on a table in such a way that half looked delicious and appetizing while the other half were crushed and unappealing. The experimenters detonated this volatile situation by contriving for the Red Devils to arrive at the party first. The experimenters were not disappointed when nature took its course and the early arriving Red Devils grabbed the best half of the refreshments for themselves and sat down to enjoy them. The consequences were even better than Mephistopheles could have anticipated. Sherif and Sherif (1956, p. 296) wrote:

> When the "Bull Dogs" arrived a short time later and saw the sorry-looking refreshments left, they immediately protested. The "Red Devils" justified their actions with "first come, first served," which became the standardized justification for all "Red Devils." The "Bull Dogs" proceeded to eat their refreshments, hurling taunts, insults, and names at the "Red Devils." Particularly common was the term "pigs." Among the names used by most "Bull Dogs" for "Red Devils" on this and later occasions were "pigs," "dirty bums" or "red bums," "jerks," and several more objectionable terms.
>
> The next morning the "Red Devils" retaliated by deliberately dirtying their breakfast table to make K.P. duty harder for the "Bull Dogs." Upon seeing the dirty table, the "Bull Dogs" decided to mess it up further and leave it. All "Bull Dogs" joined in by smearing the table with cocoa, sugar, syrup, and the like, and leaving it alive with bees and wasps. The "Bull Dogs" hung the walls with threatening and derogatory posters against the "Red Devils."
>
> At lunch that day the hostility between the groups increased to such a point throughout the meal that they soon were lined up on opposite sides of the mess hall calling names and then throwing food, cups, tableware, etc. The fight was broken up. Neither group was sure who started the fight, but each was sure it was someone in the *other* group.

Given this blow-by-blow description of events, it seems superfluous to report the results of a sociometric test which was administered by the experimenters to determine whether they had been successful in creating friendship bonds within each in-group and animosity toward members of the out-group. Suffice it to say that the results of this test indicated that few Red Devils counted any Bull Dogs among their bosom buddies.

REDUCTION OF HOSTILITY

After the successful creation of intergroup hostility, the experimenters proceeded to investigate the effectiveness of various hostility-reduction techniques.

Encouraging the Campers to Share Good Times

Reinforcement theorists, such as Lott and Lott (1974), would propose that the more good times people share, the more they will like one another.

The investigators wanted to examine how useful Reinforcement principles might be to reducing hostility between groups. Thus, they gave members of rival groups such as the Red Devils and the Bull Dogs an opportunity to make social contact with each other in pleasant, and presumably rewarding, situations. The consequences of the experimenters' use of this approach demonstrate the distance which sometimes exists between the laboratory and field situations (Sherif and Sherif 1956, p. 296):

> There were seven different contact situations, including eating together in the same dining room, watching a movie together, and shooting firecrackers in the same area. These contact situations had no effect in reducing intergroup friction. If anything they were utilized by members of both groups as opportunities for further name-calling and conflict. For example, they used mealtimes in the same place for "garbage fights," throwing mashed potatoes, left-overs, bottle caps, and the like, accompanied by the exchange of derogatory names.

It is not surprising that the experimenters concluded that contact between groups does not in itself produce a decrease in an existing state of intergroup tension.

The investigators also concluded that their results cast doubt upon the hypothesis that the reward of engaging in a pleasant activity will become conditioned to others who are in the immediate vicinity. It should be observed, however, that the "pleasant activities" Sherif and Sherif describe are complicated as far as an analysis of the reinforcements involved is concerned. Though the situations were *intended* to be rewarding experiences which the rival groups would share, it is possible that the hostile behavior of the rival groups (i.e., name-calling, etc.) made the shared situations unpleasant. If so, the rival groups shared noxious, rather than pleasurable, experiences. It is also possible that such activities as the "garbage fights" were themselves sources of fun. If so, perhaps the boys were inadvertently rewarded *for* hostile behavior toward the out-group. Such reward would, of course, be expected to *increase* the hostility toward the out-group.

It is also possible that such activities as the "garbage fights" were themselves sources of fun.

Whatever the correct explanation, the first technique to reduce hostility the investigators tried, having the boys share an experience they hoped would be pleasant, did not decrease intergroup tension.

Encouraging the Campers to Cooperate

Since cooperation toward common goals had been effective in forming the two in-groups originally, the experimenters reasoned that they might reduce hostility by creating one large in-group from the two smaller in-groups. They could accomplish this, they hoped, by bringing both groups together to participate in cooperative activities. One such situation involved a campwide softball game in which selected members of both groups competed against an outside group of boys from a nearby town. This "common enemy" approach was found to be effective in reducing the hostility between campers. The experimenters, however, did not pursue this technique further since, although it reduced hostility between the smaller groups, it was clear that it eventually would lead to an equal, or even greater, amount of hostility between the larger group units. The experimenters did not want to simply transfer intergroup hostility from one group to another; rather they wanted to find out how to *eliminate* intergroup hostility.

The effect of participation in cooperative situations, which did not involve a common human enemy, was investigated next. Camp activities and events were planned in such a way that desirable goals could not be achieved by the efforts of one in-group alone; they could be achieved only if members of both groups cooperated toward the common goal. One goal involved repairing the water-supply system (which the experimenters had arranged to sabotage). Another was cooperating to obtain money to secure a movie that both groups wanted to see. And still another involved getting a truck to move, which had suddenly broken down (the experimenters again) on its way to bring food for a camp-out.

After the campers achieved all these goals by cooperative activity, a sociometric test was administered to both groups. The results clearly revealed that attitudes toward members of the out-group had changed. Although friendship choices were primarily within each in-group, choices of out-group members as friends had increased. In addition to the increased tendency to choose out-group members as friends, the experimenters found a significant reduction in the number of rejections of members of the out-group as disliked persons.

Why Should People Like Those with Whom They Cooperate?

Why should cooperation lead to greater liking? There are two possible explanations for their finding:

1   **A reinforcement theory explanation** Learning theorists, such as Lott and Lott, would contend that, through conditioning, one comes to like those who are present at the time of reward and to dislike those present at the time of punishment. If this learning factor is the only reason why cooperation is effective in increasing esteem, then cooperation should create attraction between cooperating people *only* when the cooperative effort culminates in reward.

2   **A cognitive dissonance theory explanation** A number of cognitive consistency theorists would take a more optimistic view of the relationship between cooperation and liking. Festinger's (1957) theory of cognitive dissonance, for example, suggests that even if a cooperative effort fails, it should produce increased interpersonal attraction.

A Theory of Cognitive Dissonance

The basic unit with which cognitive dissonance theory works is the "cognition." "Cognition" is simply a shortened way of indicating any knowledge, opinion, or belief persons might hold about their environment, about themselves, or about their behavior.

Dissonance theory is concerned with the relationship that an individual's ideas (or cognitions) have with one another. The theory states that three types of cognitive relationships are possible: dissonance, consonance, or irrelevance.

Cognitions are said to be in a *dissonant* relationship whenever they are incompatible. Cognitions can be dissonant for several reasons. First, cognitions can be incompatible because they contradict one another on logical grounds in the individual's own thinking system. For example, if a person believes that there is no such thing as a bad boy, and at the same time believes that criminal character is hereditary, that person should experience dissonance. Second, cognitions can be dissonant because they oppose one's past experience about the necessary relationship between events. For example, suppose a climber slipped and fell at the summit of a mountain. If, while falling, the climber noticed that the trees below him were *receding* further and further in the distance, the climber should experience dissonance (as well as relief).

Cognitive elements are in a *consonant* relationship if one follows from the other on logical or experiential grounds.

Finally, cognitions can be *irrelevant* to one another. For example, the cognitions "The English are very proud of their gardens" and "Hotel rooms never have enough coat hangers" would probably be judged by nearly everyone to be totally irrelevant to one another.

According to dissonance theory, the presence of dissonance gives rise to pressures to reduce or eliminate that dissonance and to avoid the increase of dissonance. In addition, the theory states that the more dissonance one is experiencing, the more anxious one will be to reduce one's existing dissonance.

What predictions can we derive from dissonance theory as to the effect that human cooperative efforts should have on liking? According to dissonance theorists, most people would agree to expend effort on a cooperative project only if they believed the project would be successful in the end. If they are wrong, if the project is unsuccessful, they should experience dissonance. Several experimenters (e.g., Aronson and Mills 1959) have demonstrated that people who have cooperated in an unsuccessful project often will try to reduce their dissonance by trying to convince themselves that the futile effort was really "worth it" anyway. Since the other cooperating people are usually an extremely salient aspect of an unfruitful cooperative situation, one might expect that individuals whose cooperative efforts fail might justify their efforts by exaggerating the other benefits associated with the situation—such as the development of friendships with others in the situation. A man who works two years on a novel and then finds that no one will publish it may decide that the project nevertheless had some merit because it gave him the chance to spend time with his secretary.

Cooperation may, of course, promote liking even before it is known whether the cooperative effort will result in success or failure. The reader will recall from the discussion of research in Chapter 3 that Heider would expect individuals in close proximity to one another, and who are working on similar projects, to perceive themselves as a "unit." Individuals have been found to increase their liking for those they perceive as being in a unit relationship with themselves. (See Berscheid, Boye, and Darley 1968.)

Frustration and Aggression

It is clear that we generally like those with whom we cooperate. In this section we shall examine the complement of this principle: We generally dislike those who frustrate our attempts to secure desired goals.

Most research on the relationship between frustration and aggression has been inspired and influenced by a book written in 1939 by Dollard, Doob, Miller, Mowrer, and Sears. Their book, *Frustration and Aggression*, provided a theoretical framework which enabled investigators to predict the effect frustration should have on attraction.

In order to understand the vast amount of research which has been conducted on the relationship between frustration and aggression, we must first understand how these theorists defined the terms, "frustration" and "aggression." Frustration was defined (Dollard *et al.* 1939, p. 7) as "an interference with the occurrence of an instigated goal response at its proper time in the behavior sequence" In other words, a "frustration" is a condition or event which prevents an individual who has begun progressing toward a goal from reaching that goal. Aggression was defined (p. 9) as "any sequence of behavior, the goal response to which is the injury of the person toward whom it is directed." In other words, persons are aggressing if, and only if, by their fantasies, plans, or actions they *intend* to injure another.

Dollard *et al.* originally contended that frustration was a necessary and sufficient condition for aggression. Specifically, they stated (p. 1) "Aggression is always a consequence of frustration . . ." and ". . . whenever frustration occurs, aggression of some kind and of some degree will inevitably result."

In arguing that a frustrated individual *always* reacts with aggression, these theorists did not overlook the fact that we often have to learn to suppress and restrain our overt aggressive reactions. They simply argue that even though we may restrain ourselves from committing certain aggressive actions, we will express our aggression in some other form. They argue (p. 2), "It has been found that although these reactions may be temporarily compressed, delayed, disguised, displaced, or otherwise deflected from their immediate and logical goal, they are not destroyed."

Several critics have quarrelled with the strong statement that frustration is a necessary and sufficient condition for aggression. (For example, see Bandura 1973; Bandura and Walters 1963; Baron and Eggleston 1972; Darley, Chereskin, and Zanna 1975; Miller 1941; and Tedeschi, Smith, and Brown 1974, for an elucidation of the various objections that have been raised.) Though many theorists would agree that the connection between frustration and aggression is not as inevitable as Dollard *et al.* originally proposed, they would also probably agree that frustrated individuals are, in general, more likely to aggress against others than those who aren't frustrated. Much experimental research supports this point of view. (Relevant research has been conducted by Berkowitz 1965; Berkowitz and Green 1962; Berkowitz and Holmes 1960; Berkowitz and Rawlings 1963; Burnstein and Worchel, 1962; Elbert and Ulrich cited in Ulrich 1966, p. 660; Hamblin 1958; Hamblin, Bridger, Day and Yancey 1963; Hokanson 1961; Horwitz 1958; and Mallick and McCandless 1966.)

What Determines How Frustrating an Experience Is?

The Yale group hypothesized that "the strength of instigation to aggression varies directly with the amount of frustration" (p. 28). This means that the more individuals are frustrated, the more aggressive they will be. But what determines how frustrated individuals are? According to these authors, the amount of frustration one experiences, and thus the strength of one's instigation to aggress, is a positive function of three factors: (1) "the strength of the instigation to the frustrated response"; (2) "the number of frustrated response-sequences"; and (3) "the degree of interference with the frustrated response."

1 The notion that the stronger the drive one thwarts, the more frustrated the thwarted individual will be, and thus the more aggression the individual will demonstrate, receives some support from an experiment conducted by Sears and Sears (cited in Dollard *et al.* 1939, pp. 28–29.) This proposition makes intuitive sense. We are undoubtedly more frustrated when a talkative salesperson corners us on our way to dinner than when we are on our way to a boring lecture.

2 In arguing that frustration is a positive function of the number of frustrated response-sequences, the authors are merely hypothesizing that frustration is cumulative. Relatively minor frustrations, when close together in time, should produce an aggressive response greater in strength than would be expected from one minor frustrating event alone. For example, they report that a man who had previously been a willing subject in several very trying and arduous experiments, when asked to free-associate to 50 words, lost his temper. This last irritation was obviously "the straw that broke the camel's back."

3 The hypothesis that the more one interferes with an individual's progress toward a goal response, the more frustrated and aggressive the thwarted individual will be, has received support from several correlational studies. These studies gained widespread attention because the variables they utilize have great social significance.

Hovland and Sears (1940), for example, argued that "aggressive acts should be more numerous during years of depression than during years of prosperity," since during an economic depression many of an individual's needs are thwarted. The worse the economic conditions are, the less money individuals have to buy the things that they desire, and the more frustrated they should be. Hovland and Sears proposed, then, that there should be a negative correlation between economic prosperity and group aggression.

To test their hypotheses, the authors chose the annual per-acre value of cotton in 14 Southern states for the years 1882–1930 as their index of economic prosperity. As a measure of aggression they chose the number of lynchings in these same fourteen states during the same period. The data revealed that during the period when economic prosperity was steadily increasing (from 1882–1930), the number of lynchings steadily decreased, as the authors expected.

Hovland and Sears also made a more crucial test of their hypothesis. They considered not just the general upward or downward trends of prosperity and lynchings, but also the effect that *unexpected* recessions or prosperity had on aggression. They first calculated the extent to which economic conditions or lynching frequencies deviated from the general trend lines. Then they correlated these corrected scores. The authors found that the correlation between the value of cotton and the total number of lynchings was −.63.

Hovland and Sears (1940, pp. 308–309) report additional intriguing evidence in support of the frustration–aggression hypothesis. Thomas (1925) found that economic indices and "property crimes with violence" were correlated −.44. Frustration may produce aggression toward politicians as well as toward blacks. Writing during a period in which the country was more rural and more dependent on farming than it is today, Marshall (1927) noted that politicians were regularly voted out of office following periods of deficient rainfall. He said:

> Over a sixty-year period, in seven cases out of eight (Presidential elections) when the rainfall was greater than normal, the party in power, regardless of which one it was, continued to stay in power. On the other hand, in six cases out of seven when the rainfall was less than normal, a new swarm of political parasites descended on Washington.

James C. Davies (1962) provides the most intriguing historical evidence in support of the frustration–aggression hypothesis. Frustration–aggression theorists have been careful to point out that "deprivation" is not synonymous with "frustration." If a deprived man is resigned to his fate, and makes no attempt to attain a better life, he cannot be said to be "frustrated." It is only when a deprived man tries to better his lot, when he tries to reach for a goal, and is thwarted, that he is "frustrated."

Simple *deprivation* should not lead to aggression. *Frustration* always should. Berkowitz (1969, pp. 15–16) provides a concise statement of this argument.

> Poverty-stricken groups who had never dreamed of having automobiles, washing-machines, or new homes are not frustrated because they had been deprived of these things; they are frustrated only after they had begun to hope. If they had dared to think they might get these objects and had anticipated their satisfactions, the inability to fulfill their anticipations is a frustration. Privations in themselves are much less likely to breed violence than are the dashing of hopes.

Davies (1962), too, in "Toward a theory of revolution," agrees that it is not deprivation, but frustration, that sparks revolutions. Davies points out that it is *not* a people who have long endured crushing poverty who are most likely to revolt. There are several reasons why this is so: First, the people's physical and mental energies may be totally expended in the process of merely staying alive; they have no energy left with which to foment a revolution.

Second, as Soule (1935, p. 20) has noted:

> When the people are in their most desperate and miserable condition, they are often least inclined to revolt, for then they are hopeless.

Or, as Davies (1962, p. 7) puts it:

> When it is a choice between losing their chains or their lives, people will mostly choose to keep their chains, a fact which Marx seems to have overlooked.

When *are* people likely to rebel? According to Davies, it is when a people simply takes it for granted that their reasonable expectations *will* be met—if not this year, then certainly next year—and for some reason their expectations are seriously frustrated. It is *then* that they revolt.

> Revolutions are most likely to occur when a prolonged period of objective economic social development is followed by a short period of sharp reversal. The all-important effect on the minds of people in a particular society is to produce, during the former period, an expectation of continued ability to satisfy needs—which continue to rise—and, during the latter, a mental state of anxiety and frustration when manifest reality breaks away from anticipated reality.

The Davies model is diagrammed in Fig. 7.1.

Davies systematically charts the conditions preceding several revolutions, the American Revolution of 1776, the French Revolution in 1789, Dorr's Rebellion in 1842, the Russian Revolution in 1917, the Egyptian Revolution in 1950 . . . and a variety of civil disturbances. He concludes that, in every case, the economic data mirror the inverted J-Curve model diagrammed in Fig. 7.1.

THE INHIBITION OF AGGRESSIVE ACTS

As Davies observes, people do not overtly aggress every time they are frustrated, even when the aggression is not likely to cost the aggressors

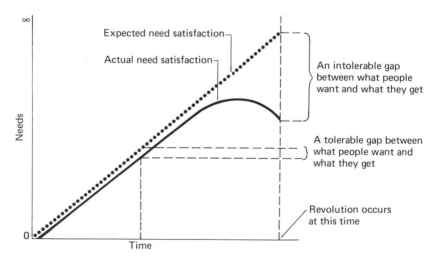

Fig. 7.1 Need satisfaction and revolution.

their lives. We can probably all agree, for example, that if a student speeding to a final exam was stopped by a policeman, and given a ticket and a long lecture on reckless driving, the student would be frustrated. We can also agree, however, that the probabilities are very low that the student would hit the policeman or run him over with the car or even call the policeman names.

Dollard and his colleagues (1939) recognized that anticipated punishment would inhibit overt aggression. They proposed (p. 33) that "the strength of inhibition of any act of aggression varies positively with the amount of punishment anticipated to be a consequence of that act." These theorists predicted that *specific* aggressive acts which are followed by punishment would come to be suppressed. They did *not* imply that individuals punished for aggression learn never to be aggressive, but rather that they learn to express their aggression in other forms (say, in aggressive fantasies).

The fact that anticipated punishment merely causes frustrated individuals to suppress their aggressive responses, and does not eliminate the tendency to aggress, is often overlooked. When the threat of possible punishment for antisocial behavior is removed, we are sometimes surprised to discover that a person we have always categorized as mild-mannered emerges as a pugnacious combatant. When placed in a punishment-free environment, the Walter Mittys among us, previously forced to confine our aggression to fantasy, are given an opportunity to live our aggressive dreams. It surely cannot be entirely coincidental that the favorite song of many women's liberationists and sympathizers is "Jenny's Song" from the Three-Penny Opera.

There is some research to support the observation that normally staid individuals will act in more socially unacceptable ways when placed in a punishment-free environment than they will in their normal environments. Festinger, Pepitone, and Newcomb (1952) observed that conservative American Legionnaires have been known to turn into boisterous and riotous individuals at their national conventions. Away from their homes, in a city where nobody knows them, part of a large, anonymous, and perceptually homogenous group, many of them may feel safe to indulge in activities that they would normally have to suppress. Festinger *et al.* labeled this process of losing identity "deindividuation." A great deal of research supported the notion that individuals will express more overt aggression than they normally would if others are not able to easily identify them. (See, for example, Festinger *et al.* (1952), Gergen and Gergen (1971), Maslach (1972), or Zimbardo (1969).

THE TARGET OF AGGRESSION

Who, or what, will be the target of aggression? The authors of *Frustration and Aggression* argued that the most satisfying target for aggression is the frustrating agent (p. 40). It is not always possible or practical to aggress against the frustrating agent, however. Sometimes we are unable to identify the source of our frustration. Sometimes it is socially inappropriate to aggress against our frustrator. (It is unacceptable, for example, to hit the octogenarian wearing glasses and a hearing aid who accidentally crushes our foot with his leg braces.) Sometimes, as we discussed earlier, we are afraid to aggress against our frustrator who is stronger and more powerful than we are. For example, a child is often frustrated by its parents. The child soon learns, however, that if it aggresses directly against the source of the frustration, it will be punished. "Honor thy father and thy mother" is a rule congenial to parents, and it is a rule that they generally take the trouble to enforce.

When we are inhibited from aggressing directly against the source of our frustration, we have a tendency to perform less direct acts of aggression —to "displace" our aggression by directing it toward someone or something which is not responsible for our frustration. That we do often displace our aggression is obvious. The man who is frustrated at the office is afraid to yell at his boss so he may yell at his wife; she, in turn, may pick on the children who may kick the dog who chases the cat. . . .

People who are unable or afraid to aggress directly against their frustrator may choose to aggress instead against others who are *similar* in some way to their frustrator, but against whom it is less *frightening* to aggress. (See Miller 1944 and 1951 for a detailed discussion of how people may select the target for displaced aggression. According to Miller, which of the many substitute targets is chosen depends on how frustrated individuals are, how frightened they are of aggressing against their frustrator, and on how similar various potential targets are to their frustrator.)

A graphic example of the way aggression can be displaced along the lines of similarity is provided by Mowrer (as reported in Dollard *et al.* 1939, p. 49):

> A small boy in an institution displayed unusually strong aggression against adults. This took the form of biting, pinching, and hair-pulling. Under the severe discipline of the institution, this overt aggression was soon inhibited by expectation of punishment. Then the child began running after other children, biting them, pinching them, pulling their hair. These manifestations of aggression were in turn eliminated, in fact so thoroughly that the child ceased biting altogether, even refusing to bite into solid food. Then the child commenced to pinch himself, bang his

TRUDY

head and to pull out his own hair. These actions were so injurious that he created bad sores on his body and two large bald spots on his head. . . .

According to the authors:

. . . this case appears to present a picture of frustration imposed by adults, aggression against adults, inhibition of this aggression and displacement of it to other children, inhibition of the aggression against other children and turning of it, still with much the same responses, against the self.

Many experiments have demonstrated that frustrated individuals will displace aggression to minority groups who are less likely than the frustrator to retaliate against them. One such classic experiment was done by Miller and Bugelski (1948). Their subjects were boys in the Civilian Conservation Corps who were working in an isolated area. The boy's main entertainment each week was attending Bank Night at a movie in town. One Bank Night, before it was time to leave for the movie, the boys were required to take some very difficult tests. Included in the tests were items intended to measure their attitudes toward various nationality groups, including Mexicans and Japanese. As the time for the movie approached and then passed, the tests kept coming. Missing the movie was undoubtedly a severe frustration for the boys. Since they could not directly attack the experimenters, the researchers expected that the boys would displace their aggression to members of the salient minority groups. The data supported this hypothesis. After it became obvious that the movie had been missed, the boys were again asked some questions about their attitudes toward minority group members. The questionnaire results indicated that the boys expressed more unfavorable attitudes toward minority groups after the frustrating experience than they had expressed previously.

Cowen, Landes, and Schaet (1959) replicated these results. They found that people who had been insulted expressed more hostile attitudes toward blacks than did individuals who had not been frustrated.

There is also correlational evidence that people who are frustrated by unknown or invulnerable sources do tend to express more aggression toward individuals who are not responsible for their frustration. Bettelheim and Janowitz (1950) interviewed World War II veterans, and classified them as to their hostility toward Jews and blacks. Prejudiced attitudes were found to be related to a deterioration in the veterans' social status. Those men who held jobs of a lower social status after the war than they had before the war were more hostile toward minority group members than were veterans whose occupational opportunities had improved.

Further, a survey conducted by Campbell (summarized in G. W. Allport

1954, p. 224), found that people who were dissatisfied with their jobs were more anti-Semitic than were people who were contented with their employment.

Frustrated people do not inevitably aggress against minority groups, however. Stagner and Congdon (1955) angered college students and found that these students did not dislike minority group members more than a control group which was not angered.

We have stated previously that frustrated individuals who cannot aggress against their frustrator directly may displace their aggression to someone who is similar to their frustrator in some way. Obviously substitute targets can be similar to the frustrator along a wide variety of dimensions. It is surprising to discover, however, that similarities which we might think of as very minor are often important determinants of where frustrated individuals will displace their aggression.

Berkowitz (1968) reports two ingenious studies done in collaboration with Knurek which document this point. In one experiment, men were prevented from winning money by the incompetence of their partners. Subsequently, the frustrated men were asked to evaluate a second person. Men were found to attribute more unfavorable characteristics to the innocent bystander if he happened to possess the same first name as the frustrator than if the bystander possessed a neutral name. Similarly, in a second experiment, people who were insulted by another were subsequently given an opportunity to administer electric shocks to a third person who was innocent of doing any injury to anyone. Frustrated persons (compared to non-insulted control persons) gave more shocks to the innocent third person only when that person had the same name as their frustrator.

The Social Learning View of Aggression

It is clear that the relationship between frustration and aggression is not as simple and straightforward as the original frustration-aggression hypothesis depicted. As research on aggression has accumulated, we have seen that the frustration–aggression formulation has undergone considerable modification (and even the modifications have been themselves modified as new findings have emerged).

Recently, more and more investigators of aggression have shunned the frustration–aggression hypothesis altogether and have taken a different theoretical approach to understanding aggressive behavior. Many take the position that aggressive behavior toward others is learned just as other kinds of behavior are learned. Albert Bandura (1973), one of the leading proponents of the social learning view of aggression, has argued that people need not be angered or aroused emotionally in order to behave aggressively. The social learning analysis of aggression emphasizes that a society can produce highly aggressive people simply by valuing aggressive accomplishments, by furnishing successful models of aggression, and by ensuring that aggressive actions secure rewarding effects. Thus, we may behave in an aggressive or unfavorable manner toward others even though we do not particularly dislike them nor even because we necessarily wish to hurt them. Rather, we may behave in a harmful manner toward them because doing so is valued by society in general, or by the groups to which we belong in particular, or because behaving in a negative or harmful manner toward those persons helps us to achieve desirable goals.

One implication of the social learning view of aggression toward others, then, is that we cannot always correctly conclude from the fact that a person has hurt another, that the person disliked and intended to harm the other. But even when the harm (or the help) we do others is accidental, it may have consequences for our subsequent attraction to the person we have hurt. In the next chapter, we shall examine some of these consequences.

Summary

In this chapter we reviewed the theories and evidence which suggest that we tend to like those who cooperate with us in our attempts to gain reward for ourselves . . . and to dislike those who compete against us for rewards.

First we reviewed two major theories of interpersonal attraction:

1 **Reinforcement theory** The Reinforcement theorists contend that not only do we like people who intentionally reward us, and dislike those who intentionally punish us but that we also feel strongly toward those who are merely *associated* with joy or pain.

2 **Cognitive dissonance theory** According to Dissonance theory, people seek consonance and avoid dissonance. According to Dissonance theory, if people spend a great deal of effort working together on a project, they should come to like one another, whether the project is successful or not. If they spend a great deal of effort competing against one another, they should come to dislike one another.

Cooperation We began by reviewing the study by Sherif *et al.* of the Bull Dogs and the Red Devils. Sherif and his colleagues provide compelling naturalistic evidence that cooperation breeds liking.

Competition We began by considering the classic work, *Frustration and Aggression*, by Dollard *et al.* which argued that frustration always leads to aggression.

Finally, we considered three questions:

1 What determines how frustrating an experience is? Theorists such as James C. Davies have been careful to point out that deprivation is not synonymous with frustration. If deprived persons are resigned to their fate, and make no attempt to attain a better life, they cannot be said to be frustrated. It is only when deprived persons try to better their lot and are thwarted that they're frustrated. In *Toward a Theory of Revolution*, Davies presents some evidence that it is not deprivation, but frustration, that breeds revolution.

2 What determines whether or not we inhibit our aggressive acts? Frustration does not inevitably breed physical aggression. Frustration may also generate aggressive plans or fantasies.

3 What determines whom we pick to aggress against? If it were possible, the frustrated would probably always direct their anger to the cause of their problems. However, it is not always possible or practical to do so. All we can do is displace our aggression.

The Reinforcement theorists began with a simple postulate: people are inveterate reward-seekers. They like those who reward them and dislike those who punish them.

equity theory and attraction

In Chapters 3 through 7, we found that this simple principle can tell us a great deal about human behavior. So far, so good.

Now for the next step. Thus far, we have talked about individuals as if they are in isolation from one another. But they are not. Humans are social animals. Society is composed of men and women—*all* trying to get all they can out of life. However, the physical environment is finite. There are fixed quantities of love, respect, food, and land. There is not enough to go around. It follows, then, that every society has to hammer out certain rules for deciding who gets what when.

What Equity theorists have studied, then, is (1) how people go about deciding who deserves what . . . when, and (2) how people react when they feel they are getting more . . . or less . . . than they deserve out of life.

Let us begin by reviewing Equity theory.[1] Then we can proceed to discuss some of the Equity theorists' intriguing research findings.

Equity theory is a strikingly simple theory. Essentially it consists of four propositions:

1 *Individuals will try to maximize their outcomes (where "outcomes" equals the rewards a person experiences minus the cost he endures).*

2 *A group of people can maximize their collective reward by developing an agreed-upon system for "equitably" apportioning the available rewards and costs among the group members. Thus, groups will evolve such systems of equity and will attempt to induce all individual members to accept and adhere to these systems once they are established. They*

---

1.   For a complete description of Equity theory, see E. Walster, G. W. Walster, and E. Berscheid, *Equity: Theory and Research*, Allyn and Bacon, 1978.

will generally reward an individual member of the group who treats the others equitably and will generally punish (increase the costs for) a group member who behaves inequitably.

3 When a person finds himself participating in an inequitable relationship with another/or a group of others, he becomes distressed. Further, the more inequitable his relationship, the more distress that individual will feel.

4 A person who discovers he is in an inequitable relationship will attempt to eliminate his distress by restoring equity to the relationship. The greater the inequity that exists, the more distress he will feel, and the harder he will try to restore equity.

Essentially, then, the Equity argument runs as follows:

People are motivated by self-interest. But "people-in-society" soon learn that they can probably come closest to getting what they want if they play according to society's rules . . . or at least appear to be doing so.

Thus, Equity theory argues that, all in all, humans feel most content when they are getting exactly what they think they deserve out of life—no more and certainly no less. Any time individuals exploit others, or allow themselves to be exploited, they will experience distress. (Such "distress" reactions have been labeled by different theorists in various ways. The *exploiter's* distress has been labeled "guilt," "shame," "dissonance," "empathy," "conditioned anxiety," or "fear of retaliation." The *victim's* distress has been labeled "anger," "shame," "humiliation," "dissonance," or "conditioned anxiety.") Regardless of how the distress is labeled, the evidence suggests that people generally *do* feel uncomfortable when they find themselves involved in an exploitive relationship.

How do exploiters and their victims handle these feelings of distress? Now, there's the rub. Humans may reduce their distress via two techniques:

Restoration of Actual Equity

One way an exploiter can restore equity to an unjust relationship is by volunteering to compensate the victim. Similarly, a victim can restore equity by demanding restitution. Many studies indicate that a harmdoer will often exert considerable effort to make restitution. (See, for example, Walster and Prestholdt 1966; Berscheid and Walster 1967; and Schmitt and Marwell 1972.) Parallel evidence indicates that a victim's first response to exploitation is often to seek restitution (see Leventhal and Bergman 1969, and Marwell, Schmitt, and Shotola 1971).

Restoration of Psychological Equity

When individuals find themselves in inequitable relationships, they can reduce distress in a second way. They can distort reality and convince themselves (and perhaps others as well) that really they *are* getting just what they deserve.

A variety of studies document the imaginative techniques both exploiters and victims use to justify injustice. Studies have demonstrated, for example, that we rationalize the harm we have accidentally done another by derogating our victim, by denying responsibility for our act, or by minimizing the victim's suffering. (See Brock and Buss 1962; Glass 1964; and Sykes and Matza 1957.) There is even some sparse experimental evidence that, under the right circumstances, victims will justify *their own* exploitation. (See Austin and Walster 1974, and Leventhal and Bergman 1969.)

Actual vs. Psychological Equity Restoration

At this point, Equity theorists confront a crucial question. When will individuals try to restore actual equity to their relationship? When will they settle for restoring psychological equity instead? Equity theory predicts that individuals will follow a "Cost-Benefit" strategy when deciding how they should respond. Whether individuals respond to injustice by attempting to restore actual equity, by distorting reality, or by doing a little of both, has been found to depend on the costs and benefits they think will be associated with each strategy. (See, for example, Berscheid and Walster 1967; Berscheid *et al.* 1968, or Weick and Nesset 1968.)

According to both Equity theory and Dissonance theory (which we reviewed in Chapter 7), whether participants decide to treat others fairly (or treat them inequitably, and then justify it) should have a marked effect on their relationships.

In this chapter we will see that the way in which we treat others may deeply affect our subsequent feelings toward them; we often come to dislike the people we exploit, and to like the people we benefit, as well as the other way around. We will also discover that, paradoxically, the more responsible we feel for our decision to treat the other person harshly or generously, the more we should like the person we benefited and to dislike the person we hurt.

Exploiters' Reactions to Their Victims

EVIDENCE THAT EXPLOITERS WILL MAKE RESTITUTION TO THEIR VICTIMS

It has not often been observed that it is a principle of human nature for the exploiter to make restitution to the exploited. Junius's cynical comment in his *Letters* that "A deathbed repentance seldom reaches to restitution" is a common observation. In spite of the cynicism of philosophers, exploiters do often attempt to restore equity to a relationship by making restitution to their victims. Some of the conditions under which a harmdoer attempts to compensate the victim has been investigated by Walster, Walster, Abrahams, and Brown (1966), Walster and Prestholdt (1966), Berscheid and Walster (1967), Freedman, Wallington, and Bless (1967), Carlsmith and Gross (1969), and Berscheid, Walster, and Barclay (1969).

EVIDENCE THAT EXPLOITERS WILL JUSTIFY THEIR HARMDOING

There is voluminous evidence that exploiters often attempt to reduce their distress in the second way—by convincing themselves that their behavior actually *was* justified. That we often justify our cruelties to others was apparent even to the ancients. Tacitus argued, "It is a principle of human nature to hate those whom you have injured."

Denigration of the victim is, of course, only one way by which exploiters can justify their harmdoing. They can also justify their exploitation by denying that they are responsible for the victim's suffering, by insisting that the victim deserved to suffer, or by minimizing the degree to which the victim actually did suffer from their actions.

One of the first experiments to demonstrate that we justify the harm we do another was conducted by two investigators who were testing predictions they derived from Dissonance theory. Davis and Jones (1960) reasoned that since most of us think of ourselves as kind and fair persons, we should experience dissonance anytime we realize we have deeply hurt another. Ironically, one way that we "kind and fair" persons can make ourselves feel a little better is by deciding that our hapless victims "deserved what they got." Davis and Jones also argued that the more responsible we feel for our decision to hurt another, the more dissonance we'll feel, and the more eager we will be to reduce our cognitive discomfort by denigrating our victim.

Finally, these investigators were interested in the fact that in some situations we can sometimes "withdraw" or take back cruel behavior. When we have hurt others by insulting them, we can say "I didn't mean it," or "I was playing a joke," and thereby partially eliminate the harm we have done. Davis and Jones hypothesized that when such "taking back" is possible, we will not denigrate the victim, but rather will choose to make amends.

To test these hypotheses, the authors conducted an experiment. College students were recruited to take part in an experiment on first-impression formation. Their main task was presumably to form a first impression of a man in an adjoining room. While the student listened, the experimenter interviewed the man. The interviewee was actually a confederate who attempted to answer all questions in a friendly way; he seemed slightly nervous and quite involved in creating a favorable yet honest impression of himself. When the interview was over, the experimenter asked the student to rate the confederate. (This gave the experimenter some idea of how the student felt about the soon-to-be victim.)

At this point the experimenter explained to the student that he was also interested in how people respond to extremely flattering or extremely negative evaluations of themselves. He then showed the student two prepared evaluations. One was complimentary; it contained such statements as "You sound like one of the most interesting persons that I have met since I came to Duke; I would really like to get to know you better." The other evaluation was negative; it contained statements such as "My overall impression was not too favorable" and "I wouldn't go out of my way to get to know you." The experimenter explained that the student should read one of these evaluations to the other person so that both the student and the experimenter could observe how he would react to the flattering or disparaging evaluation.

Choice vs. no choice The experimenter tried to cajole half of the students (those in the Choice condition) into *volunteering* to read the incredibly harsh evaluation to their fellow student. (The experimenter told them that they could choose *either* evaluation to read to the other student, but that he would appreciate it if they would choose the negative one. This request was effective in getting nearly all students to agree to read the negative evaluation.) The experimenter tried to *force* the remaining students (those in the No-Choice condition) to read it. (He simply told them they *must* read the negative evaluation.)

Anticipation vs. nonanticipation The experimenter wanted to lead some of the students to believe they would be able to meet the other person later (and thus they could explain they hadn't really meant their harsh criticism) . . . and half to believe that a subsequent meeting was impossible (and thus there was no way the injury could be undone). If the student had been assigned to the "Anticipation" of interaction condition, the experimenter said that after they studied the other's reaction to the negative evaluation, the student would have an opportunity to explain things to the other. If the student had been assigned to a "Nonanticipation" of interaction condition, the experimenter said that the student would not be able to tell the other how the student really felt.

The negative evaluation which all of the participants in this experiment read to the interviewee was harsh. It said:

> I hope that what I say won't cause any hard feelings, but I'll have to say right away that my overall impression was not too favorable. To put it simply, I wouldn't go out of my way to get to know you. Maybe I'd change my mind if we could talk together in more natural surroundings, but from the way you speak, not so much what you said but how you said it, I'd guess that you'd have some personal problems that it would make it hard for us to get along very well. Your general interests, and so on, just strike me as those of a pretty shallow person. To be more specific, frankly, I just wouldn't know how much I could trust you as a friend after hearing your answers to those moral questions. You took the easy way out every time. I guess I should point out that some of the things you said made a good impression on me, but that would be kind of a waste of time, since the general impression that I have is not too good. That's all I have to say.

After the student read the negative evaluation to the other, the experimenter asked the student to rate the other's likability, warmth, conceit, intelligence, and adjustment.

How did students feel about the other *after* insulting him?

Figure 8.1 illustrates how students felt about their partners *before* the harm was done, and how their feelings changed after they had insulted and demeaned them. Davis and Jones expected those in the Choice condition to "put down" their victim more than would those in the No-Choice condition, and those in the Nonanticipation of interaction condition to denigrate the victim more than those in the Anticipation condition. Thus, those in the "Choice–Nonanticipation" condition should "put down" the victim the most; those in the "No-Choice–Anticipation" condition should put him down the least.

It is clear from inspecting Fig. 8.1 that only the first portion of this hypothesis was confirmed. It is somewhat surprising to note that the No-Choice–Anticipation condition, expected to produce the least dissonance, is very similar to the two moderate dissonance conditions. Apparently, whether or not the student had any freedom to read the negative evaluation was not related to the production of dissonance as long as the student felt it possible to retract the harmful act in a future meeting with the victim.

On the basis of this evidence, the authors concluded that we are most likely to derogate our victim when we: (1) believe that we had some freedom not to behave in the harmful manner, and (2) realize that we cannot easily disclaim the behavior in the eyes of the person we have hurt. (These findings were replicated by Davidson 1964.)

Glass (1964) has added to our understanding of the denigration process. Glass hypothesized that the higher our self-esteem, the more likely we will

	Condition			
	Choice		No choice	
	Anticipation	Nonanticipation	Anticipation	Nonanticipation
Before $\overline{M}$	51.0	55.5	48.0	54.7
Change $\overline{M}$	−1.8	−7.7	−2.2	−1.7

Fig. 8.1 Mean before and change scores of summary rating evaluation. **Note:** The lower the before score, the more favorable the rating. A negative change score indicates change toward a less favorable impression. From K. E. Davis and E. E. Jones, p. 406. © 1960 by the American Psychological Association. Reprinted by permission.

be to derogate someone we victimize. Glass points out that if persons have low self-esteem (i.e., believe that they have a preponderance of unfavorable characteristics), the knowledge that they have injured another should not be especially dissonance-arousing. It is true that they have behaved in a socially disapproved way; however, their cruel acts are consonant with their general low self-regard. When persons believe they are fine, kind, and intelligent, however, knowledge of their aggression causes both a serious conflict with social norms *and* with their self-images. Thus, Glass concludes, the higher our self-esteem, the more we should be motivated to explain away our cruel behavior by derogating our victim.

Glass tested this hypothesis in a straightforward way. Two weeks before the experimental session, Glass gave students a series of psychological tests. He returned the test results to students at the beginning of the experimental session. Unknown to them, however, the results they received were false. Actually, only two personality reports were given out. Half of the students' reports were favorable and designed to raise their self-esteem. (They were told that they were personable, mature, mentally alert, intelligent, and that they had a concern for the feelings of others.) Half of the reports were designed to lower their self-esteem.

Students then began working together on a concept-formation task. They were asked to teach fellow students a series of concepts. Students were instructed to administer a 100-volt shock to their partners each time the partner made an error. Half of the "experimenters" (those in the Choice condition) were given the option of refusing to administer a series of electric shocks to the other person. The remaining "experimenters" (those in the No-Choice condition) were simply directed to administer the shocks.

The concept-formation task consisted of 60 learning trials. The confederate pretended to make 24 incorrect responses. Each time the student punished the confederate for the error, the confederate gasped and moved in discomfort in order to lead the student to believe that the student was causing the confederate considerable pain. When the learning trials were complete, the students were asked to indicate their attraction for the victim. They were also asked how they felt about the use of electric shock in experiments, to estimate how painful the shocks they had administered to the confederate actually were. Glass's hypothesis was confirmed. There was a significant interaction between the Choice and Self-esteem treatments: when students had had a *choice* about whether or not to harm the other person, those who possessed high self-esteem *did* denigrate the victim, but those who possessed low self-esteem did not. When students had been *forced* to harm their victims, no denigration occurred in either self-esteem condition.

Think about your own behavior. How do you feel when you know in your heart that you've treated another shamefully? Terrible? Determined not to admit it? If so, you're like everyone else. What do you do about it? You may try to convince yourself that the victim "had it coming." (We've already discussed *that*.) Or you may adopt two other diversionary strategies: (1) You may attempt to deny responsibility for the victimization; (2) you may try to deny that the victim *really* suffered. Brock and Buss (1962 and 1964) investigated these justification techniques. In what was presumably a learning experiment, they required participants to teach another person a concept and to administer a shock whenever an incorrect response was made. Those investigators varied the degree of choice the person had about whether or not to shock the victim–learner, the amount of justification the person was given for acting as a supervisor, the amount of shock he administered to the victim, the extent to which the participant was allowed to communicate with the victim, and the sex of the participant and of the victim. Brock and Buss examined how these variables affected how much obligation persons said they felt they had been under to shock the victim, how painful they perceived the shocks delivered to the victim to be, and the extent to which they justified the use of shock in experiments. The results of this experiment are multitudinous and too complex to allow more than a few of the findings to be summarized here. First, Brock and Buss (1962) found some evidence that the more choice people had as to whether or not to administer shock, the more distress they felt, and the harder they worked to reduce the distress; "Choice" students reduced their distress by minimizing the painfulness of the shocks they delivered, but their "No-Choice" counterparts did not (in fact, these students seemed to *exaggerate* the painfulness of the shocks they were required to administer).

Brock and Buss also found that those who were asked to give strong shocks to the victim reported later that they felt quite obligated to administer shock; those who were asked to give weaker shocks did not report such strong obligation. (It should be noted the experimenter's request to the person to administer shock to the learner was phrased exactly the same, regardless of the amount of shock the person was asked to deliver. Brock and Buss (1964) later replicated this finding.)

The preceding evidence provides compelling support for the notion that people often justify their cruelties; we have seen that exploiters may react to injustice by insisting that *they* were not the ones who hurt the victim, that the victim was not really hurt, or that the victim deserved to suffer.

COMPENSATION OR JUSTIFICATION? A COST–BENEFIT ANALYSIS

Operating from different theoretical positions, experimenters have proposed and demonstrated that people may react in two quite different ways to harming another: They may compensate the victims for the harm they have suffered . . . or they may justify their harmful action.

Obviously it is important to be able to predict when persons are likely to react to their harmful acts by compensating the victim and when they are likely to justify the victim's suffering instead. This is especially true since the two different reactions have diametrically opposed consequences for the victim. For example, if the harm-doers compensate the victims for their suffering, they accept responsibility for their harm-doing, they try to make up for their unacceptable behavior, and presumably they would be less willing to do the same thing again. On the other hand, when the harm-doers justify the harm they have done, they deny responsibility for it, they convince themselves that their behavior was acceptable, and presumably they should be more willing to engage in the behavior a second time (Berscheid, Boye, and Darley 1968).

According to equity theory, two situational factors should be crucial determinants of exploiters' response to inequity:

1 The *adequacy* of the possible techniques for restoring equity;

2 The *cost* of the possible techniques for restoring equity. People should prefer techniques that completely restore equity to techniques that only partially restore equity; further, they should prefer techniques associated with little material or psychological cost to techniques with greater cost.

More precisely, equity theorists would expect that, (1) *Other things being equal, the more adequate an exploiter perceives an available equity-restoring technique to be, the more likely he will be to use this technique to restore equity.* Equity theorists would also expect that, (2) *Other things being equal, the less costly an exploiter perceives an available equity restoring technique to be, the more likely he will be to use this technique to restore equity.*

Researchers have found that cost–benefit factors *do* seem to determine whether harm-doers respond to their victims with justice or with justification. We will review some of this research below.

THE ADEQUACY OF EQUITY-RESTORING TECHNIQUES

The Adequacy of Available Compensations

By "adequacy of compensation" is meant the extent to which a compensation benefits the victims, relative to the harm done to them. According to this definition, an available compensation may lack adequacy for two reasons: It may be inadequate to cover the harm done, or it may be an excessive restitution relative to the harm done.

There is a considerable amount of evidence demonstrating that harm-doers are more likely to make compensation if they can conceive of an adequate compensation than if they can only conceive of compensations that would be "too little" or "too much."

Berscheid and Walster (1967) and Berscheid, Walster, and Barclay (1969) attempted to explain why harm-doers would be reluctant to make either inadequate or excessive compensations. They reasoned that—from the harm-doer's point of view—making a partial compensation is an unsatisfactory way to restore equity. By itself, the partial compensation cannot restore equity; even after the compensation has been made, the victim is still in a deprived state. Similarly, excessive compensation cannot, by itself, eliminate the harm-doer's distress. An excessive compensation eliminates one kind of inequity, only to produce another. For these reasons, the authors predicted (and found) that people are more likely to compensate their victims (and presumably less likely to justify their victim's suffering instead) when they can conceive of an adequate compensation than when all of the compensations available to them are either inadequate or excessive.

In the experiment conducted with women's church groups (Berscheid and Walster 1967), women were led to deprive a fellow parishioner of trading stamps, which she desperately wanted to secure a birthday present for her son, in a vain attempt to win additional stamps for themselves. (Interviews with the women revealed that they felt guilty when they later ruminated on their actions.) When the women were subsequently given an opportunity to compensate their victim, at no cost to themselves, it was found that the adequacy of the available compensation was of crucial importance in determining whether or not the women would choose to compensate. Those women who had an opportunity to give their victim an adequate compensation—one which would exactly replace the number of trading stamps their fellow parishioner had lost—were much more likely to compensate than were those women who were limited to giving an insufficient compensation (a few stamps) or an excessive compensation (a great many stamp books). In the "control" conditions in which women were given an opportunity to award trading stamps to a person she had not injured, this tendency did not exist. This finding was replicated by Berscheid, Walster, and Barclay (1969).

If we accept these findings at face value, they have some surprising implications. In the hope of eliciting as much restitution as possible, people who have been victimized will often try to impress upon those in a position to make restitution how much they have suffered. They naturally assume that the better the case they make for their claim of extensive suffering, the more likely it is that they will be compensated. The preceding research, however, indicates that in some instances, victims might fare better if they *minimized* the degree to which the harmful act caused them to suffer. Increasing the amount of debt claimed might be an effective way to secure increased benefits *if* the harm-doer can conceivably make a restitution adequate to cover the suffering described. If, however, the suffering is aggrandized to such an extent that it exceeds the highest level of compensation available to the harm-doer, the victim may increase the chances of receiving no compensation at all—and, worse, of the harm-doer's creating justifications for the victim's suffering instead.

Victims might fare better if they minimized the degree to which the harmful act caused them to suffer.

The Adequacy of Available Justifications

There is also some sparse evidence that persons are more likely to choose to restore equity by justifying the harm they have done, if they can conceive of adequate justifications. An "adequate" justification is one which: (1) sufficiently justifies the performance of the harmful act, and (2) which is also plausible to the harm-doer, the victim, and to others.

The *sufficiency* of a justification can be defined as the extent to which the explanation, or reason for performing the act which harmed the victim, restores psychological equity to the relationship between the harm-doer and the victim. Consider the following example: A baseball player trips a member of the rival college team during a ball game. He later claims that he "did it" because the rival's pitches were "too close for comfort." Most people would probably consider this excuse to be fairly "reasonable," if somewhat unsporting. If instead of tripping the rival, however, the player brutally stabs the rival pitcher and claims he did it for the same reason, we are puzzled. Alternative "justifications" such as, "My mother likes my sister more than she likes me" or "The sun was shining in my eyes" sound equally bizarre to us.

Unfortunately, little is known about the determinants of whether a justification will be seen as "sufficient" or "insufficient" in relation to the performance of a harmful act.

Scientists do know a great deal, however, about the factors which determine whether a given justification will be judged to be *credible* by others. (See, for example, McGuire in Lindzey and Aronson 1968).

One factor which may help determine whether harm-doers will construct justifications—even when these involve massive self-delusion—is whether harm-doers are confident that others will never challenge their justificatory slight of hand. Because the severest critic of the credibility of the harm-doers' justifications is likely to be their victim, harm-doers will be much more likely to justify the suffering of their victim when they expect the victim will never see or interact with them again; harm-doers should be less likely to justify the suffering of a victim with whom they anticipate future interaction.

There are at least two reasons why individuals who hurt a person with whom they expect to have a great deal of subsequent contact should be more reluctant to distort their victim's characteristics than those of a person they expect never to see again.

First, of course, the more intimate we are with someone, the more likely we are to possess voluminous information about that person (whether we want it or not). Thus, if harm-doers try to distort an intimate's characteristics, they will soon find themselves in trouble; their fine rationalizations and justifications will keep bumping up against recalcitrant facts. However, it will be easy for their fantasies about a victim whom they will never see again to proliferate without the deterrent of hard information.

Second, harm-doers should expect more difficulty *maintaining* an adequate distortion when the distortion involves an intimate than when it involves a stranger. They must anticipate that if they engage in a massive distortion of an intimate's character (or of the circumstances surrounding the harmful act), their intimate-victim will have many opportunities (at least many more opportunities than a victim they'll never see again) to confront them, to challenge the credibility of their rationalizations, and—if the justifications seem "incredible"—to perhaps retaliate against them.

For two reasons, then, anticipation of future interaction with the victim should breed accuracy of perception and should discourage these justifications as a distress-reducing technique.

Evidence that men and women do engage in such "cold-blooded" calculations, when deciding whether to perceive others clearly—or "through a glass, darkly," comes from Pannen (1977).

We stated that there are two important determinants of a harm-doer's choice of equity restoring techniques: The *adequacy* of the available techniques for restoring equity and the *cost* of these techniques. In this section we reviewed evidence that adequate compensations and justifications are preferred to inadequate ones. In the next section, we will consider the evidence which indicates that the greater the cost of an equity-restoring technique, the less likely persons are to use it to restore equity to their relationship with others.

THE COST OF EQUITY-RESTORING TECHNIQUES

There is some experimental evidence to support the contention that the less costly exploiters perceive an available equity-restoring technique to be, the more likely they are to use that technique to restore equity.

The Cost of Available Compensations

Few will disagree that people are most likely to volunteer to compensate a person they've hurt when they can do so at a relatively low cost to themselves. A tipsy guest, who accidentally breaks a wine glass, is fairly likely to try to make amends by sending apologies along with a replacement if a duplicate wine glass can be purchased at a nearby store; the guest is less likely to attempt compensation if a trip to Iran is necessary to get the replacement. If any doubting Thomases need documentation of this point, they should be reassured that there *is* evidence that cost factors do influence a harm-doer's willingness to make restitution. (See Weick and Nesset, 1968.)

The Cost of Available Justifications

Parole boards have observed cynically: "On death row, everyone is innocent." And there's a reason. Sometimes it is inordinately costly to admit you're wrong . . . and "take it like a man." It is far easier to try to persuade, if not yourself, then at least others, that you're innocent.

For example, researchers have found that while we are frequently willing to admit to *ourselves* that we were wrong, we are surprisingly reluctant to admit *to others* that we were mistaken. Perhaps we are reluctant to expose ourselves to the "costs" of social disdain; it may be less costly to try to explain away our errors instead.

An experiment conducted by Walster and Prestholdt (1966) with social work trainees illustrates this tendency to justify our errors when it would be costly for us to admit them. The trainees were told they would be working on an actual case, with actual clients. Ostensibly, the trainees' job was to listen to case history reports in which different social workers discussed two clients—a daughter and her mother. It was the trainees' job to make a realistic, honest, and accurate evaluation of each client.

Before the trainees heard the first report, they were given some background information concerning the clients. Control group trainees were warned that the report which they would soon hear was not entirely correct, that certain events were so misleading that if they were taken at face value they would lead one to make an overly generous evaluation of the mother and an overly harsh evaluation of her daughter. Experimental group trainees were not given this warning.

Trainees then heard the first social workers' report, wrote an evaluation of both clients, and made a recommendation as to the type of treatment they should receive. Trainees in the Control condition, who had been warned to disregard certain false information, naturally wrote a fairer evaluation of the clients. Trainees in the Experimental condition, who had not received complete information, usually wrote an unjustly harsh evaluation of the daughter and an overly generous evaluation of the mother.

After completing their evaluations, half of the trainees received a treatment which strongly committed them to their initial evaluations; these trainees were required to sign their evaluations, their instructor then read them, and finally, the evaluations were sent to the clients' psychiatrist. The other half of the trainees were not committed to their evaluations. The uncommitted trainees were allowed to keep their evaluations; in fact, they were told they could simply rip them up and throw them away.

Trainees then heard the second case report which argued that the first report was misleading and which presented information contradicting the impression of the clients provided in the first report. After the trainees heard the second report, the experimenter asked the trainees to make a final and anonymous evaluation of the clients.

The authors found that commitment was a crucial variable in determining whether trainees would change their minds in the face of new information or would attempt to justify their unfair treatment and continue to treat the client unjustly. Committed trainees continued to adhere to their overly harsh or overly favorable evaluations long after receiving the correct information. Uncommitted trainees were quite willing to change their minds. (In fact, uncommitted trainees seemed to bend over backwards to be fair after their initial error; they were even more favorable to the daughter and more harsh to the mother than were Control trainees.)

The authors were also interested in whether or not the predicted variations in liking would affect the trainees' behavior toward the clients. Thus, immediately after the trainees had evaluated the clients for the last time, the instructor mentioned that social work volunteers were now needed to assist the clients. The trainees' liking for the clients *was* strongly linked to their willingness to help them.

Benefactors' Reactions to Their Beneficiaries

Until now we have concentrated entirely on how persons will respond to someone that they have unjustly injured. However, we are also interested in the question, "How will individuals respond after conferring an undeserved benefit on someone?"

Both equity and cognitive consistency researchers have suggested that a benefactor should experience at least some twinges of distress after dispensing benefits to another who is undeserving of them. If we believe, as most of us do, that people should get what they deserve and *only* what they deserve, and yet we find ourselves in the position of gratuitously rewarding an undeserving person, we should experience distress. One way we can reduce our distress is to convince ourself that the recipient of our benefits is in fact more deserving of them than we initially thought.

The notion that doing a favor for others may increase our attraction to them is not new with the equity and the cognitive consistency theorists. Gerard (1966) points out that Aristotle and Aquinas both believed that benefactors come to love the recipients of their favors. Both asked and attempted to decide "Whether a man ought to love more his benefactor than one he has benefited." The reasons these philosophers give for why we should come to love persons we have benefited (while we oftentimes come to resent the person who has benefited *us*) sound very much like those of contemporary psychological theorists. For example, Aristotle says:

> . . . it is more difficult to give than to receive favors: and we are most fond of things which have cost us most trouble, while we almost despise what comes easy to us.

Jecker and Landy (1969) conducted an ingenious experiment to test this hypothesis. They proposed that when we expend effort, time, or material possessions in order to benefit another person—especially when we dislike that person—we experience cognitive dissonance. When we do not particularly like a person, and have no reason to suspect that the person will reciprocate our kindness, we have little justification for performing the favor. They predicted then, that if people were led to help someone they disliked, they would try to justify doing the undeserved favor by increasing their attraction for the other. They also proposed that the larger the favor people performed, the more dissonance they would experience, and the more they would increase their liking for the initially disliked other.

To test their hypotheses, students were recruited to participate in a concept formation task. Throughout their performance of this task, the ex-

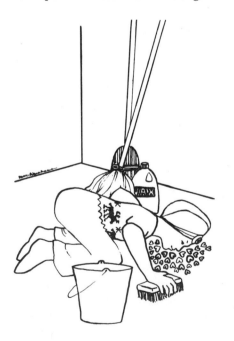

. . . *benefactors come to love the recipients of their favors.*

perimenter behaved in a uniformly rude and brusque way toward them. When they finished, and by design, the students had won either 60 cents or three dollars at the task.

Students were then randomly assigned to one of three conditions. In one condition, they were prodded into doing a favor for their disagreeable experimenter. The experimenter said to these students, "I wonder if you could do me a favor. The funds for this experiment have run out and I'm using my own money to finish the experiment. As a favor to me, would you mind returning the money you won?" If students hesitated to return the 60 cents or three dollars they had won, the experimenter said "I can't make you return the money, but I wish you would as a favor to me." The students were then thanked for participating in the experiment and asked to report to the psychology department secretary.

Students in another condition did a favor for someone other than the experimenter, i.e., the "psychology department." Students who were assigned to this condition were not asked by the experimenter to return the money they had won; they were simply thanked for their participation in the experiment and, like all of the other students, were asked to report to the department secretary. However, when they got there, the departmental secretary asked them to do a favor for the psychology department. She said: "The money Mr. Boyd is using comes from the psychology department's research fund, which is running extremely low. The *department* would appreciate your doing it a favor by returning the money to the fund."

The remainder of the students, who were assigned to a No-Favor condition, were thanked for their participation, instructed to report to the departmental secretary, but were not asked to do a favor for anyone.

Before they left, students in all conditions were asked by the secretary to fill out questionnaires, purportedly designed by the psychology department to find out how students felt about the experiments in which they were participating. Actually, this questionnaire contained the dependent measure; as part of the questionnaire, students were asked to rate their personal liking for the experimenter.

Jecker and Landy found, as predicted, that those students who returned the money to the experimenter liked him *better* than did those students who returned their money to the psychology department. The authors also found some support for their hypothesis that the bigger the favor students performed for the experimenter, the greater would be their liking for him; students who returned the three dollars to the experimenter tended to like him more than students who returned only 60 cents, but the difference, while in the predicted direction, was not statistically significant.

The Effect of Chance Consequences

It is popularly believed that "Nothing succeeds like success" and that "Everybody loves a winner." Is it true that we like those who have fortuitously succeeded? that we dislike those who have accidentally failed? If so, why do we so frequently allow the caprices of chance to determine our esteem for another?

One reason why we may praise or blame others for the accidental consequences they have enjoyed or suffered through no action or fault of their own is that we may automatically assume that people get what they deserve. Since we know that many of the things that happen to persons are in some way a consequence of their own actions, our best guess—particularly in an ambiguous situation—is that the persons are probably at least partially responsible for their fate. When individuals admit to us that everyone is out to get them, and that all their attempts to improve their lot are blocked by a malevolent fate, we become suspicious; we reject the possibility that, through no fault of their own, the last dozen people they met happened to be sadists. It is possible, of course, that an individual would have such a run of bad luck, but it is so unlikely that we do not really seriously consider the possibility.

There is a second reason why we may praise or blame others for consequences over which they had no control and are in no way responsible for. Our assumption that "people get what they deserve" also may be motivated by our desire to believe that the world is a predictable, and an equitable, place.

Walster (1966) proposed that it is particularly comforting for us to believe the world is predictable and equitable when we contemplate the very severe consequences which others may suffer. She hypothesized that when we hear about an accident, we often want to blame someone (preferably the victim) for the accident. Our desire to assign responsibility for the accident should be especially strong when the consequences of the accident are very serious. When we hear that others have suffered a very small loss, it is easy to feel sympathy for them, to ascribe their misfortune to chance, and to acknowledge that unpleasant things can happen to persons through no fault of their own. But as the magnitude of the misfortune increases, it becomes more and more unpleasant to acknowledge that "this is the kind of thing that could happen to anyone." Such an admission implies that a serious catastrophe could happen to us. If we can convince ourselves that the serious accident was the victim's fault, it is reassuring. Then we need only assure ourselves that we are a different kind of person from the person the victim is, or that we would behave differently under the circumstances which produced the accident, and we can then feel protected from catastrophe.

Walster tested this hypothesis by describing a young man's driving habits to groups of judges. In her description, she varied the degree of seriousness of the accident which was said to have resulted from the same pre-accident behavior. Her findings showed that the more serious the consequences were said to be, the more "morally unacceptable" the youth's behavior was judged to be, and the more responsible he was considered to be for the accident.

Lerner and his associates have conducted several experiments to test the hypothesis that we need to believe in an equitable and just world, and that we will distort reality, if necessary, in order to maintain our belief that principles of equity rule our lives. Lerner (1965) reasons that a belief in a just world is a prerequisite for survival. He says:

> ... if people did not believe they could get what they want and avoid what they abhor by performing certain appropriate acts, they would be virtually incapacitated. It seems obvious that most people cannot afford, for the sake of their own sanity, to believe in a world governed by a schedule of random reinforcements.

There is considerable support for the proposal that observers will convince themselves that chance occurrences to others were actually deserved. Lerner (1965) asked people to observe two men performing a task together. They were told at the outset that one of the two workers would be selected by *chance* to receive a sizable amount of money for his efforts whereas the other worker would get nothing. In spite of this information that reward was randomly given, once the outcome was known to the observers they tended to persuade themselves that the worker who had been awarded the money by chance really had earned it after all.

In many of Lerner's experiments, the participants gather in a waiting room a few minutes before the scheduled experiment and are joined by a confederate (the "victim"), a person of their own age. The participants then learn that they are to take part in a study of the perception of emotional cues; the victim is to take part in a different study, a study on human learning, with another experimenter and in another room. They discover that in the learning study, the other will be punished by receiving an electric shock every time an incorrect response is made. The experimenter explains that the participants are to judge the victim's emotional state while she is participating in the learning experiment by viewing the other's performance via a television monitor. Actually, participants watch not a live closed-circuit television performance, as they expect, but a standard videotape. All participants, in all conditions, see the same videotape; all see the victim receive several apparently painful electric shocks for making incorrect responses, and they see the victim react to the shocks with expressions of pain and suffering. Finally, the participants are asked to describe their reactions to the victim. This basic experimental paradigm has been used to test several hypotheses.

Lerner and Simmons (1966) suggest there are two ways in which we can maintain our belief that the world is indeed a just place even when faced with the fact that an innocent person has been injured. First, we can convince ourself that the victim deserved to suffer because he or she did not behave in an "appropriate or commendable fashion." Or, secondly, we can convince ourself that the victim deserved to suffer because he or she is an undesirable individual. In either case, our esteem for the victim ought to be lowered as a result of his or her suffering an accidental misfortune.

Lerner and Simmons hypothesized that observers would feel more compelled to justify victims' suffering, and thus would derogate the victims more when they believed that the victims' suffering would continue, than if they believed that the suffering was at an end (or had occurred in the past). The authors varied the preceding design slightly to test this notion. They led one group of observers to believe that the videotape they saw represented only the first half of an experiment; ostensibly, the victim was going to continue to be shocked even after the observers had completed their ratings. In other conditions, the videotape was said to represent the complete experiment. In still other conditions, the videotape was said to have been made some time ago.

The results supported the authors' hypothesis. The observers derogated the victim more when her suffering was only half over than when it was at an end or when the videotape was acknowledged to be several months old.

The authors' second hypothesis is the more surprising. Most of us would assume that people will admire and feel compassion for a person who has suffered for the sake of others—a person who is a martyr. For example, the sympathy Roman observers felt when observing the suffering of the Christian martyrs is often assumed to have encouraged the spread of Christianity. However, Lerner and Simmons point out that the suffering of someone who has acted out of altruistic motives should be extremely threatening to our belief in a just world. A martyr, by virtue of goodness, does not deserve to suffer. Thus, observers should reject the willing martyr even more than the innocent victim.

This hypothesis was tested by altering the preceding experimental paradigm slightly. In the martyr condition, the victim claimed to be afraid of electric shock and did not want to participate in the experiment. At the

experimenter's urging the victim agreed to go on so that the other participants could make their observations and thereby satisfy their course re-
quirement. The observers subsequently evaluated the martyr as less attractive than a victim who had *not* expressed fear of shock and agreed to go on
in order to help the observers.

Summary

We began this chapter by reviewing Equity theory. The theory consists of
four propositions:

1 Individuals try to maximize their outcomes.

2 A society can maximize collective reward by developing an agreed on
system for equitably apportioning rewards among members.

3 When people follow society's dictates, they feel fine. When they find
themselves treating others inequitably, they feel vaguely uneasy.

4 Thus, when persons realize they have exploited . . . or lavishly over-
benefited others . . . they will try to "set things right." They will try to restore either actual, or psychological, equity.

According to Equity theory, two factors should determine how persons
respond to when they realize they have treated another unjustly: (1) The
adequacy of the possible techniques for restoring equity, and (2) the cost of
the possible techniques for restoring equity. People naturally prefer to use
techniques that completely restore equity to those that only partially restore
it. They prefer to use techniques that are associated with little psychological
or material cost to others.

We then proceeded to consider the evidence that the way in which we
treat another person may deeply affect our feelings toward the other. We
often come to dislike the people we exploit and like the people we benefit.

Exploiters Come to Dislike Their Victims

Davis and Jones and Glass provide evidence that, anytime we have deeply
hurt others, we feel guilty. Ironically, one way we can make ourselves feel
a little better is by convincing ourselves and others that those we have hurt
are repulsive, stupid, persons—who deserve to suffer.

Benefactors Come to Like Their Beneficiaries

Researchers also provide *some* evidence that anytime we realize we have
lavishly dispensed benefits to someone who really doesn't deserve them, we

feel some twinges of remorse. Jecker and Landy document that one way we reduce our distress is to convince ourselves that the other is really deserving . . . and more likable than we had thought.

In a final section, we considered the effect that purely chance events have on our liking for others. Is it true that "Everybody loves a winner"? Do we really like those who—strictly by chance—succeed? Is it true that "Nobody likes a loser"? Do we really dislike those who, just by chance, fail? The answer is "Yes." There are two reasons why this is so: (1) Perhaps, in life, people really do *usually* get what they deserve. Thus, in the absence of any knowledge, we may tend to assume that "He who has, deserves" and "He who doesn't, doesn't." (2) Perhaps we believe that "This is a just world" because that's what we *want* to believe. Lerner provides considerable evidence for this latter hypothesis.

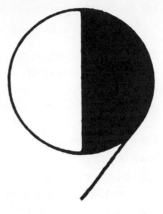

Introduction

the beginnings: romantic love

*Love is such a tissue of para-
doxes, and exists in such an
endless variety of forms and
shades, that you may say almost anything about it that you please, and it
is likely to be correct.*   (FINCK 1902, p. 224.)

Finck was a Victorian era author who had a good deal to say about love in
his treatise *Romantic Love and Personal Beauty: Their Development, Causal
Relations, and Historic and National Peculiarities.*

A good deal is still being said. In the latter half of the 20th century,
commentators of all stripes and persuasions are pleased to address the topic
of love. From song-writers to politicians, from novelists to editors to astro-
nauts to students, from the lady from Dubuque to the man on the street,
all feel compelled to give the subject of romantic love their personal attention, and to offer to all who are willing to read, listen, or watch, their unique
theories and opinions of the importance—or nonimportance—of love, the
antecedents of love and the impossibility of identifying the determinants of
love, the consequences of love, the feeling of love, love "in an endless variety of forms and shades."

And all are just as likely to be correct as they were in Finck's day. At
least no one can yet say to them "nay," for there still does not exist a mature
body of literature representing the fruits of systematic and scientific investigation of the most interesting of all varieties of interpersonal attraction.

Historical Deterrents to the Study of Romantic Love

The lack of empirical information about romantic love is surprising since it
assumes great importance in our culture. Love not only qualifies as one of
the most talked about, written about, and sung about human phenomena,

147

but the feeling of romantic love for another is generally regarded as the sine qua non for marriage in our society. That romantic love should be a precondition for matrimony is often debated but that it is, is generally recognized. As Waller and Hill observed in their classic text, *The Family* (1951, p. 115), "In our culture one marries because one has fallen in love." Or, as Burgess and Wallin (1953), authors of another classic text in the field of marriage and the family, *Engagement and Marriage*, put it, "The expected, approved, and sanctioned precondition to marriage in American society is falling in love. According to our mores, love is the only right basis for marriage."

Burgess and Wallin backed up their observation with data. They asked approximately 1000 young men and women who were engaged to be married, "Do you think that a person should ever marry one whom he or she does not love?" Eighty-two percent of the men and 80 percent of the women said "No"; only 12 percent of the men and 15 percent of the women said "Yes." (The remainder were "undecided.")

Kephart (1967) asked approximately 1000 college students an even more stringent question, "If a man (woman) had all the other qualities you desired, would you marry this person if you were not in love with him (her)?" Even if a woman fit their marital specifications exactly, eleven percent of the men said "Yes" they would marry her, 24 percent weren't certain what they would do, 65 percent said "No." The women in Kephart's sample were somewhat less romantic; while only four percent said they would marry a man who exactly fit their personal specifications for a husband if they didn't love him, a whopping 72 percent said they were "undecided" and only 24 percent gave a flat "No."

If love is the ground upon which a marriage is built and children are typically conceived and born and raised, if it is the foundation of the family, the nuclear unit of our society, why has love not received the scientific attention it would seem to deserve? Why has such a distinguished psychologist and humanist as Abraham Maslow (1954, p. 235) found it necessary to admonish his colleagues for their neglect of love:

> It is amazing how little the empirical sciences have to offer on the subject of love. Particularly strange is the silence of psychologists, for one might think this to be their particular obligation. . . . Sometimes this is merely sad or irritating, as in the case of the textbooks of psychology and sociology, practically none of which treats the subject. . . . More often the situation becomes completely ludicrous. One might reasonably expect that writers of serious treatises on the family, on marriage, and on sex should consider the subject of love to be a proper, even basic, part of their self-imposed task. But I must report that no single one of the volumes on

these subjects available in the library where I work has any serious mention of the subject.

There are probably three main reasons why researchers neglected the study of love.

First, as Burgess and Wallin (1953, p. 11) noted, until as recently as the 1950s:

> Love and marriage were regarded as belonging to the field of romance, not of science. The theory of romantic love held full sway. The predominant view was that in some mysterious, mystic and even providential way a person was attracted to his or her pre-destinate. The general assumption was that young people fell in love, married and lived happily ever afterwards, as a result of some mystic attraction. Even when marriages turned out unhappily, the disillusioned partners explained the failures as being due to their having mistaken infatuation for love. Or else they placed the blame on bad luck or fate.

For some time the popular, but erroneous, belief that human behavior is not subject to scientific study and prediction acted as a deterrent to the study of love.

Researchers neglected the important topic of love for a second reason: until fairly recently, experimental research into romantic love was "taboo." For example, in the 1920s a professor at the University of Minnesota was fired because he approved of a questionnaire on attitudes toward sex. (Clear evidence of the researcher's depravity was provided by the fact that he had asked respondents such personal questions as "Have you ever blown into the ear of a person of the opposite sex in order to arouse their passion?")

Burgess and Wallin (1953) argue that before World War I young people would have refused to answer questions on the subjects of marriage and love, considering them too intimate, personal, and sacred. They would certainly have considered questions about sex to be beyond the pale. It took the pioneering work of Kinsey and his colleagues, and more recently that of Masters and Johnson (1966), to remove the shroud of mystery and myth from human sexuality, and to help make it possible to study related topics.

Finally, there is a third reason why researchers neglected the study of love—they weren't quite sure how to go about it.

Interestingly enough, Maslow tempered his harsh criticism of those who had neglected the study of love, as soon as he tried to investigate the topic himself. He notes (p. 235), somewhat poignantly:

> I must confess that I understand this better now that I have undertaken the task myself. It is an extraordinarily difficult subject to handle in any tradition, and it is triply so in the scientific tradition. It is as if we were at

the most advanced position in no-man's-land, at a point where the conventional techniques of orthodox psychological science are of very little use. And yet our duty is clear. We *must* understand love...."

Today, probably all scientists agree that love does exist, that it can be studied, and that it is critical that we do so.

But before we smile too smugly at the "know-nothing" attitudes of our predecessors, let us admit that our "enlightenment" is rather precarious. Even today, politicians can still make political hay by attacking the teacher or researcher who dares to discuss questions of love and sex.

For example, in 1975, a prominent Midwestern senator denounced the National Science Foundation for encouraging researchers to study romantic attraction. The senator's objections to "squandering" money on such research were twofold: (1) he was convinced that scientists could never find an answer to the "mystery" of love, and (2) even if they did, the senator didn't want to hear it—and he was confident that no one else did either:

> I believe that 200 million other Americans want to leave some things in life a mystery, and right at the top of things we don't want to know is why a man falls in love with a woman and vice versa.... So National Science Foundation—get out of the love racket. Leave that to Elizabeth Barrett Browning and Irving Berlin. Here, if anywhere, Alexander Pope was right when he observed, 'If ignorance is bliss, 'tis folly to be wise.'

It apparently escaped the senator's attention that the American public voluntarily and spontaneously spends millions each year on books and

'Ignorance is bliss! That'll be five cents, please.
Cartoon by Sanders in the Milwaukee (Wisc.) Journal.

magazine articles which expound theories about the causes and cures of romantic love, and yet millions more to psychiatrists, psychologists, and other therapists, as well as to fortune-tellers, astrologers, and other members of the occult, in return for their "answers" to questions about love and related matters. The "love business" has been booming for quite awhile and indicates that answers to questions about love are right at the top of things we *do* want to know.

The fact that, until, recently, love and sex were assumed to be too unscientific, too sacred, or too difficult to study explains why there is a dearth of information about these varieties of interpersonal attraction. What *do* we know about love?

Romantic Love[1]

We began our book by defining Interpersonal Attraction:

An individual's tendency or predisposition to evaluate a person or a symbol of that person in a positive or a negative way.

We observed that "Interpersonal Attraction" included a variety of very special human feelings—friendly liking, romantic and passionate love, companionate love, parental love, love of humankind, love of country, love of God. Initially, psychologists focused almost entirely on Interpersonal Attraction's gentlest variety—liking. Recently, however, psychologists began to explore Interpersonal Attraction's more exotic and intense varieties—romantic (or passionate) love and companionate love.

What is passionate love, anyway?[2]

According to Walster and Walster (1978) *passionate* (i.e., romantic) *love* is:

A state of intense absorption in another. Sometimes "lovers" are those who long for their partners and for complete fulfillment. Sometimes "lovers" are those who are ecstatic at finally having attained their partners' love, and, momentarily, complete fulfillment. A state of intense physiological arousal.

Few scientists have explored this intense variety of attraction. However, readers who have carefully worked their way through Chapters 1 through 8 may well ask if their knowledge of the antecedents and consequences of

---

1. For a fuller discussion of romantic and passionate love, see Elaine Walster and G. William Walster. *Love*. Reading, Mass.: Addison-Wesley, 1978.
2. In Chapter 10 we will focus on passionate love's gentle cousin—companionate love.

attraction *in general* doesn't tell them all they need to know about romantic love. After all, romantic love is simply intense liking, isn't it?

The question of whether romantic love is qualitatively different from other forms of attraction—or whether it's simply very intense attraction—is one that scientists have spent a good deal of time thinking and debating with each other about.

Most of the theorists we have discussed so far have assumed that their attraction theories are equally applicable to mild attraction *and* to intense, passionate love. They have taken the position that mild liking and love are *not* qualitatively different.

Nevertheless, some investigators are uneasy about simply assuming that the same Reinforcement theories, unmodified, can explain both mild attraction and the overwhelming and consuming variety of attraction known as romantic love.

For example, Berscheid and Walster (1974) outline some of the important ways in which romantic love and liking differ:

The Importance of Fantasy in the Generation of Romantic Love

> When two mouths, thirsty each
>   for each, find slaking,
> and agony's forgot, and hushed
>   the crying
> of credulous hearts, in heaven—
>   such are but taking
> Their own poor dreams within
>   their arms and lying
> Each in his lonely night, each
>   with a ghost.   *Rupert Brooke*

Reinforcement theorists have generally assumed that it is the rewards, or punishments, one *actually* receives from another which create liking. It seems doubtful, however, that lovers are so reality-bound. When lovers close their eyes and daydream, they can summon up a flawless partner—a partner who instantaneously satisfies all unspoken, conflicting, and fleeting desires. Compared with these grandiose fantasies, the rewards we receive in our real interactions are dismayingly sparse. As a consequence, sometimes the most extreme passion is aroused—not by real-life love objects—but by partners who are barely known . . . or who exist only in imagination.

Theorists interested only in liking, then, can possibly afford to focus entirely on the impact *actual* reward has on liking. In contrast, it seems likely that romantic love theorists will be forced to consider both the re-

Compared with these grandiose fantasies, the rewards we receive in our real interactions are dismayingly sparse.

wards lovers receive in fantasy and rewards they fantasize they might receive in future interaction with their partners.

Romantic love: the fantasy Theorists generally agree that romantic love is inexorably tied up with fantasy. Waller and Hill, for example, state flatly (1951, p. 120) that, "Idealization is an essential element in romantic love."

According to clinical psychologist Theodor Reik, it is when we are most dissatisfied with ourselves that we are most vulnerable to love. It is when we are most dissatisfied with ourselves that we engage in wish-fulfilling fantasies—we think of all the things we would like to be (but are not) and all the things we would like to have (but do not). Eventually, according to Reik, we more or less "drape" this fantasy structure around another person; we convince ourselves that this idealized person has all we want or desire.

Social psychologists have found some evidence that Reik's hypothesis is correct. Acute deprivation does seem to set the stage for passionate fantasies. It has been frequently demonstrated, for example, that when people are sexually aroused, they normally have sexual fantasies (e.g., Lehman and Epstein 1961). There is also some evidence that, as Reik hypothesizes, these fantasies sometimes get all mixed up with the reality of another person.

Let us consider a typical experiment.

Stephan *et al.* (1971) proposed that when we are sexually aroused, our minds wander, and pretty soon our dazzling fantasies lend sparkle to drab reality. Stephan *et al.* tested this proposition in a simple experiment. The authors contacted college men, and asked if they'd be interested in participating in a study of college dating practices. They wanted to find out how men felt about a blind date they'd picked for them. While the men waited to give their first impression of their date-to-be, they were given some reading material to while away the time. The "reading material" was designed to dampen the sexual feeling of some of the men, and to stimulate the sexual feelings of the others. In the Non-aroused condition, men were given a boring treatise on the sex life of the herring gull to read. In the Highly-aroused condition, men were given a romantic story of sexual seduction.

When the waiting period was up, the experimenter called the men in, presumably to tell them a little about their date, and to get their initial reaction to her. In all cases, the same date was described to the men. They were shown the picture of a pretty blonde. They were also given her background questionnaire. From the woman's self-description, it was evident that she was active, fairly intelligent, easy to get along with, and moderately liberal. Then the men were asked what they thought of her.

Stephan *et al.* speculated that when men were sexually aroused their fantasies should be stimulated. They should begin to "idealize" their prospective date—exaggerating both her sexual *desirability*, and her sexual *receptivity*. They found that they were right. The more aroused a man was, the more beautiful he thought his date was. In addition, the more aroused he was, the more likely he was to assume that his date would be sexually receptive. Aroused men rated their dates as being more amorous (vs. non-amorous), immoral (vs. moral), willing (vs. unwilling), promiscuous (vs. unpromiscuous), unwholesome (vs. wholesome), careless (vs. careful), nasty (vs. nice), durable (vs. delicate), and not very inhibited (vs. inhibited).

Stephen *et al.* provide yet other evidence consistent with the hypothesis that the greater one's needs, the more one will fantasize about people or·objects which might satisfy these needs. They speculated that men who were able to satisfy their sexual needs routinely would have little need to "idealize" their forthcoming date. Men who were sexually deprived should be very motivated to fantasize that *this* date would be able and willing to satisfy their sexual longings. The authors (p. 100) found some support for this contention:

> The more sexually experienced males in our study (determined by self-report of frequency and recency of sexual experience) found the stimulus girl *less* attractive than did the inexperienced males.

There is evidence, then, that aroused, but unfulfilled, needs may arouse need-related fantasy and suggestive evidence that unfulfilled sexual needs may be an especially frequent instigator of romantic idealization of a member of the opposite sex.

Ambivalence of Emotion in Romantic Love

Liking generally seems to be a straightforward and sensible phenomenon. As the research described in the previous chapters well documents, we like those who reward us and we dislike those who thwart our desires. Unfortunately, romantic love, that exotic variety of attraction, does not fit very neatly into the Reinforcement paradigm. It is true that some practical people manage to fall in love with beautiful, wise, entertaining, and wealthy people who bring them happiness. Many of us, however, with unfailing accuracy, seem to fall passionately in love with people who are almost guaranteed to bring us suffering. The plaint that "I can't live with him and I can't live without him," an intense approach–avoidance dilemma, seems to be far more frequently heard in reference to "romantic love relationships."

Observers disagree, then, about the nature of the emotional states which are most conducive to passion. Some insist that passionate love is inexorably entwined with fulfillment and the anticipation of fulfillment. Others insist that passionate love is virtually synonymous with agony. (Indeed, the original meaning of passion was "agony"—as in "Christ's Passion.") College students evidently share the theorists' confusion as to whether passionate love is a joyous state or a painful one. Students at several universities were allowed to ask psychologists one question about romantic love. Among the most frequent questions was "Can you love and hate someone at the same time?"

As we noted in Chapter 1, most researchers of interpersonal attraction have presumed that our evaluative feelings toward another are unidirectional—the more we like a person, the less we dislike him or her. Theorists of romantic love, however, must try to account for the vacillation between positive and negative affect, the ambivalence that sometimes seems to be characteristic of passionate love relationships.

The Effect of Time upon Loving and Liking

The passage of time seems to affect romantic love and liking differently; liking appears to be more durable. One of the "laws" of liking, expressed by Homans (1961, p. 203), is that ". . . other things equal, the more a man interacts with another, the more he likes him." In stark contrast to this statement is the observation that "The history of a love affair is the drama of its fight against time." Most authors of marriage and family texts agree. Williamson (1966), for example, warns that romantic love is a temporary phenomenon and cautions that although intense passion may be a prerequisite for marriage, it is bound to dwindle after lengthy interaction. Reik (1944), too, warns that the very best one can hope for after several years of marriage is an "afterglow."

The diminishing of romantic love over time seems predictable to the extent it is based on fantasy and idealization of the romantic partner. In time, one's fantasies, and along with them, one's love, are bound to be eroded. To the extent that liking is based on more realistic grounds, it should not be as vulnerable to deterioration from continued interaction with the partner.

It should be explicitly noted that there is little or no research investigating the stability of passionate attraction, or even mild attraction, over substantial periods of time.

These dissimilarities between romantic love and liking are some of the reasons some attraction researchers are reluctant to conclude that romantic love is simply an intense form of liking. They continue to entertain the possibility that the investigation of the antecedents of romantic love may require us to supplement the general Reinforcement theories (which have directed research on the milder forms of attraction) with special theories focused directly upon this phenomenon.

Theories of Romantic Love

There *are* psychological theories of romantic love available. For example, we referred to Theodor Reik's theory earlier. Most, if not all, of these theories, however, have been developed by clinical psychologists who—drawing upon their clinical and therapeutic work with clients and their personal observations of human behavior—have constructed theories about the determinants of romantic love.

CLINICAL THEORIES OF LOVE

Many of these theoretical treatises on romantic love are woven with the thread of "psychological dependency." A crucial relationship is believed to exist between our dependence upon another for our comfort, well-being, and happiness, and our love for him or her.

Abraham Maslow calls it "D-love" (1954). "Deficiency-love," he theorized, springs from our needs for love, for security, and for belongingness; when another gratifies our "deficiency" needs, we love the other in return. According to Maslow, there is another kind of love—"B-love." But while all of us can aspire to love another simply for the other's "being" rather than for the satisfactions the other provides, only very few exceptional, "self-actualized" individuals may ever actually experience such love. The kind of love most of us experience in our lifetime is, in Maslow's view, D-love.

Several other theoreticians agree. Cashler (1969), for example, speculates that love grows out of our needs for security, sexual satisfaction, and social conformity. Klein and Riviere (1953) also believe that love has its genesis in our dependency upon other people for the satisfaction of our needs. And Reik (1944), too, hypothesizes that a sense of our own deficit —a dissatisfaction with ourselves and our state in life—is our spur to love another.

The soil of romantic love, then, according to these theorists, is our own unfulfilled needs, our deficiencies, our dissatisfaction with ourselves. Those who are satisfied, those who do not need, are not candidates for the experience of love.

The notion that love springs from unfilled needs is compatible with the observation that romantic love feeds on fantasy and idealization of the other since it has been documented that unfulfilled needs are the wellspring of much wish-fulfilling fantasy. This conception of romantic love also is consistent with the observation that ambivalence of emotion often characterizes love relationships, for to grow dependent upon another for our happiness may not be an unalloyed delight, particularly when one can't be certain that the other reciprocates our attraction to the other (cf. Berscheid and Fei 1976).

The clinical theories of romantic love have not yet stimulated a great deal of research. They are often written loosely and unsystematically and do not always invite empirical test. Nevertheless, there is evidence for their central notion that romantic love for another is associated with high degrees of dependency on the other. Rubin (1970), who has developed a scale to measure love (See Chapter 1), found that one of love's components is "affiliative and dependent need." Berscheid and Fei (1976), who have developed a scale to assess degree of dependency upon another in a particular relationship, found that the higher a man or woman scores on the scale which measures his or her dependence on the other, the more likely he or she is to report that he or she is "in love" with the other. Further, the men and women who said they were "in love" were significantly more dependent upon the person they were in love with than were those who "didn't know" whether they were in love with the other. In turn, those people who said they "didn't know" if their relationship was love, scored significantly higher on the Dependency Scale than did those men and women who were confident that they were "not in love."

THE TWO-COMPONENT THEORY OF PASSIONATE LOVE

In 1964, Schachter proposed a new theory of emotion. Schachter argued that both mind and body make a critical contribution to a person's emotional experiences:

Mind. According to Schachter, our semiconscious assumptions about what we should be feeling in a given situation have a profound impact on what we do feel in that situation. A person learns—from society, parents, friends, and from personal experience—what emotions, if any, it is appropriate to feel in various settings. We know that we *should* feel "joyous excitement" when a friend comes to visit . . . and *should* feel "anxiety" when an enemy swaggers into town. (The untutored may well experience the very same physiological *feelings* on both occasions, a sort of "hyper" state.) According to Schachter, our assumptions as to what it is *appropriate* to feel have a critical impact on what we do feel.

Body. Schachter argues that persons can experience an emotion only if they *have* some "feelings." They must be aroused physiologically.

Schachter argues that both mind and body make an indispensable contribution to our emotions. Our minds determine what specific emotion we will feel. Our bodies determine whether or not we will feel any emotion at all.

Schachter and Singer (1962) tested the theory in an ingenious series of experiments:

Manipulating appropriate cognitions According to Schachter and Singer, people feel what it's *appropriate* to feel.

If everyone around you is euphoric, caught up in a wild, abandoned water fight, celebrating a Rose Bowl victory, celebrating a friend's engagement, you think that it's appropriate to feel "happy."

If everyone around you is furious—your roommate has stuck you with the dishes, again—you've been told there will be a surprise quiz the day before Christmas—you think that it's appropriate to be "angry."

If, on the other hand, you're in a medical setting, you think it's appropriate to have "symptoms." The last thing you think it is reasonable to be is "euphoric" or "angry."

To test the notion that we feel what we're supposed to feel, Schachter and Singer arranged for students to be in a euphoric setting, angry setting, or a medical setting, at the time they became physiologically aroused.

Manipulating physiological arousal Schachter and Singer's next step was to manipulate the second component of emotion—physiological arousal. Schachter and Singer injected volunteers with a substance that they claimed

GRIN AND BEAR IT   by Lichty & Wagner

"I thought I was having a great day until I looked at my mood ring."

GRIN AND BEAR IT by George Lichty and Fred Wagner. Courtesy of Field Newspapers Syndicate.

was Suproxin, a new vitamin compound whose effects upon vision was said to be of interest to the experimenters. In reality, the researchers injected half of the students (those in the *Unaroused* group) with a saline solution placebo. They injected the remaining students (those in the *Aroused* groups) with an arousing drug—epinephrine. (Epinephrine is an ideal drug for producing a "high." Its effects mimic the discharge of the sympathetic nervous system. Shortly after persons receive an epinephrine injection, they experience palpitations, tremor, flushes, and accelerated breathing. In short, they experience the same physiological reactions which accompany a variety of natural emotional states.) What happened?

The data supported Schachter and Singer's (1962) hypothesis: they found that both physiological arousal and appropriate cognitions *are* indispensable components of a true emotional experience. It was the students who were in a setting where it was *appropriate* to feel euphoria or anger, *and* who were physiologically *aroused*, who experienced the most intense emotions.

Evidence from Schachter and Wheeler (1962) and Hohmann (1962) has provided additional support for the two-component theory of emotion.

SCHACHTER'S TWO-COMPONENT THEORY OF PASSIONATE LOVE

Walster and Berscheid (1974) and Walster and Walster (1978) speculated that perhaps Schachter's two-component theory would be a useful blueprint for assembling the apparent jumble of redundant, inconsistent, and implausible pieces of the passionate love puzzle.

According to Schachter, both our minds *and* our bodies have a critical impact on our emotions. Thus, we should be especially vulnerable to love any time (1) our hazy, jumbled, inconsistent ideas as to what love is combine to tell us that "this may be love," and (2) we are intensely physiologically aroused—for whatever reason. (In Schachter's paradigm, then, it is no longer difficult to understand why passionate love can be intensified by intensely pleasurable *or* intensely painful experiences. Both delight and suffering are physiologically arousing.)

Let us see if Schachter's Two-Component theory gives us any insight into romantic and passionate love.

Understanding Romantic Love: Our Ideas Influence Our Emotions

Most people share some rough ideas as to what romantic love is. (Of course, they sharply disagree on the details.) Probably most of us can resonate to some extent with Walster and Walster's (1978) definition:

Passionate (i.e., Romantic) Love:
A state of intense absorption in another. Sometimes "lovers" are those who long for their partners and for complete fulfillment. Sometimes "lovers" are those who are ecstatic at finally having attained their partners' love, and, momentarily, complete fulfillment. A state of intense physiological arousal.

Where do people pick up their general ideas as to what love is?

It starts with our culture It is our culture that determines whether or not we will ever fall in love. Anthropologists insist that, in some primitive societies, passionate love doesn't even exist. When anthropologists ask such tribespeople about their passionate feelings, they are incredulous. They never heard of anyone who felt like *that*. Our culture, however, takes it for granted that, sooner or later, almost everyone will fall in love. We are obedient: we do.

In 1936, anthropologist Ralph Linton (p. 175) made this point in a harsh observation:

All societies recognize that there are occasional violent emotional attachments between persons of the opposite sex, but our present American culture is practically the only one which has attempted to capitalize on these and make them the basis for marriage. The hero of the modern American movie is always a romantic lover, just as the hero of an old Arab epic is always an epileptic. A cynic may suspect that in any ordinary population the percentage of individuals with capacity for romantic love of the Hollywood type was about as large as that of persons able to throw genuine epileptic fits.

Not only does our culture tell us that love exists, it also gives us a rough idea as to when it's appropriate to feel love, and when it isn't.

It's not true that only the external appearance of a woman matters. The underwear is also important.

Firestone 1970, p. 134

I took one look at you and then my heart stood still In our culture, people assume that only attractive human beings should inspire passionate fantasies. If persons admit that they are sexually attracted to a hunchback, to an octogenerian, or to someone with no nose, they are branded as sick or perverse.

The evidence suggests that most individuals docilely accept the prescription that beauty and sexual and romantic passion are inexorably linked. The best evidence we have suggests that teenagers and young adults are more enamored by the physical attractiveness of their dating partners than by the partners' intelligence, personality, or similarity.

In a typical study, Berscheid, Dion, Walster, and Walster (1971) took Polaroid snapshots of college men and women. Judges categorized each photo as attractive or unattractive. The experimenters then asked students about their dating histories. The authors found that *women's* physical attractiveness was strongly related to their popularity. Attractive women had more dates within the past year ($r = .61$), the past month ($r = .50$), and the past week ($r = .44$). For *men*, there was only a slight (but insignificant relationship between physical attractiveness and dating frequency (past year $r = .25$; month $r = .21$; and week $r = .13$.)

Byrne, Ervin, and Lamberth (1970) conducted a field study to determine the extent to which beauty and romantic attraction were related. Students were invited to participate in a study of computer dating; they were told that they had been matched by the computer with a partner who was similar or dissimilar in attitudes to themselves. During this initial interview, the experimenter unobtrusively evaluated the man and woman's physical attractiveness. The partners were introduced to one another and asked to spend the next 30 minutes on a coke date in the student union. They were told they should then return to the experimental room so that the experimenter could ask them about their first impressions of one another. All participants indicated how sexually attractive their partner seemed, how much they thought they would enjoy dating him or her, and how much they would like this person as a spouse.

Once again, the authors found that men and women's physical attractiveness was strongly associated with how desirable they were as dates. The more handsome a male, the higher his partner evaluated his sexual desirability (.70), his databality (.57), and his marriageability (.55). The more beautiful the woman, the higher her partner evaluated *her* on the same three dimensions.

Walster, Aronson, Abrahams, and Rottman (1966) assessed the physical attractiveness of 752 college freshmen. (A panel of college sophomores rated them; they had only five seconds or so in which to rate the freshmen's attractiveness.) A good deal of data concerning the freshmen's intelligence, personality, and attitudes were also assembled in subsequent university-wide testing. Freshmen were then randomly assigned a date for a large computer dance. During intermission, the freshmen were asked to say how satisfied they were with their computer date. The authors discovered that the sole determinant of how much students liked their date, how eager they were to date their partner again, and how often they subsequently asked their partner out for a date (it was determined later) was simply the physical attractiveness of the partner. The more physically attractive the date, the more he or she was liked and the more he or she was pursued. Efforts to find additional factors that would influence attraction failed. For example, students with exceptional social skills and intelligence levels were not liked any better than were students less fortunate in this regard. It seems, then, that it is helpful to be beautiful if you wish to inspire passion in your contemporaries.

Our society provides us with an avalanche of inconsistent ideas as to what love is. From *Snow White, Cinderella,* and *Rapunzel,* and later on from *Cosmopolitan* and *Ladies Home Journal,* women learn that, if they're just beautiful enough, and sweet enough, a handsome prince will chance along and change their lives. From *The Bell Jar* and *Jennie, The Feminine Mystique,* and our consciousness-raising group, women learn that maybe he won't.

From the sunny lyrics of "What a day this has been; what a rare mood I'm in; why it's almost like being in love . . ." we learn that love is a positive experience—that it's associated with esthetic reverence, sexual ecstasy, excitement, and joy. From the down-and-out lyrics of "Can't help lovin' dat man . . . ," we learn that love is a painful experience—a state inexorably linked to sexual deprivation, longing for appreciation, and the shame of rejection and neglect.

We form our general, culturally shared ideas as to what love is like from this jumble of day-to-day experiences. (No wonder, then, that we find love confusing.)

It continues in the family In the family, children are painstakingly taught what emotions are appropriate in which situations.

The child's world is an emotionally confusing one. Envision, for example, a little boy who is playing with a truck while his mother greets a newly arrived neighbor and her infant daughter. He is rubbing his eyes; he has missed his nap. Soon it will be dinner time; he experiences vague hunger pangs. While absorbed in the visitor's movements, he accidentally runs his truck over his hand; it hurts. He watches his mother talking and gesturing to the visitor and her little girl. Her voice seems unusually high and animated. They all look at him. His nose tickles.

In response to this *complex* of factors, the boy becomes momentarily overwrought. He hides his face in his mother's skirt for a few seconds, and then peers out. What caused him to hide his face? What emotion is he feeling? Is he jealous of the little girl? Is he afraid of strangers? Is he playing a game? Is he angry because the truck hurt his hand? Is he trying to get attention?

His mother provides an answer for him. She says, "Don't be shy, John. Susan won't hurt you. Come out and meet her." His mother reduces a chaotic jumble of stimuli to manageable size. She instructs him that it is Susan's appearance that has caused his emotional agitation. She informs him that when one has an emotional reaction in the presence of strangers it is called "shyness." She also communicates that the other stimuli, his sore hand, for example, are not responsible for his aroused state.

In childhood, we are painstakingly taught when the words "joy" and "grief," "fear" and "anger," "excitement" or "boredom" are appropriate.

There is one exception, however. Parents rarely give us any *direct* instruction as to the nature of love. No parent ever says to her child: "I think you're probably deeply in love with Mrs. Glass," or "You know what you're feeling? You're feeling sexy, that's what." Parents simply assume that ("Thank God") children don't have feelings like that—or if they do, it's better not to talk about them.

Instead, we pick up our families' ideas about the nature of love and sex almost by osmosis. We quietly observe what our parents say and what they do, when they forget that we're listening and watching. We listen to the advice our mother gives our rowdy Aunt Bessie when she cries that Jim is seeing another woman, and asks if she should leave him. We watch our parents kiss, hug, and touch—or fail to touch—one another.

Thus, in our families we absorb still other ideas about love and sex. We can't even put most of these ideas into words. They are caught from the shadowy, confused world of childhood—where fantasy is mixed with fact —where events are only dimly perceived—where everything is terribly confusing—and where there's no way to check on your perceptions by asking. Our early ideas may be hazy and confused, but they're etched into our minds, and they have a profound impact on our notions as to what love is.

ATTITUDES TOWARD DEPENDENCY AND LOVE

Dependency is an important theme in much of the romantic love literature. When one imagines the flawless partner, or is lucky enough to find in real life a person who can satisfy many of one's desires, an awareness of the extent to which one could be dependent on that other, how much one needs the other, is a frequent concomitant. But when lovers realize they are about to become or have become dependent on the loved one, they may experience conflicting reactions.

On one hand, their awareness of how much joy the loved one may bring them should cause lovers to further appreciate each other. On the other hand, their awareness of dependency may be upsetting. First, the more benefits the loved one provides, the more the dependent lover has to fear should the loved one stop returning the love. Second, adults are supposed to be independent; weak, dependent adults are scorned. Maslow (1954) exemplifies the subtle way we cast aspersions on a person who reveals dependency. The reader will recall that Maslow argued that there are two types of love: (1) that rare and superior type of love characteristic of "self-actualized" people, "B-love," or love for the other's being, and (2) an *inferior* type of love characteristic of "nonactualized," ordinary mortals, "D-love," or deficiency love, where one loves another for what the other can do for one.

Because dependency is both delightful and disturbing, most individuals are intensely ambivalent about becoming dependent on another. A number of romantic love theorists have commented upon this ambivalence. For example, Blau (1964) noted that in romantic love, dependency "has a frightening aspect." Reik (1963) and Klein and Riviere (1953) associated "anxiety of dependency" and "fear of dependency" with love. Thibaut and Kelley (1959, p. 66) describe the "ambivalence which a person tries to delay before it overwhelms him." Those individuals who associate romantic love with dependency and who have learned to fear deep reliance upon another person should be less vulnerable to passionate love.

It ends with our own experiences Finally, our own romantic experiences have a special impact on how we think about love. Most of us don't have very many romantic experiences. (For example, the "average" woman receives only two proposals of marriage in a lifetime—and she accepts one.) Our experience is limited but it's potent and, for good or ill, it has a deeply felt impact on our ideas about love.

It should come as no surprise to us, then, that researchers such as Lee (1974) find that people associate the label "love" with markedly different experiences.

Understanding Romantic Love: Our Bodies Count Too

According to Schachter, both our *minds* and our *bodies* influence our emotions. In the previous section, we focused on our *minds*—and on the impact that our semiconscious ideas about love and sex have on our intimate relations. But what about our *bodies?* What sorts of experiences are most likely to arouse us?

Observers disagree, passionately, about the types of emotional experiences which are most likely to fuel passion. Some observers insist that passionate love is inexorably entwined with joy and fulfillment. Other, more cynical, observers insist that passionate love is just as frequently linked to pain and suffering. Most social psychologists would acknowledge that both intense joy and intense suffering can contribute to passion. Both intensely joyous and intensely painful experiences are physiologically arousing. Thus, according to the social psychologists, under the right conditions, both joy and anguish should have the potential for deepening our passion.

Does any evidence exist to support the contention that, under the right conditions, both intense joy *and* intense suffering may deepen passion? Yes.

In the next section, we will look at the dazzling side of love. We'll consider the evidence that the delight we share with others helps kindle our passion. In the final section of this chapter, we'll look at the murkier side of love. We'll consider the evidence that sometimes we love someone passionately—not *in spite* of suffering our loved one causes us, but *because* of it.

Pleasant Emotional Experiences: Facilitators of Passion?

We have a staggering number of needs and desires. The first psychologist to write a social psychology text, William McDougall (1908), compiled an almost endless compendium of human needs. By 1962, Henry Murray had pared the list down to 28. Many of our needs are unfulfilled much of the time. Now and then we encounter someone who, in fantasy or in reality, promises to satisfy our long-unfilled needs. When this happens, we are likely to have a strong emotional response. Such joyous reactions may provide the fuel for passion.

Let us consider some of the reinforcements that can have a potent impact on love.

Sexual gratification Freud, and a host of others, have assumed that *inhibited* sexuality is the foundation of romantic feelings. It may well be that *gratified* sexuality is an equally strong stimulant to passion. Sex is arousing. When we're caught up in a sexual encounter, our face flushes, our heart pounds, and we become *very* aroused. (Or, in Masters and Johnson's (1966) terms: sexual intercourse induces hyperventilation, tachycardia, and marked increases in blood pressure.)

In brief, sexual experiences and the anticipation of such experiences are generally arousing. And religious advisors, school counselors, and psychoanalysts to the contrary, sexual gratification has probably incited as much passionate love as sexual frustration has.

Valins (1966) has demonstrated that even the erroneous belief that someone has excited us sexually can facilitate our attraction to the other.

Valins recruited college men, ostensibly to determine how they would react physiologically to sexual stimuli. The men were told that their heart rate would be amplified and recorded while they viewed ten seminude *Playboy* photographs. The feedback the men received was experimentally controlled. They were led to believe that when they examined slides picturing some of the *Playboy* bunnies, their heart rate altered markedly; when they examined others, they had no reaction. (Valins assumed that men would interpret any alteration in heart rate—either a marked speed up or a precipitous "standing still"—as enthusiasm for the bunny, and no change in heart rate as disinterest.)

The men's liking for the arousing vs. unarousing slides was assessed in three ways: (1) They were asked to rate how attractive and appealing each of the pinups was; (2) They were offered a photograph of a pinup in remuneration for participating in the experiment; and (3) A month later, in a totally different context, they were interviewed, and were asked to rank the attractiveness of the pinups. In all cases, men markedly preferred the pinups they thought had aroused them to those they thought had not.

Security vs. excitement As Masters and Johnson (1975) observed, we are all faced with a wrenching dilemma: everyone needs security—we are all attracted to the mate who understands us, who cares for us, and who is guaranteed to be around, through thick and thin, until we're old. At the same time, we all long for excitement, novelty, and danger. We're tossed between our need for one and our longing for the other.

Psychologists know full well how desperately humans need security. Developmental psychologists *once* believed in the "cupboard theory" of infant love: they thought that infants became attached to their mothers because they received milk from them. The pioneer observations of Harry and Margaret Harlow (1974) showed they were wrong. Food is important— but what's really important for the development of love is that the mother be soft, warm, and rocking; someone to cling to . . . especially when you're uncertain about the world. (It doesn't even matter if she's a bogus "mother" —made of wire and cloth. If she's clingable, she's lovable.)

We all need someone who understands us . . . someone to share our triumphs . . . and to be around when things go wrong . . . desperately wrong.

On the other hand, once we become really secure, we stop focusing on what we have—security—and start longing for what we don't have— excitement.

Dangerous experiences are arousing. For some peculiar reason, psychologists almost inevitably assume that the arousal one experiences in dangerous settings is entirely negative. Thus, they typically label the physiological reactions which are provoked by dangerous experiences as "fear," "stress," or "pain." They then focus upon ways individuals can learn to foresee and avoid actual danger, or to overcome unrealistic fears. (They almost seem to equate "excitement seeking" with wickedness. For example, in *Human Sexual Response,* Masters and Johnson (1966) reassured readers that "mere thrill seekers" were scrupulously prohibited from participating in their research. Presumably, one has to be properly respectful about sex before being entitled to assist in scientific discovery.)

Almost never do psychologists acknowledge that it is sometimes fun to be frightened; that it is enjoyable to have a strong emotional response; that reactions to danger can be labeled in positive, as well as in negative, ways; that excitement is an antidote to boredom. One pioneer, Berlyne (1960), has recognized that "danger and delight grow on one stalk," and has systematically explored the conditions under which novelty and excitement are especially attractive to people.

Nonscientists appear to believe that arousal can be fun. Parachuting, skiing, and sportscar racing are valued by sports enthusiasts for the danger they provide. Passionate affairs are valued by many for their excitement. Individuals who realize that they are on dangerous ground may label the rush of passion that they experience as "love," as well as "anxiety."

For most people, passionate love *is* stimulated by joy and happiness. What about the darker side of love? As psychologists point out, painful experiences are physiologically arousing, too. And, under the right conditions, painful experiences, such as anxiety and fear, frustration, jealousy, and

Presumably, one has to be properly respectful about sex before being entitled to assist in scientific discovery.

anger, and total confusion, should have the potential for deepening our passion. Is there any evidence that men and women often love others, not *in spite of* the fact that the others cause them anguish, but *because* they do? Yes.

Unpleasant Emotional Experiences: Facilitators of Passion

Negative reinforcements produce arousal in all animals (see Skinner 1938). For human beings there is some evidence that under certain conditions, unpleasant experiences may enhance romantic passion.

Fear When persons are frightened, they become intensely physiologically aroused for a substantial period of time (Wolf and Wolff 1947; Ax 1953; Schachter 1957).

In a series of experiments in British Columbia, psychologists Donald G. Dutton and Arthur P. Aron (1974) discovered a close link between fear and sexual attraction.

In one experiment, the authors invited men and women to participate in a learning experiment. The men were introduced to their partner—a beautiful woman. Now for the bad news. The men discovered that by signing up for the experiment, they'd gotten into more than they'd bargained for. The experimenter was studying the effect of electric shock on learning. Sometimes the experimenter quickly went on to reassure the men they'd been assigned to sort of a "control group"—that they'd be receiving a barely perceptible "tingle" of a shock. Other times, the experimenter tried to terrify the men. He warned them that they'd be getting some pretty painful electrical shocks. Privately, the experimenter approached the man and asked how he felt about the beautiful woman. (He ruefully observed that sometimes things like that affect task performance.) He asked the man to tell him, in confidence, how attracted he was to his partner (e.g., "How much would you like to ask her out for a date?" "How much would you like to kiss her?").

The investigators predicted, as any good social psychologists would, that fear would facilitate attraction. And, it did. The terrified men found the woman a lot sexier than the calm and cool men did.

In another series of experiments, Dutton and Aron found some naturalistic evidence in support of the contention that fear and sex are linked. The psychologists compared the reactions of young men crossing two bridges in North Vancouver. The first, Capilano Canyon Suspension Bridge, is a 450-foot-long, five-foot-wide span that tilts, sways, and wobbles over a 230-foot drop to rocks and shallow rapids below. The other bridge, a bit farther upstream, is a solid safe structure; it sits solidly 10 feet above a shallow rivulet which runs into the main river.

As each young man crossed the bridge, a good-looking college woman approached him. She explained that she was doing a class project and asked if he would fill out a questionnaire for her. When the man had finished, the young woman offered to explain her project in greater detail "when there was more time." She wrote her telephone number on a small piece of paper, and handed it to the man, so he could call her if he wanted more information.

Who called? Why, the men who met the young woman under frightening conditions, of course. (Nine of the 33 men on the suspension bridge called her. Only two of the men on the solid bridge called. Needless to say, when a *man* was the interviewer, virtually none of the men bothered to call him to "discuss the experiment.")

Rejection Rejection is always disturbing. When persons are rejected, they generally experience a strong emotional reaction. They are humiliated and angry. There is some evidence that a rejected person is a volatile person.

The reader will recall that, in Chapter 7, Reinforcement theorists (Dittes 1959; Walster 1965; Jacobs *et al.* 1971) proposed that when our self-esteem is low, when we're discouraged and upset, our emotions are quixotic. We respond to love with unusual appreciation and to rejection with unusual resentment and hostility.

These results, too, suggest that under the right conditions, the highly aroused person may interpret confused feelings as love, or as hatred.

Frustration and challenge Khrushchev, depicting the Russian character, said (in Galbraith 1969, p. 110):

> When the aristocrats first discovered that potatoes were a cheap way of feeding the peasants, they had no success in getting the peasants to eat them. But they knew their people. They fenced the potatoes in with high fences. The peasants then stole the potatos and soon acquired a taste for them.

Theorists seem to agree that the obstacles lovers encounter in their attempt to possess another intensify love.

Sexual Frustration. Sexual inhibition is often said to be the foundation of romantic feelings. For example, Freud (1925, p. 213) argued:

> Some obstacle is necessary to swell the tide of libido to its height; and at all periods of history whenever natural barriers in the way of satisfaction have not sufficed, mankind has erected conventional ones in order to enjoy love.

Presumably, when sexual energy is bottled up, it will be sublimated and expressed as romantic longing, rather than sexual longing.

Experimental evidence concerning the impact of other kinds of obstacles to love on the intensity of the lovers' romantic feelings comes from Walster, Walster, Piliavin, and Schmidt (1973) and from Driscoll, Davis, and Lipitz (1972).

The Hard-to-Get Girl. Socrates, Ovid, the Kama Sutra, and "Dear Abby" are in agreement about one thing: a girl who is hard to get inspires more passion than does a girl who "throws herself" at a man. Socrates (in Xenophon 1923, p. 247) advises Theodota, a *hetaera:*

> They will appreciate your favors most highly if you wait till they ask for them. The sweetest meats, you see, if served before they are wanted seem sour, and to those who had enough they are positively nauseating; but even poor fare is very welcome when offered to a hungry man [Theodota inquires] And how can I make them hunger for my fare? [Socrates' reply] Why, in the first place, you must not offer it to them when they have had enough—by a show of reluctance to yield, and by holding back until they are as keen as can be, for then the same gifts are much more to the recipient than when they are offered before they are desired.

Ovid (1963, pp. 65–66) remarks:

> Fool, if you feel no need to guard your girl for her own sake, see that you guard her for mine, so I may want her the more. Easy things nobody

wants, but what is forbidden is tempting. . . . Anyone who can love the wife of an indolent cuckold, I should suppose, would steal buckets of sand from the shore.

Bertrand Russell (in Kirch 1960, pp. 10–11) argues:

The belief in the immense value of the lady is a psychological effect of the difficulty of obtaining her, and I think it may be laid down that when a man has no difficulty in obtaining a woman, his feeling toward her does not take the form of romantic love.

To find authors in such rare accord on an aspect of passionate love is refreshing. Better yet, their observation seems to provide support for the two-component theory. Unfortunately for the theory (but fortunately for the easy-to-get men and women), the data suggest that hard-to-get men and women do not inspire especially intense liking in their suitors. (See Walster, Walster, and Berscheid 1971; and Walster, Berscheid, and Walster 1973.)

Walster *et al.* (1973) report several experiments designed to demonstrate that a challenging girl will be a more dazzling conquest than a readily available girl. All experiments secured negative results.

In the first set of experiments, college males were recruited for a computer date-match program. The program was ostensibly designed to evaluate and improve current computer matching programs. In an initial interview, men filled out a lengthy questionnaire.

Two weeks later, the men were asked to drop by to collect the name and telephone number of their date-match. The "matchmaker" asked them to telephone her, to arrange a date from her office, so that they could report their first impressions of the date after the call. Actually, each man was provided with the telephone number of the same woman—an experimental confederate.

In the *Easy-to-get* condition, the woman was obviously delighted to receive his telephone call and grateful to be asked out. In the *Hard-to-get* condition, the woman accepted a coffee date with some reluctance. She seemed to have many other dates, and was not sure whether or not she really wanted to get involved with someone new.

The results of this and other similar experiments failed to support the "hard-to-get" hypothesis; it was found that men had an equally high opinion of the hard-to-get and the easy-to-get women.

A further study—a field experiment—also failed to support the hypothesis. In this study, a prostitute serving as the experimenter, delivered the experimental communication while she was mixing drinks for her clients. Half the time she played hard to get. She indicated that she could only see a limited number of clients and, thus, she had to be very selective about whom she could accept as a customer. Half of the time (in the easy-to-get condition) she allowed the clients to assume that she would accept all customers. Then she had sexual intercourse with the clients.

The client's liking for the prostitute was assessed in three ways: (1) the prostitute estimated how much the clients seemed to like her; (2) she recorded how much he paid for the 50-min hour; and (3) she recorded how soon he called her for a second appointment.

The hard-to-get hypothesis was *not* supported. Clients appeared to like the selective and unselective prostitute equally well.

Faced with this firestorm of evidence that a hard-to-get date does *not* seem to inspire more passion than the easy-to-get one, Walster and her co-workers reconsidered their hypothesis. First, they systematically recorded the advantages and disadvantages a man might associate with a generally hard-to-get or a generally easy-to-get partner. For example, an "easy-to-get" woman, while perhaps desperate for company because she is unattractive, might be a friendly and relaxing date; a "hard-to-get" woman, while having the advantage of being a challenge, might be unfriendly and ego-crushing. In previous research, they thought, perhaps the hard-to-get and easy-to-get women's assets and liabilities balanced each other out. The women, whether easy or hard to get, had potentially attractive assets and potentially unsettling liabilities. What would the perfect date be like? What kind of a woman would possess most of the advantages, but few of the disadvantages, of both the hard-to-get and the easy-to-get woman? A woman who is crazy about you (she is easy for *you* to get), but is hard for anyone else to get should be maximally rewarding.

Walster and her co-workers then tested the hypothesis that the selectively hard-to-get woman would be preferred to a generally hard-to-get woman, to a generally easy-to-get woman, or to a control woman (a woman whose general hard-to-getness or easy-to-getness was unknown) in the following way: once again they recruited men to participate in a computer date-match program. The men filled out questionnaires, and then waited several weeks for the computer to match them with potential dates. When they reported to the office for the name of their date, they were told that the computer had selected five women's names. The men examined biographies of these women, so that they could choose which one they wanted to date. The women's biographies described their backgrounds, interests, attitudes, etc. Attached to the biography was each woman's evaluation of the dates that had been assigned to her. Each man (who knew his own code number) could thus discover how each woman had rated him as well as the four other men with whom the computer had matched her. (Presumably, her evaluations were based on the biographies she had been shown.)

These ratings constituted the experimental manipulation. One woman made it evident that she was *generally easy to get*. (She indicated that she was "very eager" to date every fellow the computer had assigned to her.) A second woman made it evident that she was *generally hard to get*. (She indicated that she was willing, but not particularly eager, to date the five fellows assigned to her.) One of the women made it evident that she was *selectively hard to get*. (Although she was very eager to date the man, she was reluctant to date any of his rivals.) Two of the potential dates were *control* women. (The experimenter said that they had not yet stopped in to evaluate their computer matches, and, thus, no information was available concerning their preferences.)

These data provided strong support for the revised hypothesis. The selectively hard-to-get woman was uniformly the most popular woman. She was liked far more than her competitors. Men liked the generally hard-to-get, the generally easy-to-get, and control dates equally.

Parental Interference. Driscoll, Davis, and Lipitz (1972) observed a fascinating paradox. Parents interfere in a love relationship in the hope of destroying it. But, the authors observed, more often than not parental interference in a love relationship intensifies the feelings of romantic love between members of the couple. The authors begin their delightful article by surveying the extent to which parental opposition and intense love have been pitted against one another. They remind readers that Romeo and Juliet's short but intense love affair took place against the background of total opposition from the two feuding families. The difficulties and separations which the family conflict created appear to have intensified the lovers' feelings for each other.

Finally, the authors remind us that de Rougemont (1940), in his historical analysis of romantic love, emphasized the persistent association of obstacles or grave difficulties with intense passion. They conclude that an affair consummated without major difficulty probably lacks zest.

The authors distinguish between romantic love (for example, infatuation, passionate love) and conjugal love. They point out that romantic love is associated with uncertainty and challenge. Conjugal love, on the other hand, is more likely to be related to trust and genuine understanding. Conjugal love evolves gradually out of mutually satisfying interactions and from increasing confidence in one's personal security in the relationship.

The authors tested their hypothesis that parental opposition would deepen romantic love (as opposed to conjugal love) in the following way: The authors invited 91 married couples and 49 dating couples (18 of whom were living together) to participate in a marital relations project. Most married couples had been married about four years. Most of the dating couples had been going together for about eight months. All of the 49 dating couples were seriously committed to one another.

During an initial interview, all the couples filled out three scales:

Assessment of parental interference: This scale asked couples to estimate the extent to which their parents interfered and caused problems in their relationship. Each person was asked whether or not they had ever complained to their mate that her (his) parents interfere in their relationship, are a bad influence, are hurting the relationship, take advantage of her (him), don't accept him (her), or try to make him (her) look bad.

Conjugal love scale: This scale measured the extent to which participants loved, cared about and needed their partner, and felt that the relationship was more important than anything else.

Romantic love scale: The researchers rescored the Conjugal Love Scale in order to obtain "a purified index of Romantic Love." (This index was constructed by partialing out of the Love Scale that portion of variance which could be counted for by trust—a characteristic the authors felt more typical of conjugal love than of passionate love.)

Driscoll *et al.* found that parental interference and passion were related as they expected them to be. Parental interference and romantic love were correlated 0.24 for the married sample and 0.50 for the unmarried sample. Parental interference and romantic love *were* positively and significantly related.

Next, the authors investigated whether *increasing* parental interference would provoke increased passion. Six to ten months after the initial interview, the authors invited all of the couples back for a second interview. During this second interview, they asked couples to complete the Parental Interference, Conjugal Love, and Romantic Love Scales once again. By comparing couples' initial interview responses with the later ones, Driscoll *et al.* could calculate whether the couples' parents had become more or less interfering in the relationship, and how these changes in parental interference had affected the couples' affair. The authors found that as parents began to interfere more in a relationship, the couple appeared to fall more deeply in love. If the parents had become resigned to the relationship, and had begun to interfere less, the couples began to feel less intensely about one another.

Since the data from the Driscoll *et al.* study are correlational, rather than experimental, alternative explanations for these findings are, of course, possible. The authors specifically mentioned two other plausible explanations.

First, perhaps the results are due to the selective attrition of participants from the study. A couple with a weak relationship may stop seeing one another as soon as parents voice disapproval. Only couples who are very much in love may be willing to defy strong parental opposition. Thus, parental interference and love may seem to be related, only because the sample does not include couples who were low in love and high in parental interferences.

Second, parental interference may not be a *cause* of, but rather a *reaction* to, the couple's commitment to marry. When parents realize that the couple is deeply in love, they may begin to interfere. Thus, it is not interference that deepens love, but deepening love that stimulates worried parents to interfere.

The authors attempted to test the validity of these alternative explanations with other available data and concluded that these alternative explanations were not reasonable explanations for the results.

The data indicating that parental interference breeds passion are fascinating. When parents interfere in an "unsuitable" match, they interfere with the intent of destroying the relationship, not of strengthening it. Yet, these data warn parents that, if the relationship survives, interference is likely to boomerang. It may foster desire rather than divisiveness.

The preceding data lend some credence to the argument that the juxtaposition of agony and ecstasy in passionate love may not be entirely accidental. Although most people assume that agony follows love, it may be that it precedes it and provides the ground in which it can flourish. Loneliness, deprivation, frustration, hatred, and insecurity all appear capable—under certain conditions—of supplementing a person's romantic feelings. Passion demands physiological arousal, and unpleasant experiences are arousing.

Summary

It is paradoxical that, although scientists would surely agree that love is more interesting than liking, they have spent a great deal of time and effort studying liking, and very little studying love. As a consequence, we know a great deal about liking, and very little about love.

There are probably three reasons why early researchers neglected the study of love: (1) Scientists thought that researchers could *never* penetrate the "mystery" of love. (2) It was taboo to study love and sex. (3) Even if it weren't taboo, researchers weren't sure *how* to go about studying it.

Recently, however, researchers have begun to focus on love. We began our discussion of romantic love by distinguishing it from its cousins: "liking" and "companionate love."

Romantic or Passionate Love. "A state of intense absorption in another. Sometimes "lovers" are those who long for their partners and for complete fulfillment. Sometimes "lovers" are those who are ecstatic at finally having attained their partner's love, and, momentarily, complete fulfillment. A state of intense physiological arousal."

Liking. "The affection we feel for casual acquaintances."

Companionate Love. "The affection we feel for those with whom our lives are deeply intertwined."

In this chapter, we focused on passionate love. We speculated that perhaps Schachter's two-component theory of emotion might give us a way of understanding passionate feelings. Schachter argues that both the mind and body make a critical contribution to a person's emotional experience. We speculated that mind and body might be critically important in determining our romantic feelings, too.

Mind. According to Schachter, our semiconscious assumptions about what we should be feeling in a given situation have a profound impact on what we do feel in that situation.

Where do people pick up their general ideas as to what love is? We found from three sources: the most general guidelines as to what love is come from our culture; our families, and our own experiences, fill in the details.

Body. According to Schachter, persons can experience an emotion only if they *have* some feelings. They must be physiologically aroused. We asked: What sorts of experiences are most likely to arouse us? First we considered the dazzling side of love. We found that romantic love *is* associated with intense pleasure. However, love has a darker side. Sometimes it is those who arouse us by causing us anxiety and fear, frustration, jealousy, anger, or even total confusion who spark passion.

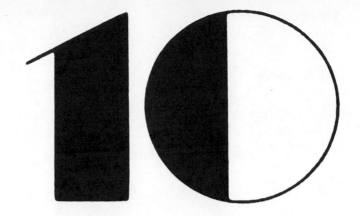

So far, we have focused entirely on the most exotic variety of love —passionate love. Passionate love is a wildly emotional state: tender and sexual feelings, elation and pain, anxiety and relief, altruism and jealousy coexist in a confusion of feelings. Passionate love is an exotic and rare flower.

companionate love

Companionate love is a more familiar variety. It will be recalled that *liking* was defined as "the affection we feel for casual acquaintances"; *companionate love* as "the affection we feel for those with whom our lives are deeply intertwined." We may speculate that the only real difference between liking and loving is in the intensity of our feelings, and in the extent to which our lives are intertwined with another's.

George Levinger (1974) provides a visual illustration of the variety of relationships we can have with others, from the most fleeting, half-realized encounters to the deepest of relationships.

Zero Contact

In our lifetime, we come into contact with only a very few of the earth's 4.15 billion people. The rest of humanity is forever lost to us.

Awareness (Level 1)

Levinger (1974, p. 101) observes:

> As I write this, I glance outside my window into the dusk and see a stranger walking past. He is silhouetted in the light of a street lamp. His image is that of a college student, a bit on the stocky side, carrying a stack of books. He walks slowly and deliberately up the path, his eyes fixed on the ground ahead of him. I see him as a representative of the other students on campus; beyond that impression, I experience little sense of knowing him.

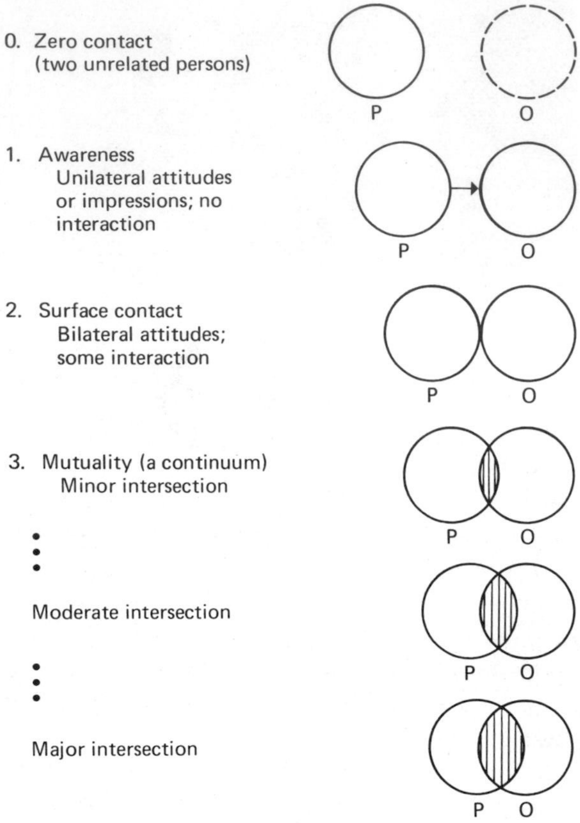

0. Zero contact
   (two unrelated persons)

1. Awareness
   Unilateral attitudes
   or impressions; no
   interaction

2. Surface contact
   Bilateral attitudes;
   some interaction

3. Mutuality (a continuum)
   Minor intersection

   .
   .
   .

   Moderate intersection

   .
   .
   .

   Major intersection

Fig. 10.1 Levels of pair relatedness. (Reproduced from Huston 1974, p. 102)

> The largest portion of our relations with others consists of such momentary impressions of which the perceived other is not aware.

Psychologists have generally focused on just such fleeting "relations." For example, consider Byrne's experiments. Typically, Byrne asks students how they feel about a fellow student, whose attitudes are presumably similar or dissimilar to their own. They are "unilaterally aware" of his existence. They think they know something about him. He knows nothing of them.

Surface Contact (Level 2)

We have a multitude of transitory meetings with others every day. We meet people in classes, at bus stops, in the university book store, at large mixers. We hardly remember their names. We run into the bus driver, the building custodian, the student in the room down the hall, again and again, but we still continue to exchange little more than a token "hello." (Social psychologists, in laboratory experiments, usually study people caught up in such superficial relationships.)

Sometimes, for some reason or other, we begin a real relationship with someone.

Mutuality (Level 3): Minor Intersection

In the early stages of a relationship, we are usually wary. Altman and Taylor (1973, pp. 136–141) provide a compelling description of the early stages of mutuality:

> Whether at a cocktail party, a small social gathering, or on a first date, individuals make only a small part of themselves accessible. . . . Their responses are not very rich or broad, are often stereotyped, reflect only the most superficial aspects of their modes of response, and demonstrate little personal uniqueness . . . they smile graciously and easily, are quick to nod agreement and understanding, offer greetings without hesitation, and exhibit a range of behaviors to present the image of a pleasant, understanding, likable person.

Major Intersection

Sometimes our early tentative pokings into friendship are so satisfying that we decide to take a chance: we begin to tell our friend about ourselves . . . and begin to find out what our friend is really like.

Altman and Taylor (1973, pp. 136–141) provide a compelling description of the later stages of mutuality:

> *Stable exchange:* Achieved in only a few relationships, stable exchange continues to reflect openness, richness, spontaneity, and so on in public areas. . . . Dyad members know one another well and can readily interpret and predict the feelings and probable behavior of the other. . . . For the first time, perhaps, there is a considerable richness of communication in the central core areas and a high degree of mutual spontaneity, permeability, and dyadic uniqueness. In addition to verbal levels, there is a great deal of exchange of nonverbal and environmental behaviors, and less restrictiveness in facial expressions, gestures, body movements, touching and so on. They are more willing to allow each other to use, have access to, or know about very private apparel and belongings.

In the past five years, researchers have begun to intensively study the self-disclosure process. (See, for example, research by Huesmann and Levinger 1976; Jourard 1971; Kurth 1970; and Worthy, Gary, and Kahn 1969.) These researchers have found that, in casual relations, we rarely reveal much of ourselves. It is only in intimate relationships that we become willing to exchange the most personal of information. For most people, one of the nicest things about companionate love is the realization that we know almost all there is to know about another human—and that the other human knows all there is to know about *us*, warts and all.

Theories of Mate-Selection

In our culture, people often associate romantic and companionate love with marriage. Thus, until recently, the questions "Who falls in love with whom?" and "Why?" generally come out as "Who marries whom?" and "Why?"

Winch's Theory of Complementary Needs

Winch's (1958) Theory of Complementary Needs (which we presented in some detail in Chapter 5) was one of the earliest and most influential theories of mate selection. You will recall that Winch's basic hypothesis is that an individual chooses from a field of eligible candidates that person who is most likely to provide him or her with need-gratification.

The concept of a "field of eligibles" was elaborated by Kerckhoff (1974). Kerckhoff points out that society specifies a "field of desirables"; that is, society makes it very clear *who* constitutes a desirable mate. A desirable mate should be someone of our own age, socioeconomic class, religion, educational level, and, until recently, race.

Society also restricts our "field of availables." We necessarily spend most of our time associating with people who are very like ourselves. We rarely bump into people from strikingly different backgrounds.

Kerckhoff argues that both these influences may be responsible for the strong evidence of homogamy in mating. Like may marry like because our culture decrees that similarity between spouses on a variety of social characteristics is desirable. Like may also marry like because the "field of availables" is generally made up of people very similar to ourselves; we simply do not have much of an opportunity to meet, much less fall in love with and marry, people who are different from ourselves.

Winch argues that we choose from this broad field of eligibles, a mate whose personality is *complementary* to our own.

Murstein's Stimulus–Value–Role Theory

Recently, Murstein (1976) has proposed the "Stimulus–Value–Role" theory of marital choice.

Murstein theorizes that, at first glance (in the "Stimulus" stage), all we *can* know about a person is what kind of first impression the person makes. We know what the person looks like, sounds like, what other people say about the person . . . and not much else. Murstein (pp. 116–117) points out that the stimulus stage is of crucial importance:

> For, if the other person does not possess sufficient stimulus impact to attract the individual, further contact is not sought. The "prospect" in question might make a potentially exemplary, compatible spouse, he might manifest value consensus and superb role compatibility with the perceiver. But the perceiver, foregoing opportunities for further contact, may never find this out.

Murstein admits that it is not fair that physical attractiveness should count so much in determining who gets to know whom . . . but it does.

Later in the relationship (in the "Value" stage), the couple begins to discover whether or not they share similar attitudes and values. Murstein observes that the more a couple agrees about what is important in life, the more likely their relationship is to survive.

Finally, if the couple has managed to weather the first two stages, Murstein hypothesizes that they enter a "Role" stage: the couple begin to find out whether they function well in the various roles they play. Survival of this stage, he predicts, is preliminary to marriage.

Murstein (1976) provides considerable evidence in support of the idea that in different stages of a relationship, different things become important.

Equity Theory*

In *Equity: Theory and Research,* Equity theorists argue that Equity theory provides some insights, not just into our casual relations, but into our romantic and marital relationships as well. They argue that equity considerations are important determinants of who dates whom and who marries whom. They argue that couples will not even initially enter into a relationship, much less stay in it, unless it is profitable to *both* of them.

For example, Blau (1968) observes that people end up with the mates they "deserve." He points out that if one hopes to reap the benefits of associating with another, one must offer one's partner enough benefits to make it worthwhile for him or her to stay in the relationship. The more desirable

---

*   See Chapter 8 for a review of Equity theory.

a suitor is, the more desirable a partner he can attract. His less desirable fellow will have to settle for a less desirable "leftover." Thus, Blau argues, market principles ensure that each person gets as desirable a mate as he or she deserves.

Goffman (1952, p. 456) puts the matter even more bluntly. He notes:

A proposal of marriage in our society tends to be a way in which a man sums up his social attributes and suggests to a woman that hers are not so much better as to preclude a merger or partnership in these matters.

On the basis of such reasoning, equity theorists proposed a "matching hypothesis": they proposed that the more equitable a romantic relationship is, the more viable it will be.

The hypothesis of matching in social choice was first explored by Walster, Aronson, Abrahams, and Rottman (1966). They proposed two hypotheses: (1) The more "socially desirable" an individual is (e.g., the more physically attractive, personable, rich, famous, considerate an individual is), the more socially desirable he or she will expect a "suitable" partner to be. (2) Couples who are similar in social desirability will better like one another and will have a more enduring relationship than will couples who are markedly mismatched. Figure 10.2 depicts graphically these predictions.

These hypotheses were tested in a field study. Seven hundred and fifty-two college freshmen were recruited to attend a Computer Date-Match Dance. They were told their partner would be assigned by a computer.

The freshmen's "Social Desirability" was roughly tapped by assessing one social input, their physical attractiveness. The four ticket sellers, themselves students, evaluated each freshman's looks as he stood in line to purchase a ticket to the dance. (One's "social desirability" is of course made up of many things besides his physical attractiveness. The authors chose physical attractiveness as the indicator of the freshman's social desirability because this particular trait could be quickly assessed under standard conditions by the student's peers. Data indicate that physical attractiveness ratings are strongly related to one's own perception of one's social desirability, so such an index appears to be an appropriate one.)

Freshmen filled out several questionnaires which provided a great deal of other information about them. They recorded their age (nearly all were 18), height, race, and religious preference. They also filled out Self-esteem and Popularity measures. The experimenters secured several additional measures from the University of Minnesota's statewide testing service program. The student's high school academic percentile rank, his *Minnesota Scholastic Aptitude Test* (*MSAT*) score, his *Minnesota Multiphasic Personality In-*

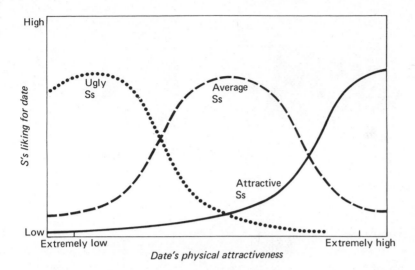

Fig. 10.2 Amount of liking predicted for dates of varying attractiveness by ugly, average, and attractive subjects (*Ss*).

ventory (*MMPI*) scores, and his *Minnesota Counseling Inventory* (*MCI*) scores were secured.

Two days after the students completed their questionnaires, they were randomly assigned to a date. The dance was held in a large armory. The couples generally arrived at the dance at 8:00 P.M. and danced or talked until the 10:30 P.M. intermission. During intermission, students' impressions of their dates were assessed. How often couples actually dated later was determined six months after the dance.

First, the authors predicted that students would *expect* the "all-knowing" computer to assign them partners of approximately their own social desirability. At the time the Attractive, Average, or Unattractive freshmen signed up for the dance, they were asked how physically attractive, how personally attractive, and how considerate they expected their date to be. The authors predicted that the more attractive the freshmen, the more desirable they would expect an "appropriate" date to be. This prediction was confirmed.

Secondly, the authors predicted that the more equitable a computer match was, the more viable the relationship would be. The freshmen who signed up for the dance were randomly assigned to a date. It was hypothesized that those students who obtained, by chance, dates of their own social desirability level—whether high, medium, or low—would like each other more than those who received dates whose social desirability level was far inferior or far superior to their own.

Courtesy of Mell Lazarus and Field Newspaper Syndicate.

The validity of this hypothesis was tested in three ways. First, during intermission, students were asked how much they liked their date. Second, they were asked how eager they were to continue the dating relationship. Third, the authors interviewed all participants six months after the dance, in order to determine whether or not the couples had actually continued to date.

This time, the authors found no support for the matching hypothesis. All those involved, *regardless of their own social desirability*, liked the most desirable dates. The more physically attractive the date, the more he or she was liked. The Walster *et al.* results, or lack thereof, were subsequently corroborated by other investigators who tested the hypothesis in similar computer dance situations (e.g., Brislin and Lewis 1968; Walster 1970; Tesser and Brodie 1971).

The Walster *et al.* conclusions drew a flurry of protest. Subsequent investigators pointed out that the computer dance situation was *not* an optimal setting in which to test the matching hypothesis.

For example, Berscheid *et al.* (1971) pointed out that in a normal dating situation, students must be concerned with whether or not their partner is a "good match." If they approach a too-desirable partner, they run the risk of being rejected. If they approach a partner who is far less desirable than themselves, they may end up "stuck" with a less desirable date than they could have had. The computer dance setting, the authors argue, may have short-circuited these normal processes. When a computer pairs you up with someone, you might take it for granted that it knows what it's doing. You might take it for granted that it has provided you with a good match.

Berscheid *et al.* conducted two experiments to determine if the matching principle would reveal itself under more realistic circumstances. They hypothesized that: (1) when a man was required to actively *choose* a dating partner (rather than evaluate one already secured), and (2) when he knew that the chosen date might possibly reject him, he would be concerned about finding a good match.

The results of both experiments found support for the matching principle. As in Walster *et al.*, everyone greatly preferred the physically attractive dates. *Within* this general trend, however, it was clear that highly attractive men and women *did* tend to choose more attractive dates than did less attractive individuals.

The Berscheid *et al.* study had one perplexing result, however. The authors had tried to vary students' concern with rejection. Some students were told that there was no chance they would be rejected (duplicating, the authors thought, the computer date setting). Some students knew that their partners could reject them if they felt like it (duplicating, the authors thought, a normal dating setting). Berscheid *et al.* expected students to be relatively unconcerned with matching in the first setting. They expected students to be very concerned with matching in the second setting. To their surprise, they found that students in all groups took matching principles into account when making their choices.

Recently, Huston (1973) and Stroebe, Insko, Thompson, and Layton (1971) have tested, and supported, the matching hypothesis.

Kiesler and Baral (1970) were the first to confirm equity "matching" predictions in an experimental setting. The authors hired college men to see how well they could do on a "new" intelligence test. In the Raised Self-Esteem condition, men were led to believe that they were doing extremely well. (The experimenter smiled and nodded and mentioned how extraordinarily well they were doing.) In the Lowered Self-Esteem condition, men were led to believe that they were doing badly on the test. (The experimenter made it apparent that he was displeased with their performance. He frowned, looked away, and mentioned that other men had performed better.)

During a break in testing, the experimenter and the student visited a nearby canteen to relax. When they entered the canteen, the experimenter recognized a woman seated at a nearby table and greeted her. (The woman was actually a confederate.)

The woman's attractiveness was sytematically varied. In one condition, the Attractive condition, the confederate was made up to be very physically appealing; she wore becoming makeup and fashionable clothing. In the Unattractive condition, an attempt was made to reduce her real attractiveness; she wore no makeup, heavy glasses, and had her hair pulled back with a rubber band. Her skirt and blouse clashed and were arranged sloppily. After the couple was introduced, the experimenter excused himself briefly. The woman began talking to the man in a friendly, accepting, and interested way.

What Kiesler and Baral were *really* interested in was how much interest men displayed in the confederate. If he asked the woman for a date, asked for information which presumably would lead to a date (e.g., asked for her phone number), offered to buy a snack or coffee for her, or ignored her when she said she should "get back to work," he was given points on an Index of "romantic behavior."

Kiesler and Baral found strong support for the matching contention that the more desirable a man feels, the more attractive a woman he will feel entitled to. When the men's self-esteem had been raised, they behaved more romantically toward the attractive confederate. But when their self-esteem had been lowered, they behaved more romantically with the less attractive confederate.

Matching: Fait Accompli

There is still other evidence that men and women of equal physical attractiveness tend to pair up.

Silverman (1971) tried to determine whether dating couples tend to be of similar attractiveness. Teams of observers went to such dating habitats as bars, social events, and theater lobbies, where they could watch young dating couples. Silverman and his associates found that dating partners were extraordinarily similar in physical attractiveness.

The observers observed how "intimate" the couples seemed to be (i.e., did they hold hands, touch one another, etc.?) during the period of observation. Silverman hypothesized that couples more similar in attractiveness would be happier with each other, and this would be reflected in their degree of physical intimacy. He found that he was right. Sixty percent of the couples who were highly similar in physical attractiveness engaged in intimate physical contact of some kind. Only 46 percent of the moderately similar couples and 22 percent of those in the lowest similarity group did so.

In a more tightly controlled study, Murstein (1972) also found evidence of matching. Murstein examined the correspondence between the physical attractiveness levels of 99 couples who were engaged or going steady. The degree of matching exhibited by the dating couples was compared to that of a control group of couples which was formed by randomly pairing the physical attractiveness scores of the 99 men and women with each other. Photographs were taken of each of the dating couples, and ratings of the physical attractiveness of each member of each couple were made. According to Murstein, judges did not know which partner belonged to whom when they made their attractiveness judgments.

Murstein found evidence of matching along the physical attractiveness dimension; the physical attractiveness level of the engaged or steadily dating couples was significantly less discrepant than those of the artificially paired couples. Murstein (p. 11) concluded:

> Individuals with equal market value for physical attractiveness are more likely to associate in an intimate relationship such as premarital engagement than individuals with disparate values.

Matching: More Complex Cases

Thus far, we've reviewed only that evidence which documents that people tend to pair off with partners who possess similar traits. It is clear, however, that couples can be "matched" in a variety of ways. For example, the handsome man (who is not especially dependable, warm, etc.) *may* use his assets to capture a beautiful partner, *or* he may decide to pursue a partner who is far plainer than himself, but who is far more dependable and warm than he is. Murstein *et al.* (1974, pp. 3–4) provide a compelling description of the way such complex matching might operate:

> A handsome man is seen with a woman of mediocre attractiveness. "I wonder what he sees in her?" may be the quizzical question of a bystander. Quite possibly, she possesses compensating qualities such as greater intelligence, interpersonal competence, and wealth than he, of which the bystander knows nothing. . . .
>
> Another case of compensatory exchange might be indicated if an aged statesman proposed marriage to a young beautiful woman. He would probably be trading his prestige and power for her physical attractiveness and youth.

There is some evidence in support of the contention that people do engage in such complicated balancing and counterbalancing in selecting mates. (See Walster *et al.* 1977, for a review of this research.)

For example, Elder (1969) proposed that beautiful women have an advantage in attracting highly successful mates.

In the 1930s, the Oakland Growth Study rated fifth and sixth grade girls' physical attractiveness; they rated the girls' coloring, goodness of features, goodness of physique, goodness of grooming, and sex appeal. Years later, Elder tracked down the girls, and found out what had become of them. He found that the more attractive the adolescent, the "better" she had done. The beautiful girls apparently used their beauty to "capture" mates whose "mobility potential" and "social status" far exceeded their own.

Berscheid *et al.* (1973) interviewed 2000 men and women about their current dating, mating, or marital relations. Forty-five percent of the men and women were 24 years old or younger, 25 percent were between 25 and 44, and the rest were 45 or older.

Berscheid *et al.* argued that if a person is vastly "superior" to his partner in one sphere—say physical attractiveness—he will be able to attract and keep a partner who has more to contribute in other spheres. The authors tested their hypothesis in the following way: First of all, the authors asked men and women how attractive they and their partners were:

- Much more physically attractive than I
- Slightly more physically attractive than I
- As attractive as I
- Slightly less attractive than I
- Much less attractive than I

On the basis of the respondents' replies, they divided respondents into three groups: individuals who were far more attractive than their partners, those who were just about as attractive as their partners, and those who were far less attractive than their partners.

As predicted, the authors found that the more attractive a person is compared to his or her partner, the richer, the more loving, and the more self-sacrificing his or her partner was likely to be. It appears, then, that the asset of beauty *can* be used to attract a beautiful partner, or it can be used to attract a partner who possesses quite different assets.

One recent study directly tested the hypothesis that equitable relationships are stable relationships. Researchers at the University of Wisconsin interviewed 511 men and women who were dating casually or steadily. First the researchers tried to find out whether the couple's relationship was a fair and equitable one or not. They began by explaining:

> Recently, psychologists have become interested in "dating" and "marriage contracts." At one time, Americans' marriage contracts were fairly standard. Couples promised to "love," "honor," and "cherish" . . . and that was often all they thought about it. Recently, however, young people have started to become a bit more thoughtful about the kinds of relationships they want. They've started to think in very concrete ways about the kinds of things they're willing to put into their relationships . . . and the kinds of things they expect in return.
>
> What we'd like to do now is find out a little about how—considering what you're putting into it—your dating relationship "stacks up."

They asked men and women to consider all the things they (and their partners) could contribute to a relationship, i.e., such *personal contributions* as being a good looking person, being intelligent, having a good personality, etc.; such *emotional contributions* as being a loving person, an understanding person, etc.; such *day-to-day contributions* as being an agreeable person, helping make decisions, etc. Then they were asked to estimate how much they (and their partners contributed to the relationship:

My contribution is:	*My partner's contribution is:*
+4 extremely positive	+4 extremely positive
+3 very positive	+3 very positive
+2 moderately positive	+2 moderately positive
+1 slightly positive	+1 slightly positive
−1 slightly negative	−1 slightly negative
−2 moderately negative	−2 moderately negative
−3 very negative	−3 very negative
−4 extremely negative	−4 extremely negative

Next, they asked students to consider all the benefits, and frustrations, a person could reap from a relationship: love, respect, security, excitement, a good time, or the opposite, and then to estimate how much they (and their partner) got out of their relationship.

My outcome is:	My partner's outcome is:
+4 extremely positive	+4 extremely positive
+3 very positive	+3 very positive
+2 moderately positive	+2 moderately positive
+1 slightly positive	+1 slightly positive
−1 slightly negative	−1 slightly negative
−2 moderately negative	−2 moderately negative
−3 very negative	−3 very negative
−4 extremely negative	−4 extremely negative

From these estimates, the researchers could calculate how equitable the men and women perceived their relationship to be. Three and one-half months later, they interviewed men and women once again.

The permanence of a relationship was assessed in three different ways: (1) they asked men and women if they were going with their partner at the present time. (2) If so, they asked them how long they'd been going together. If not, they asked them how long they went together before they broke up. (3) Finally, they asked how certain they were that they would still be going together next year—and five years from now. They found that men and women in equitable relationships did have the most long-lasting relationships. (See Fig. 10.3.)

Those men and women involved in fairly equitable relationships were in relationships that were currently intact, and they expected them to remain that way. Men or women who felt they were getting far *less* than they deserved from their relationship (and who have every reason to wish that something better will come along) were naturally quite pessimistic about the future of their relationship. So were those men and women who knew that they were getting far *more* than they deserved from the relationship, and had every reason to *hope* the relationship would last. They, too, had to admit that their relationship probably would not last.

What can we conclude from the preceding studies? Two conclusions seem defensible: (1) Individuals *prefer* romantic partners who are more desirable than themselves. (2) However, individuals' romantic *choices* are influenced by equity considerations. People do seem to end up choosing partners of approximately their own "social worth." Romantic choices appear

Relationship's permanence

How equitable is subject's romantic relationship?	Are you still together?[1]		How long have you been going together?[2]	How certain are you that you'll still be going together:[3]	
	Time 1	Time 2		one year from now?	five years from now?
Person is getting far less than he or she deserves	1.41	1.31	3.93	1.33	1.03
Person is getting slightly less than he or she deserves	1.57	1.44	5.40	1.89	1.39
Person is getting just what he or she deserves	1.73	1.70	5.62	2.53	2.05
Person is getting slightly more than he or she deserves	1.71	1.61	5.23	2.21	1.63
Person is getting far more than he or she deserves	1.41	1.42	4.19	1.38	1.16

[1] A score of 1 = No; 2 = Yes.

[2] The higher the number, the longer they've been going together — or the longer they went together before the relationship died.

[3] The higher the number, the more certain the man or woman is that the relationship will last.

Fig. 10.3 The relationship between equity/inequity of a romantic relationship and its permanence.

to be a delicate compromise between our desire to capture an ideal partner and one's realization that we must eventually settle for what we can get.

Summary

In this chapter, we focused on companionate Love. *Liking* has been defined as "the affection we feel for casual acquaintances"; *companionate love* as "the affection we feel for those with whom our lives are deeply intertwined." Levinger has tried to "scale" the intimacy of relationships. We start out having "Zero Contact" with others; we move to "Awareness," through "Surface Contact," and sometimes on to real intimacy, "Mutuality."

Recently theorists have begun to explore the factors that determine who loves whom, and why. We reviewed three theories of mate selection: Winch's Theory of Complementary Needs, Murstein's Stimulus–Value–Role Theory, and Equity's Matching Hypothesis. We found that there is some evidence that equitable relationships are more viable than inequitable ones.

If we compare *Interpersonal Attraction* (1969) **epilogue**
with *Interpersonal Attraction*, Second Edition
(1978), we can see that, in the last eight years, some profound changes have occurred in the field. In 1969, Reinforcement theorists were already having a major impact on Interpersonal Attraction research. They offered a paradigm that worked. In the last eight years, Reinforcement theorists have been busy filling in the details.

It is in the areas of romantic and companionate love where the major new developments have occurred. In *Interpersonal Attraction* (1969) there was one thin chapter on "Courtship and Love." In the second edition, there are two thick chapters—one on romantic and one on companionate love.

And, if we were asked to predict what the third edition of *Interpersonal Attraction* (1985), will be like, we would predict that, by then, social psychologists will focus not just on what causes people to fall passionately or companionately in love in the first place, but one on the dynamics of continuing relationships as well. What causes love to grow? Is there anything you can do to preserve it? What causes it to wither and die? Right now most of the insights about the nature of deeply intimate relationships come from clinicians. We suspect that by the year 1980 social psychologists will have a great deal more to say on the matter.

Abrams, R. H. 1943. Residential propinquity as a factor in marriage selection. *American Sociological Review* 8: 288–294.

references

Adams, B. N. 1972. Birth order: A critical review. *Sociometry* 35: 411–439.

Adler, A. 1926. *The neurotic constitution.* New York: Dodd, Mead.

Allgeier, A. R., and D. Byrne. 1973. Attraction toward the opposite sex as a determinant of physical proximity. *Journal of Social Psychology* 1973, 90: 213–219.

Allport, G. W. 1954. *The nature of prejudice.* Reading, Mass.: Addison-Wesley.

Altman, I., and D. A. Taylor. 1973. *Social penetration: the development of interpersonal relationships.* New York: Holt, Rinehart and Winston.

Argyle, M. 1967. *The psychology of interpersonal behavior.* Baltimore, Md.: Penguin Books.

Aronson, E. 1969. Some antecedents of interpersonal attraction. In W. Arnold and D. Levine (eds.), *Nebraska symposium on motivation* (Vol. 17). Lincoln: University of Nebraska Press.

Aronson, E. 1970. Who likes whom—and why. *Psychology Today* 74 (August): 48–50.

———, and D. Linder. 1951. Gain and loss of esteem as determinants of interpersonal attractiveness. *Journal of Experimental Social Psychology* 1: 156–171.

——— and J. Mills. 1959. The effect of severity of initiation on liking for a group. *Journal of Abnormal and Social Psychology* 67: 31–36.

———, and P. Worchel. 1966. Similarity vs. liking as determinants of interpersonal attractiveness. *Psychonomic Science* 5: 157–158.

Arsenian, J. M. 1943. Young children in an insecure situation. *Journal of Abnormal and Social Psychology* 38: 225–249.

Austin, W., and E. Walster. 1974. Reactions to confirmations and disconfirmations of expectancies of equity and inequity. *Journal of Personality and Social Psychology* 30: 208–216.

Averill, J. R. 1969. Autonomic response patterns during sadness and mirth. *Psychophysiology* 5: 399–414.

Ax, A. F. 1953. The physiological differentiation between fear and anger in humans. *Psychosomatic Medicine* 15: 433–442.

Back, K. W., and M. D. Bogdonoff. 1964. Plasma lipid responses to leadership, conformity, and deviation. In P. H. Leiderman and D. Shapiro (eds.), *Psychobiological approaches to social behavior*. Stanford, Calif.: Stanford University Press, pp. 36–39.

Backman, C. W., and P. F. Secord. 1959. The effect of perceived liking on interpersonal attraction. *Human Relations* 12: 379–384.

————. 1966. The compromise process and the affect structure of groups. In C. W. Backman and P. F. Secord (eds.), *Problems in social psychology*, New York: McGraw-Hill, pp. 190–192.

Bales, R. F. 1958. Task roles and social roles in problem-solving groups. In E. Maccoby, T. M. Newcomb, and E. L. Hartley (eds.), *Readings in social psychology*. (3rd ed.) New York: Holt, pp. 437–447.

Bandura, A. 1973. *Aggression: a social learning analysis*. Englewood Cliffs, N.J.: Prentice-Hall.

————, and R. H. Walters. 1963. *Social Learning and Personality Development*. New York: Holt, Rinehart and Winston.

Banta, T. J., and M. Hetherington. 1963. Relations between needs of friends and fiancés. *Journal of Abnormal and Social Psychology* 69: 401–404.

Baron, R., and D. Byrne. 1976. *Social psychology: understanding human interaction*. (2nd ed.) Boston: Allyn and Bacon.

Bartlett, R. G., Jr., V. C. Bohr, R. H. Helmendach, G. L. Foster, and M. A. Miller. 1954. Evidence of an emotional factor in hypothermia produced by restraint. *American Journal of Psysiology* 179: 343–346.

————, R. H. Helmendach, and V. C. Bohr. 1953. Effect of emotional stress, anesthesia, and death on body temperature of mice exposed to cold. *Proceedings of Society of Experimental Biology*, N.Y., 83: 4–5.

————, R. H. Helmendach, and W. I. Inman. 1954. Effect of restraint on temperature regulation in the cat. *Proceedings of the Society of Experimental Biology* 85: 81–83.

Becker, G. 1964. The complementary–need hypothesis: authoritarianism, dominance, and other Edwards Personality Preference Schedule scores. *Journal of Personality* 32: 45–56.

Beier, E. G., A. M. Rossi, and R. L. Garfield. 1961. Similarity plus dissimilarity of personality: basis for friendship? *Psychological Report* 8: 3–8.

Bell, A. G. 1883. Upon the formation of a deaf variety of the human race. *Mem. National Academy of Sciences* 2: 179–262.

Berger, E. 1952. The relation between expressed acceptance of self and expressed acceptance of others. *Journal of Abnormal and Social Psychology* 47: 778–782.

Bergler, E. 1948. *Divorce won't help*. New York: Harper & Bros.

Berkowitz, L. 1965. Some aspects of observed aggression. *Journal of Personality and Social Psychology* 2: 359–369.

————. 1968. *The frustration-aggression hypothesis revisited*. Paper delivered at the Western Psychological Association Meetings, San Diego, Calif., March 29.

————. 1969. *Roots of aggression: a reexamination of the frustration–aggression hypothesis.* New York: Atherton.

————, and L. R. Daniels. 1963. Responsibility and dependency. *Journal of Abnormal and Social Psychology* 66: 429–436.

————, and J. A. Green. 1962. The stimulus qualities of the scapegoat. *Journal of Abnormal and Social Psychology* 64: 293–301.

————, and D. S. Holmes. 1960. A further investigation of hostility generalization to disliked objects. *Journal of Personality* 28: 427–442.

————, and E. Rawlings. 1963. Effects of film violence on inhibitions against subsequent aggression. *Journal of Abnormal and Social Psychology* 66: 405–412.

Berlyne, D. E. 1960. *Conflict, arousal, and curiosity.* New York: McGraw-Hill.

Berscheid, E., D. Boye, and J. M. Darley. 1968. Effects of forced association upon voluntary choice to associate. *Journal of Personality and Social Psychology* 8: 13–19.

————, D. Boye, and E. Walster. 1968. Retaliation as a means of restoring equity. *Journal of Personality and Social Psychology* 10: 370–376.

————, T. Brothen, and W. Graziano. 1976. Gain/loss theory and the "law of infidelity": Mr. Doting vs. the admiring stranger. *Journal of Personality and Social Psychology* 33: 709–718.

————, K. Dion, E. Walster, and G. W. Walster. 1971. Physical attractiveness and dating choice: a test of the matching hypothesis. *Journal of Experimental Social Psychology* 7: 173–189.

————, and J. Fei. 1970. Romantic love and sexual jealousy. In G. Clanton and Lynn G. Smith (eds.), *Jealousy.* Englewood Cliffs, N.J.: Prentice-Hall, pp. 101–109.

————, W. Stephan, and E. Walster. 1971. Sexual arousal and heterosexual perception. *Journal of Personality and Social Psychology* 20: 93–101.

————, and E. Walster. 1967. When does a harm-doer compensate a victim? *Journal of Personality and Social Psychology* 6: 435–441.

————, and E. Walster. 1974. Physical attractiveness. In Leonard Berkowitz (ed.), *Advances in experimental social psychology.* New York: Academic Press, 7: 158–216.

————, E. Walster, and A. Barclay. Effect of time on tendency to compensate a victim. *Psychological Reports* 25: 431–436.

————, and G. W. Walster. 1969. Liking reciprocity as a function of perceived basis of proffered liking. Reported in E. Berscheid and E. Walster, *Interpersonal Attraction.* Reading, Mass.: Addison-Wesley.

————, G. W. Walster, and E. Walster. 1969. Effects of accuracy and positivity of an evaluation on liking for the evaluator. Brief report available in E. Berscheid and E. Walster *Interpersonal attraction.* Reading, Mass.: Addison-Wesley.

Bettelheim, B., and M. Janowitz. 1950. *Dynamics of prejudice.* New York: Harper.

Blau, P. M. 1964. *Exchange and power in social life.* New York: Wiley.

————. 1968. Social exchange. In D. L. Sills (ed.), *International Encyclopedia of the Social Sciences,* New York: Macmillan, 7: 452–457.

Bogardus, E. S. 1925. Measuring social distance. *Journal of Applied Sociology* 9: 299–308.

Bonney, M. E. 1952. A study of the relationship of intelligence, family, size, and sex differences with mutual friendships in primary grades. *Child Development* 13: 79–100.

Bossard, J. H. S. 1932. Residential propinquity as a factor in mate selection. *American Journal of Sociology* 38: 219–224.

Bovard, E. W. 1959. The effects of social stimuli on the response to stress. *Psychological Review* 66: 267–277.

Bowerman, C. E., and B. R. Day. 1956. A test of the theory of complementary needs as applied to couples during courtship. *American Sociological Review* 21: 602–605.

Bramel, D. 1962. A dissonance theory approach to defensive projection. *Journal of Abnormal and Social Psychology* 64: 121–129.

————. 1969. Interpersonal attraction, hostility, and perception. In Judson Mills (ed.), *Experimental social psychology*, New York: Macmillan.

Brehm, J. W., M. Gatz, G. Goethals, J. McCrimmon, and L. Ward. 1970. *Psychological arousal and interpersonal attraction*. Mimeo. Available from authors.

Brislin, R. W., and S. A. Lewis. 1968. Dating and physical attractiveness: a replication. *Psychological Reports* 22: 976.

Brock, T. C., and A. H. Buss. 1962. Dissonance, aggression, and evaluation of pain. *Journal of Abnormal and Social Psychology* 65: 197–202.

————. 1964. Effects of justification for aggression in communication with the victim on post-aggression dissonance. *Journal of Abnormal and Social Psychology* 68: 403–412.

Broxton, A. 1963. A test of interpersonal attraction predictions derived from balance theory. *Journal of Abnormal and Social Psychology* 63: 394–397.

Burgess, E. W., and P. Wallin. 1943. Homogamy in social characteristics. *American Journal of Sociology* 49: 109–124.

————. 1953. *Engagement and marriage*. Philadelphia: Lippincott.

Burnstein, E., and P. Worchel. 1962. Arbitrariness of frustration and its consequences for aggression in a social situation. *Journal of Personality* 30: 528–540.

Byrne, D. 1961a. The influence of propinquity and opportunities for interaction on classroom relationships. *Human Relations* 14: 63–70.

————. 1961b. Interpersonal attraction and attitude similarity. *Journal of Abnormal and Social Psychology* 62: 713–715.

————. 1971. *The attraction paradigm*. New York: Academic Press.

————, and B. Blaylock. 1963. Similarity and assumed similarity of attitudes between husbands and wives. *Journal of Abnormal and Social Psychology* 67: 636–640.

————, and J. A. Buehler. 1955. A note on the influence of propinquity upon acquaintanceships. *Journal of Abnormal and Social Psychology* 51: 147–148.

————, and G. L. Clore. 1970. A reinforcement model of evaluative responses. *Personality: An International Journal* 1: 103-128.

————, C. R. Ervin, and J. Lamberth. 1970. Continuity between the experimental study of attraction and "real life" computer dating. *Journal of Personality and Social Psychology* 16: 157–165.

————, and W. Griffitt. 1966. Similarity versus liking: a clarification. *Psychonomic Science* 6: 295–296.

————, and D. Nelson. 1965. Attraction as a linear function of proportion of positive reinforcements. *Journal of Personality and Social Psychology* 1: 659–663.

————, and T. J. Wong. 1962. Racial prejudice, interpersonal attraction, and assumed dissimilarity of attitudes. *Journal of Abnormal and Social Psychology* 65: 246–252.

Cannon, W. B. 1929. *Bodily changes in pain, hunger, fear, and rage.* (2nd ed.) New York: Appleton.

Carlsmith, J. M., and A. E. Gross. 1969. Some effects of guilt on compliance. *Journal of Personality and Social Psychology* 11: 232–239.

Carnegie, D. 1937. *How to win friends and influence people.* New York: Simon and Schuster.

Casler, L. 1969. This thing called love is pathological. *Psychology Today* (December): 18–20; 74–76.

Cattell, R. B., E. F. Maxwell, B. H. Like, and M. P. Unger. 1950. The objective measurement of attitudes. *British Journal of Psychology* 50: 235–252.

Cattell, R. B., and J. R. Nesselrode. 1967. Likeness and completeness theories examined by 16 personality factor measures on stable and unstable married couples. *Journal of Personality and Social Psychology* 7: 351 361.

Clarke, A. C. 1952. An examination of the operation of residual propinquity as a factor in mate selection. *American Sociological Review* 27: 17–22.

Clore, G. L., and D. Byrne. 1974. A reinforcement–affect model of attraction. In Ted L. Huston (ed.), *Foundations of interpersonal attraction.* New York: Academic Press, pp. 143–165.

Conger, J. J., W. L. Sawrey, and E. S. Turrell. 1957. An experimental investigation of the role of social experience in the production of gastric ulcers in hooded rats. *American Psychologist* 12: 410 (Abstract.)

Coombs, C. H. 1950. Psychological scaling without a unit of measurement. *Psychological Review* 57: 145–158.

Cooper, J., and E. E. Jones. 1969. Opinion divergence as a strategy to avoid being miscast. *Journal of Personality and Social Psychology* 13: 23–40.

Cowen, D., J. Landes, and D. E. Schaet. 1959. The effects of mild frustration on the expression of prejudiced attitudes. *Journal of Abnormal and Social Psychology* 58: 33–38.

Damrosch, S. P. 1975. The effects of certainty and congruence on reactions to evaluations by others. Doctoral dissertation, University of Minnesota. (University Microfilms No. 75-21,044.)

Darley, J. M., and E. Aronson. 1961. Self-evaluation vs. direct anxiety reduction as determinants of the fear-affliction relationship. *Journal of Experimental Social Psychology Supplement* 1: 66–79.

————, and E. Berscheid. 1967. Increased liking as a result of the anticipation of personal contact. *Human Relations* 20: 29–40.

————, E. P. Chereskin, and M. P. Zanna. 1975. *Legitimating contexts for harmdoing actions: difficulties with the standard paradigm for the study of aggression.* Unpublished manuscript, Princeton University, 1975.

Davidson, J. 1964. Cognitive familiarity and dissonance reduction. In Leon Festinger (ed.), *Conflict, decision, and dissonance.* Stanford, Calif.: Stanford University Press, pp. 45–60.

Davies, J. C. 1962. Toward a theory of revolution. *American Sociological Review* 27: 5–19.

Davis, K. E., and E. E. Jones. 1960. Changes in interpersonal perception as a means of reducing cognitive dissonance. *Journal of Abnormal and Social Psychology* 61: 402–410.

Davitz, J. R., and D. J. Mason. 1955. Socially facilitated reduction of a fear response in rats. *Journal of Comparative and Physiological Psychology* 48: 149–151.

Dermer, M., and D. L. Thiel. 1975. When beauty may fail. *Journal of Personality and Social Psychology* 31: 1168–1176.

de Rougemont, D. 1940. *Love in the Western world.* (M. Belgion, trans.) New York: Harcourt, Brace and World.

Deutsch, M., and M. E. Collins. 1958. The effect of public policy in housing projects upon interracial attitudes. In Eleanor Maccoby, T. M. Newcomb, and E. L. Hartley (eds.) *Readings in social psychology.* (3rd ed.) New York: Holt, pp. 612–623.

Deutsch, M., and L. Solomon. 1959. Reactions to evaluations by others as influenced by self-evaluations. *Sociometry* 22: 93–112.

Dickoff, H. *Reactions to evaluations by another person as a function of self-evaluation and the interaction context.* Unpublished doctoral dissertation, Duke University, 1961. Also reported in E. E. Jones, *Ingratiation.* New York: Appleton-Century-Crofts, 1964.

Dion, K. L., E. Berscheid, and E. Walster. 1972. What is beautiful is good. *Journal of Personality and Social Psychology* 24: 285–290.

————, and K. K. Dion. 1973. Correlates of romantic love. *Journal of Consulting and Clinical Psychology* 41: 51–56.

Dittes, J. E. 1959. Attractiveness of group as function of self-esteem and acceptance by group. *Journal of Abnormal and Social Psychology* 59: 77–82.

Dollard, J., L. Doob, N. Miller, O. Mowrer, and R. Sears. 1939. *Frustration and aggression.* New Haven: Yale University Press.

Dorwart, W., R. Ezerman, M. Lewis, and D. Rosenhan. 1965. The effect of brief social deprivation on social and nonsocial reinforcement. *Journal of Personality and Social Psychology* 2: 111–115.

Driscoll, R., K. E. Davis, and M. E. Lipitz. 1972. Parental interference and romantic love: the Romeo and Juliet effect. *Journal of Personality and Social Psychology* 24: 1–10.

Duffy, E. 1962. *Activation and behavior*. New York: Wiley.

Dulany, D. E., Jr. 1961. Hypotheses and habits in verbal "operant conditioning." *Journal of Abnormal and Social Psychology* 63: 251–263.

Dutton, D. G. 1972. Effect of feedback parameters on congruency versus positivity effects in reactions to personal evaluations. *Journal of Personality and Social Psychology* 24: 366–371.

Dutton, D., and A. Aron. 1974. Some evidence for heightened sexual attraction under conditions of high anxiety. *Journal of Personality and Social Psychology* 30: 510–517.

Dymond, R. 1954. Interpersonal perception and marital happiness. *Canadian Journal of Psychology* 8: 164–171.

Edwards, A. L. 1941. Political frames of reference as a factor influencing recognition. *Journal of Abnormal and Social Psychology* 36: 35–50.

Edwards, A. L., and C. Kinney. 1946. A comparison of the Thurstone and Likert techniques of attitude scale construction. *Journal of Applied Psychology* 30: 72–83.

Elder, G. H., Jr. 1969. Appearance and education in marriage mobility. *American Sociological Review* 34: 519–533.

Exline, R. 1971. Visual interaction: the glances of power and preference. In J. Cole, (ed.), *Nebraska Symposium on Motivation*. Lincoln: University of Nebraska Press.

Fay, E. A. 1898. *Marriages of the deaf in America*. Washington: Volta Bureau.

Festinger, L. 1951. Architecture and group membership. *Journal of Social Issues* 1: 152–163.

———. 1952. Group attraction and membership. In D. Cartwright and A. Zander (eds.), *Group dynamics: research and theory*. Evanston, Ill.: Row, Peterson.

———. 1954. A theory of social comparison processes. *Human Relations* 7: 117–140.

———. *A theory of cognitive dissonance*. Evanston, Ill.: Row, Peterson.

———, A. Pepitone, and T. Newcomb. 1952. Some consequences of deindividuation in a group. *Journal of Abnormal and Social Psychology* 47: 382–389.

———, S. Schachter, and K. Back. 1950. *Social pressures in informal groups: a study of human factors in housing*. New York: Harper.

Finck, H. T. 1902. *Romantic love and personal beauty: their development, causal relations, historic and national peculiarities*. London: Macmillan.

Firestone, S. 1970. Love. In notes from the Second Year Women's Liberation.

Fishbein, M. 1967. *Readings in attitude theory and measurement*. New York: Wiley.

Freedman, J. L., S. A. Wallington, and E. Bless. 1967. Compliance without pressure: the effect of guilt. *Journal of Personality and Social Psychology* 7: 117–124.

Freud, S. 1925. The most prevalent form of degradation in erotic life. In E. Jones (ed.), *Collected Papers*, 4. London: Hogarth, pp. 203–216.

Fromm, E., 1939. Selfishness and self-love. *Psychiatry* 2: 507–523.

Funkenstein, D. H., S. H. King, and M. E. Drolette. 1957. *Mastery of stress*. Cambridge, Mass.: Harvard University Press.

Galton, F. 1884. Measurement of character. *Fortnightly Review 1884* 36: 179–185.

Garrison, R. J., V. E. Anderson, and S. C. Reed. 1968. Assortative marriage. *Eugenics Quarterly* 15: 113–127.

Gaynor, C., J. Lamberth, and J. C. McCullers. 1972. *A developmental study of interpersonal attraction*. Unpublished manuscript, University of Oklahoma.

Gerard, H. B. 1963. Emotional uncertainty and social comparison. *Journal of Abnormal and Social Psychology* 66: 568–573.

―――, and J. M. Rabbie. 1961. Fear and social comparison. *Journal of Abnormal and Social Psychology* 62: 586–592.

Gergen, K., and M. Gergen. 1971. *Encounter: research catalyst for general theories of social behavior*. Unpublished manuscript, Swarthmore College.

Gewitz, J. L., and D. M. Baer. 1958a. The effect of brief social deprivation on behaviors for a social reinforcer. *Journal of Abnormal and Social Psychology* 56: 49–56.

―――. 1958b. Deprivation and satiation of social reinforcers as drive conditions. *Journal of Abnormal and Social Psychology* 57: 165–172.

Glass, D. C. 1964. Changes in liking as a means of reducing cognitive discrepancies between self-esteem and aggression. *Journal of Personality* 32: 520–549.

Goffman, E. 1952. On cooling the mark out: some aspects of adaptation to failure. *Psychiatry* 15: 451–463.

Goldberg, G. N., C. A. Kiesler, and B. E. Collins. 1969. Visual behavior and face-to-face distance during interaction. *Sociometry* 32: 43–53.

―――. In press. Interpersonal attraction and situational definition as determinants of the spacing of interacting individuals. *Sociometry*.

Goldschmid, M. L. 1967. Prediction of college majors by personality tests. *Journal of Counseling Psychology* 14: 302–308.

Goldstein, J. W., and H. Rosenfeld. 1969. Insecurity and preference for persons similar to oneself. *Journal of Personality* 37: 253–268.

Goranson, R. E., and L. Berkowitz. 1966. Reciprocity and responsibility reactions to prior help. *Journal of Personality and Social Psychology* 3: 227–232.

Greenspoon, J. 1955. The reinforcing effect of two spoken sounds on the frequency of two responses. *American Journal of Psychology* 68: 409–416.

Griffitt, W. 1974. Attitude similarity and attraction. In Ted L. Huston (ed.), *Foundations of interpersonal attraction*. New York: Academic Press, pp. 285–308.

Griffitt, W., J. Nelson, and G. Littlepage. 1972. Old age and response to agreement–disagreement. *Journal of Gerontology* 27: 269–274.

Gullahorn, J. 1952. Distance and friendship as factors in the gross interaction matrix. *Sociometry* 15: 123–134.

Guttman, L. 1944. A basis for scaling qualitative data. *American Sociological Review* 9: 139–150.

Hamblin, R. I. 1958. Group integration during a crisis. *Human Relations* 11: 67–76.

———, D. A. Bridger, R. C. Day, and W. L. Yancey. 1963. The interference–aggression law? *Sociometry* 26: 190–216.

Hammond, K. R. 1948. Measuring attitudes by error–choice: an indirect method. *Journal of Abnormal and Social Psychology* 43: 38–48.

Harris, J. A. 1912. Assortive mating in man. *Popular Science Monthly* 80: 476–492.

Harvey, O. J., H. H. Kelley, and M. M. Shapiro. 1957. Reactions to unfavorable evaluations of the self made by other persons. *Journal of Personality* 25: 393–411.

Hastorf, A. H., D. J. Schneider, and J. Polefka. 1970. *Person perception.* Reading, Mass.: Addison-Wesley.

Heider, F. 1958. *The psychology of interpersonal relations.* New York: Wiley.

Hoffeditz, E. L. 1934. Family resemblances in personality traits. *Journal of Social Psychology* 5: 214–227.

Hoffman, L. R. 1958. Similarity of personality: a basis for interpersonal attraction? *Sociometry* 21: 300–308.

Hohmann, G. W. 1962. *The effect of dysfunctions of the autonomic nervous system on experienced feelings and emotions.* Paper read at Conference on Emotions and Feelings at New School for Social Research, New York.

Hokanson, J. E. 1961. The effects of frustration and anxiety on overt aggression. *Journal of Abnormal and Social Psychology* 62: 346–351.

Homans, G. C. 1961. *Social behavior: its elementary forms.* New York: Harcourt Brace and World.

———. 1974. *Social behavior: its elementary forms.* (Rev. ed.) New York: Harcourt Brace Jovanovich.

Horn, J. 1974. Sexual attraction, fear and other four-letter words. *Behavior Today,* Dec. 16, p. 329.

Horney, K. 1939. *New ways in psychoanalysis.* New York: Norton.

Horwitz, M. 1958. The verticality of liking and disliking. In R. Tagiuri and L. Petrullo (eds.), *Person, perception, and interpersonal behavior.* Stanford: Stanford University Press.

Hovland, C., and R. Sears. 1940. Minor studies in aggression: VI. Correlations of lynchings with economic indices. *Journal of Psychology* 9: 310–310.

Howard, R. C., and L. Berkowitz. 1958. Reactions to the evaluators of one's performance. *Journal of Personality* 26: 494–506.

Hudson, J. W., and L. Henzi. 1969. Campus values in mate selection: a replication. *Journal of Marriage and the Family* 31: 772–778.

Huesmann, L. R., and G. Levinger. 1976. Incremental exchange theory: a formal model for progression in dyadic social interaction. In L. Berkowitz and E. Walster (eds.), *Advances in experimental social psychology* 9: 191–244.

Hunt, A. M. 1935. A study of the relative value of certain ideals. *Journal of Abnormal and Social Psychology* 30: 222–228.

Huston, T. L. 1973. Ambiguity of acceptance, social desirability, and dating choice. *Journal of Experimental Social Psychology* 9: 32–42.

———. 1974. Editor of *Foundations of interpersonal attraction*. New York: Academic Press.

Izard, C. E. 1960a. Personality similarity, positive affect, and interpersonal attraction. *Journal of Abnormal and Social Psychology* 61: 484–485.

———. 1960b. Personality similarity and friendship. *Journal of Abnormal and Social Psychology* 61: 47–51.

———. 1963. Personality similarity and friendship: a follow-up study. *Journal of Abnormal and Social Psychology* 66: 598–600.

Jacobs, L., E. Berscheid, and E. Walster. 1971. Self-esteem and attraction. *Journal of Personality and Social Psychology* 17: 84–91.

Jecker, J., and D. Landy. 1969. Liking a person as a function of doing him a favor. *Human Relations* 22: 371–378.

Jones, E. E. 1964. *Ingratiation*. New York: Appleton-Century-Crofts.

Jones, E. E., and K. E. Davis. 1965. From acts to dispositions: the attribution process in person perception. In L. Berkowitz (ed.), *Advances in Experimental Social Psychology* 2. New York: Academic Press.

Jones, E. E., K. J. Gergen, and K. E. Davis. 1962. Some determinants of reactions to being approved or disapproved as a person. *Psychological Monographs* 76: Whole no. 521.

———, K. J. Gergen, P. Gumpert, and J. W. Thibaut. 1965. Some conditions affecting the use of ingratiation to influence performance evaluation. *Journal of Abnormal Social Psychology* 1: 613–625.

———, R. G. Jones, and K. J. Gergen. 1963. Some conditions affecting the evaluation of a conformist. *Journal of Personality* 31: 270–288.

———, and C. Wortman. 1973. *Ingratiation: an attributional approach*. Morristown, N.J.: General Learning Press.

Jones, H. E. 1929. Homogamy in intellectual abilities. *American Journal of Sociology* 35: 369–382.

Jones, R. G., and E. E. Jones. 1964. Optimum conformity as an integration tactic. *Journal of Personality* 32: 436–458.

Jones, S. C. 1973. Self and interpersonal evaluations: esteem theories versus consistency theories. *Psychological Bulletin* 79: 185–199.

———, and D. J. Schneider. 1968. Certainty of self-appraisal and reactions to evaluations from others. *Sociometry* 31: 395–403.

Jourard, S. M. 1964. *The transparent self*. Princeton, N.J.: D. Van Nostrand.

Katz, A. M., and R. Hill. 1958. Residential propinquity and marital selection: a review of theory, method, and fact. *Marriage and Family Living* 20: 327–335.

Katz, D., and E. Stotland. 1959. A preliminary statement to a theory of attitude structure and change. In S. Koch (ed.), *Psychology:' a study of a science* 3. New York: McGraw-Hill, pp. 423–475.

Katz, I., S. Glucksberg, and R. Krauss. 1960. Need satisfaction and Edward PPS scores in married couples. *Journal of Consulting Psychology* 24: 203–208.

Kelley, H. H. 1972. Attribution in social interaction. In E. E. Jones *et al.* (eds.), *Attribution: perceiving the causes of behavior*. Morristown, N.J.: General Learning Press.

Kennedy, R. 1943. Premarital residential propinquity. *American Journal of Sociology* 48: 580–584.

Kephart, W. M. 1961. *The family, society, and the individual*. Boston: Houghton Mifflin.

————. 1967. Some correlates of romantic love. *Journal of Marriage and the Family* 29: 470–474.

————. 1970. The "dysfunctional" theory of romantic love: a research report. *Journal of Comparative Family Studies* 1: 26–36.

Kerckhoff, A. C. 1974. The social context of interpersonal attraction. In T. L. Huston (ed.), *Foundations of interpersonal attraction*. New York: Academic Press.

Kerckhoff, A. C., and K. E. Davis. 1962. Value consensus and need complementarity in mate selection. *American Sociological Review* 27: 295–303.

Kiesler, C. A., and G. N. Goldberg. 1968. Multidimensional approach to the experimental study of interpersonal attraction: effect of a blunder on the attractiveness of a competent other. *Psychological Reports* 22: 693–705.

Kiesler, S., and R. Baral. 1970. The search for a romantic partner: the effects of self-esteem and physical attractiveness on romantic behavior. In K. Gergen and D. Marlowe (eds.), *Personality and social behavior*. Reading, Mass.: Addison-Wesley.

Kinsey, A. C., W. Pomeroy, C. Martin, and P. H. Gebhard. 1953. *Sexual behavior in the human female*. Philadelphia: W. B. Saunders.

Kipnis, D. M. 1957. Interaction between members of bomber crews as a determinant of sociometric choice. *Human Relations* 10: 263–270.

Klein, M., and J. Riviere. 1953. *Love, hate, and reparation*. London: Hogarth.

Klinger, E. 1971. *Structure and functions of fantasy*. New York: Wiley.

Ktasanes, T. 1955. Mate selection on the basis of personality type: a study utilizing an empirical typology of personality. *American Sociological Review* 20: 547–551.

Kurth, S. B. 1970. Friendship and friendly relations. In G. J. McCall, M. K. Denzin, G. D. Suttles, and S. B. Kurth (eds.), *Social relationships*. Chicago: Aldine.

Lacey, J. I. 1967. Somatic response patterning and stress: some revisions of activation theory. In M. H. Appley and R. Thrumbull (eds.), *Psychological stress*. New York: Appleton.

Latané, B. 1966. Studies in social comparison—introduction and overview. *Journal of Experimental Social Psychology* 2: 1–5.

———, and D. C. Glass. 1968. Social and nonsocial attraction in rats. *Journal of Personality and Social Psychology* 9: 142–146.

Lazarsfeld, P. F. 1959. Latent structure analysis. In Sigmund Koch (ed.), *Psychology: a study of a science*. Vol. 3. New York: McGraw-Hill.

Lazarus, R. S. 1968. Emotions and adaptation: conceptual and empirical relations. In W. J. Arnold (ed.), *Nebraska Symposium on Motivation*. Lincoln, Nebraska: University of Nebraska Press.

Leiman, A. H., and S. Epstein. 1961. Thematic sexual responses as related to sexual drive and guilt. *Journal of Abnormal and Social Psychology* 63: 169–175.

Lerner, M. J. 1965. Evaluation of performance as a function of performer's reward and attractiveness. *Journal of Personality and Social Psychology* 1: 355–360.

———, and C. H. Simmons. 1966. Observers reaction to the "innocent victim": compassion or rejection? *Journal of Personality and Social Psychology* 4: 203–210.

Leventhal, G. S., and J. T. Bergman. 1969. Self-depriving behavior as a response to unprofitable inequity. *Journal of Experimental Social Psychology* 5: 153–171.

Levine, J. M., and G. Murphy. 1943. The learning and forgetting of controversial material. *Journal of Abnormal and Social Psychology* 38: 507–517.

Levinger, G. 1964. Note on need complementarity in marriage. *Psychological Bulletin* 61: 153–157.

———, and J. Breedlove. 1966. Interpersonal attraction and agreement: a study of marriage partners. *Journal of Personality and Social Psychology* 3: 367–372.

———, D. J. Senn, and B. W. Jorgensen. 1970. Progress toward permanence in courtship: a test of the Kerckhoff-Davis hypotheses. *Sociometry* 33: 427–443.

Lewin, K. 1940. Formalization and progress in psychology, *University of Iowa Studies in Child Welfare* 16: 3.

Liddell, H. 1950. Some specific factors that modify tolerance for environmental stress. In H. G. Wolff, Jr., and C. C. Hare (eds.), *Life stress and bodily disease*. Baltimore: Williams and Wilkins, pp. 155–171.

Likert, R. 1932. A technique for the measurement of attitudes. *Archives of Psychology* 140: 44–53.

Lindsley, D. B. 1950. Emotions and the electroencephalogram. In M. R. Reymert (ed.), *Feelings and emotions: the Mooseheart symposium*. New York: McGraw-Hill.

Lindzey, G., and E. F. Borgatta. 1954. Sociometric measurement. In G. Lindzey (ed.), *Handbook of social psychology*, Vol. 1. Reading, Mass.: Addison-Wesley, pp. 405–448.

Loeblowitz-Lennard, H., and F. Riessman, Jr. 1946. A proposed projective attitude test. *Psychiatry* 9: 67–68.

Lott, A. J., and B. E. Lott. 1961. Group cohesiveness, communication level, and conformity. *Journal of Abnormal and Social Psychology* 62: 408–412.

———. 1974. The role of reward in the formation of positive interpersonal attitudes. In T. L. Huston (ed.), *Foundations of interpersonal attraction.* New York: Academic Press, pp. 171–189.

Lowe, C. A., and J. W. Goldstein. 1970. Reciprocal liking and attributions of ability: mediating effects of perceived intent and personal involvement. *Journal of Personality and Social Psychology* 16: 291–297.

Lundy, R. M., W. Katkovsky, R. L. Cromwell, and D. J. Shoemaker. 1955. Self-acceptability and descriptions of sociometric choices. *Journal of Abnormal and Social Psychology* 51: 260–262.

McDougall, W. 1908. *Introduction to social psychology.* London: Methuen.

McGuire, W. J. 1969. The nature of attitudes and attitude change. In G. Lindzey and E. Aronson (eds.), *The handbook of social psychology* (2nd ed.) Vol. 3. Reading, Mass.: Addison-Wesley, pp. 136–314.

Maissonneuve, J., G. Palmade, and C. Fourment. 1952. Selective choices and propinquity. *Sociometry* 15: 135–140.

Mallick, S. K., and B. R. McCandless. 1966. A study of catharsis of aggression. *Journal of Personality and Social Psychology* 4: 591–596.

Mandlebaum, D. G. 1952. *Soldier groups and Negro soldiers.* Berkeley: University of California, pp. 45–48.

Mann, J. H. 1959. The effect of interracial contact on sociometric choices and perceptions. *Journal of Social Psychology* 50: 143–152.

Manson, W. A. 1960. Socially mediated reduction in emotional responses of young Rhesus monkeys. *Journal of Abnormal and Social Psychology* 60: 100–104.

Marshall, R. 1927. Precipitation and presidents. *Nation* 124: 315–316.

Martin, R. G. 1974. *The woman he loved.* New York: Simon and Schuster.

Marwell, G. 1975. Why ascription? Parts of a more or less formal theory of the functions and dysfunctions of sex roles. *American Sociological Review* 40: 445–455.

————, D. R. Schmitt, and R. Shotola. 1971. Cooperation and interpersonal risk. *Journal of Personality and Social Psychology* 18: 9–32.

Maslach, C. 1972. Social and personal bases of individuation. Proceedings of the 80th Annual Convention of the American Psychological Association, pp. 212–213.

Maslow, A. H. 1942. Self-esteem (dominance feeling) and sexuality in women. *Journal of Social Psychology* 16: 259–294.

————. 1950. Self-actualizing people: a study in psychological health. *Personality* 1: 11–34.

————. 1954. *Motivation and personality.* New York: Harper & Row.

Masters, W. H., and V. E. Johnson. 1966. *Human sexual response.* Boston: Little, Brown.

————. 1975. *The pleasure bond.* New York: Bantam Books, 1975.

Mehrabian, A. 1968. Relationship of attitude to seated posture, orientation, and distance. *Journal of Personality and Social Psychology* 10: 26–30.

Mettee, D. R. 1971. Changes in liking as a function of the magnitude and effect of sequential evaluations. *Journal of Experimental Social Psychology* 7: 157–172.

————, and E. Aronson. 1974. Affective reactions to appraisal from others. In T. .L Huston (ed.), *Foundations of interpersonal attraction*. New York: Academic Press, pp. 235–283.

————, E. S. Hrelec, and P. C. Wilkins. 1971. Humor as an interpersonal asset and liability. *Journal of Social Psychology* 85: 51–64.

Miller, A. 1970. Role of physical attractiveness in impression formation. *Psychonomic Science* 19: 241–243.

Miller, H. L., and W. H. Rivenbark, III. 1970. Sexual differences in physical attractiveness as a determinant of heterosexual likings. *Psychological Reports* 27: 701–702.

Miller, N., D. T. Campbell, H. Twedt, and E. J. O'Connell. 1966. Similarity, contrast, and complementarity in friendship choice. *Journal of Personality and Social Psychology* 3: 3–12.

Miller, N. E. 1941. The frustration–aggression hypothesis. *Psychological Review* 48: 337–342.

————. 1944. Experimental studies of conflict. In J. McV. Hunt (ed.), *Personality and behavioral disorders*. New York: Ronald, pp. 431–465.

————. 1951. Comments on theoretical models illustrated by the development of a theory of conflict. *Journal of Personality* 20: 82–100.

————, and R. Bugelski. 1948. Minor studies in aggression: the influence of frustration imposed by the in-group on attitudes expressed toward out-groups. *Journal of Psychology* 25: 237–442.

Moreno, J. L. 1934. *Who shall survive? A new approach to the problem of human interrelation*. Washington, D.C., Nervous and Mental Disease Publishing Co.

Murstein, B. I. 1961. A complementary need hypothesis in newlyweds and middle-aged married couples. *Journal of Abnormal and Social Psychology* 63:194–197.

————. 1967. The relationship of mental health to marital choice and courtship progress. *Journal of Marriage and the Family* 29: 447–451.

————. 1970. Stimulus–value–role: a theory of marital choice. *Journal of Marriage and the Family* 32: 465–481.

————. 1976. *Who will marry whom? Theories and research in marital choice*. New York: Springer.

————, M. Goyette, and M. Cerreto. 1974. *A theory of the effect of exchange orientation on marriage and friendship*. Unpublished manuscript.

Nahemow, L., and M. P. Lawton. 1975. Similarity and propinquity in friendship formation. *Journal of Personality and Social Psychology* 32, (2): 204–213.

Newcomb, T. M. 1946. The influence of attitude climate upon some determinants of information. *Journal of Abnormal and Social Psychology* 41: 291–302.

————. 1956. The prediction of interpersonal attraction. *American Psychologist* 11: 575–586.

————. 1961. *The acquaintance process*. New York: Holt, Rinehart and Winston.

————, and G. Svehla. 1937. Intrafamily relationship in attitude. *Sociometry* 1: 180–205.

Novak, D. W., and M. J. Lerner. 1968. Rejection as a function of perceived similarity. *Journal of Personality and Social Psychology* 9: 147–152.

Nunnally, J. 1967. *Psychometric theory.* New York: McGraw-Hill.

Omwake, K. 1954. The relationship between acceptance of self and acceptance of others shown by three personality inventories. *Journal of Consulting Psychology* 18: 443–446.

Osgood, C. E., G. J. Suci, and P. H. Tannenbaum. 1957. *The measurement of meaning.* Urbana: University of Illinois Press.

Ossorio, P. G., and K. E. Davis. 1966. The self, intentionality, and reactions to evaluations of the self. In C. Gordon and K. J. Gergen (eds.), *Self in society.* New York: Wiley.

Ovid. 1963. *The art of love.* Rolfe Humphries (trans.). Bloomington, Ind.: University of Indiana Press, pp. 65–66.

Palmore, E. B. 1955. The introduction of Negroes into white departments. *Human Organization* 14: 27–28.

Pannen, D. E. 1976. *Anticipation of future interaction and the estimation of current rewards.* Unpublished doctoral dissertation, University of Minnesota.

Parrish, J. A. 1948. *The direct and indirect assessment of attitudes as influenced by propagandized radio transcriptions.* Masters thesis, Ohio State University.

Pearson, K., and A. Lee. 1903. On the laws of inheritance in man. I. Inheritance of physical characteristics. *Biometrika* 2: 372–377.

Perrin, F. A. C. 1921. Physical attractiveness and repulsiveness. *Journal of Experimental Psychology,* 4: 203–217.

Reader, N., and H. B. English. 1947. Personality factors in adolescent female friendships. *Journal of Consulting Psychology* 11: 212–220.

Reed, E. W., and S. C. Reed. 1965. Mental retardation: a family study. Philadelphia: W. B. Saunders.

Reik, T. 1944. *A psychologist looks at love.* New York: Farrar and Rinehart.

————. 1957. *The need to be loved.* New York: Farrar, Straus, and Cudahy.

Reiss, I. L. 1960. *Premarital sexual standards in America.* New York: Free Press.

Richardson, H. M. 1939. Studies of mental resemblance between husbands and wives and between friends. *Psychological Bulletin* 36: 104–120.

Rogers, C. R. 1951. *Client-centered therapy.* Boston: Houghton Mifflin.

Roos, D. E. 1956. *Complementary needs in mate selection: a study based on R-type factor analysis.* Unpublished Ph.D. dissertation, Northwestern University.

Rosow, I. 1957. Issues in the concept of need-complementarity. *Sociometry* 20: 216–233.

Rubin, Z. 1970. Measurement of romantic love. *Journal of Personality and Social Psychology* 16: 265–273.

Rubin, Z. 1973. *Liking and loving: an invitation to social psychology.* New York: Holt, Rinehart and Winston.

Russell, B. 1960. In A. M. Kirch (ed.), *The anatomy of love.* New York: Dell, pp. 10–11.

Sarnoff, I., and P. G. Zimbardo. 1961. Anxiety, fear, and social affiliation. *Journal of Abnormal and Social Psychology* 62: 356–363.

Schachter, J. 1957. Pain, fear, and anger in hypertensives and normotensives: a psycho-physiological study. *Psychosomatic Medicine* 19: 17–24.

Schachter, S. 1959. *The psychology of affiliation.* Stanford, Calif.: Stanford University Press.

————. 1964. The interaction of cognitve and physiological determinants of emotional state. In Leonard Berkowitz (ed.), *Advances in experimental social psychology,* 1. New York: Academic Press, pp. 49–80.

————, and J. Singer. 1962. Cognitive, social, and physiological determinants of emotional state. *Psychological Review* 69: 379–399.

————, and L. Wheeler. 1962. Epinephrine, chlorpromazine, and amusement. *Journal of Abnormal Social Psychology* 65: 121–128.

Schellenberg, J. A., and L. S. Bee. A reexamination of the theory of complementary needs in mate selection. *Marriage and Family Living* 22: 227–232.

Schmitt, D. R., and G. Marwell. 1972. Withdrawal and reward allocation as responses to inequity. *Journal of Experimental Social Psychology* 8: 207–221.

Schooley, M. 1936. Personality resemblances among married couples. *Journal of Abnormal Social Psychology* 31: 340–347.

Segal, M. W. 1974. Alphabet and attraction: an unobtrusive measure of the effect of propinquity in a field setting. *Journal of Personality and Social Psychology* 30: 654–657.

Selye, H. 1950. *Stress.* Montreal: Acta, pp. 267–277.

Sherif, M., and C. W. Sherif. 1956. *An outline of social psychology.* (Rev. ed.). New York: Harper and Bros.

————, O. J. Harvey, B. J. White, W. R. Good, and C. W. Sherif. 1954. Experimental study of positive and negative intergroup attitudes between experimentally produced groups. Robbers' Cave Study. Norman: University of Oklahoma. (Multilithed.)

Shrauger, J. S. 1975. Response to evaluation as a function of initial self-perception. *Psychological Bulletin* 82: 581–596.

Sigall, H., and E. Aronson. 1967. Opinion change and the gain–loss model of interpersonal attraction. *Journal of Experimental Social Psychology,* 3: 178–188.

————, and D. Landy. 1973. Radiating beauty: the effects of having a physically attractive partner on person perception. *Journal of Personality and Social Psychology* 28: 218–224.

Singer, J. L. 1966. *Daydreaming: an introduction to the experimental study of inner experience.* New York: Random House.

Socrates. 1923. In Xenophon, E. C. Marchant (trans.). *Memorabilia*, III, xi, London: Heinemann.

Soule, G. 1935. *The coming American revolution*. New York: Macmillan, p. 20.

Stagner, R., and C. S. Congdon. 1955. Another failure to demonstrate displacement of aggression. *Journal of Abnormal and Social Psychology* 51: 695–696.

Stevenson, H. W., and R. D. Odom. 1962. The effectiveness of social reinforcement following two conditions of social deprivation. *Journal of Abnormal and Social Psychology* 65: 429–431.

Stires, L. K., and E. E. Jones. 1969. Modesty versus self-enhancement as alternative forms of ingratiation. *Journal of Experimental Social Psychology* 5: 172–188.

Stock, D. 1949. An investigation into the intercorrelations between the self-concept and feelings directed toward other persons and groups. *Journal of Consulting Psychology* 13: 176–180.

Stroebe, W., C. A. Insko, V. D. Thompson, and B. D. Layton. 1971. Effects of physical attractiveness, attitude similarity, and sex on various aspects of interpersonal attraction. *Journal of Personality and Social Psychology* 18: 79–91.

Sykes, G. M., and D. Matza. 1957. Techniques of neutralization: a theory of delinquency. *American Sociological Review* 22: 664–670.

Taft, R. 1954. Selective recall and memory distortion of favorable and unfavorable material. *Journal of Abnormal and Social Psychology* 49: 23–28.

Tagiuri, R. 1958. Social preference and its perception. In R. Tagiuri and L. Petrullo (eds.), *Person, perception, and interpersonal behavior*. Stanford, Calif.: Stanford University Press, pp. 316–336.

Taylor, S. E., and D. Mettee. 1971. When similarity breeds contempt. *Journal of Personality and Social Psychology* 20: 75–81.

Tedeschi, J. T., R. B. Smith, III, and R. C. Brown, Jr. 1974. A reinterpretation of research on aggression. *Psychological Bulletin* 81, (9): 540–562.

Tesser, A., and M. Brodie. 1971. A note on the evaluation of a "computer date." *Psychonomic Science* 23: 300.

Tharp, R. G. 1963. Psychological patterning in marriage. *Psychological Bulletin* 60: 97–117.

Thibaut, J. W., and H. H. Kelley. *The social psychology of groups*. New York: Wiley, pp. 80–99.

Thomas, D. S. 1925. *Social aspects of a business cycle*. London: Rutledge.

Thompson, W. R., and R. Nishimura. 1952. Some determinants of friendship. *Journal of Personality* 20: 305–314.

Thurstone, L. L. 1928. Attitudes can be measured. *American Journal of Sociology* 33: 529–554.

Triandis, H. C., and C. E. Osgood. 1958. A comparative factorial analysis of semantic structures of monolingual Greek and American college students. *Journal of Abnormal and Social Psychology* 57: 187–196.

Ulrich, R. 1966. Pain as the cause of aggression. *American Zoologists* 6: 643–662.

Valins, S. 1966. Cognitive effects of false heart-rate feedback. *Journal of Personality and Social Psychology* 4: 400–408.

Waller, W., and R. Hill. 1951. *The family: a dynamic interpretation.* (2nd ed.) New York: Holt, Rinehart and Winston.

Walster, E. 1965. The effect of self-esteem on romantic liking. *Journal of Experimental Social Psychology* 1: 184–197.

———. 1966. The assignment of responsibility for an accident. *Journal of Personality and Social Psychology* 3: 73–79.

———. 1970. Effect of self-esteem on liking for dates of various social desirabilities. *Journal of Experimental Social Psychology* 6: 248–253.

———, V. Aronson, D. Abrahams, and L. Rottman. 1966. The importance of physical attractiveness in dating behavior. *Journal of Personality and Social Psychology* 4: 508–516.

———, and E. Berscheid. 1974. A little bit about love: a minor essay on a major topic. In T. L. Huston (ed.), *Foundations of interpersonal attraction.* New York: Academic Press, pp. 355–381.

———, E. Berscheid, and G. W. Walster. 1973. New directions in equity research. *Journal of Personality and Social Psychology* 25: 151–176.

———, and P. Prestholdt. 1966. The effect of misjudging another: over-compensation or dissonance reduction? *Journal of Experimental Social Psychology* 2: 85–97.

———, S. Sprecher, and G. W. Walster. 1977. *Equity and premarital sex.* Unpublished manuscript.

———, and G. W. Walster. 1963. Effect of expecting to be liked on choice of associates. *Journal of Abnormal and Social Psychology* 67: 402–404.

———, and G. W. Walster. 1976. Interpersonal attraction. In Bernard Seidenberg and Alvin Snadowsky (eds.), *Social psychology: an introduction.* New York: Free Press, pp. 279–308.

———, and G. W. Walster, 1978. *Love.* Reading, Mass.: Addison-Wesley.

———, G. W. Walster, D. Abrahams, and Z. Brown. The effect on liking of underrating or overrating another. *Journal of Experimental Social Psychology* 2: 70–84.

———, G. W. Walster, and E. Berscheid. 1971. The efficacy of playing hard-to-get. *Journal of Experimental Education* 39: 73–77.

———, G. W. Walster, and E. Berscheid. 1977. *Equity: theory and research.* Boston: Allyn and Bacon.

———, G. W. Walster, J. Piliavin, and L. Schmidt. 1973. Playing hard-to-get: understanding an elusive phenomenon. *Journal of Personality and Social Psychology* 26: 113–121.

Watson, W. S., and G. W. Hartman. 1939. The rigidity of a basic attitudinal frame. *Journal of Abnormal Social Psychology* 34: 314–335.

Webb, E. J., D. T. Campbell, R. D. Schwartz, and L. Sechrest. 1966. *Unobtrusive measures: nonreactive research in the social sciences.* Chicago: Rand McNally.

Weick, K. E., and B. Nesset. 1968. Preferences among forms of equity. *Organizational Behavior and Human Performance* 3: 400–416.

Weiss, W. 1953. A "sleeper" effect in opinion change. *Journal of Abnormal and Social Psychology* 48: 173–180.

Wheeler, L. 1966. Motivation as a determinant of upward comparison. *Journal of Experimental Social Psychology* 2: 27–31.

————. 1974. Social comparison and selective affiliation. In T. L. Huston (ed.), *Foundations of interpersonal attraction*. New York: Academic Press, pp. 309–328.

Williamson, R. C. 1966. *Marriage and family relations*. New York: Wiley.

Winch, R. F. 1952. *The modern family*. New York: Holt.

————. 1958. *Mate selection: a study of complementary needs*. New York: Harper & Row.

————, T. Ktsanes, and V. Ktsanes. 1954. The theory of complementary needs in mate selection: an analytic and descriptive study. *American Sociological Review* 19: 241–249.

Wolf, S., and H. G. Wolff. 1947. *Human gastric function*. (2nd ed.) London: Oxford University Press.

Worthy, M., A. L. Gary, and G. M. Kahn. 1969. Self-disclosure as an exchange process. *Journal of Personality and Social Psychology* 13: 63–69.

Zajonc, R. B. 1968. Attitudinal effects of mere exposure. *Journal of Personality and Social Psychology* 9. Monograph 1–29.

Zander, A., and A. Havelin. 1960. Social comparison and interpersonal attraction. *Human Relations* 13: 21–32.

Zimbardo, P. 1969. The human choice: individuation, reason, and order versus deindividuation, impulse, and chaos. In W. Arnold and D. Levine (eds.), *Nebraska Symposium on Motivation* 17: 237–307.

————, and E. E. Ebbesen. 1969. *Influencing attitudes and changing behavior*. Menlo Park, Calif.: Addison-Wesley.

————, and R. Formica. 1963. Emotional comparison and self-esteem as determinants of affiliation. *Journal of Personality* 31: 141–162.

Zuckerman, M. 1971. Physiological measures of sexual response in the human. *Psychology Bulletin* 75: 297–329.

index